FLEETER THAN BIRDS

Also by Doug Feldmann

*Dizzy and the Gas House Gang:
The 1934 St. Louis Cardinals and
Depression-Era Baseball*
(McFarland, 2000)

FLEETER THAN BIRDS

The 1985 St. Louis Cardinals and Small Ball's Last Hurrah

by DOUG FELDMANN

McFarland & Company, Inc., Publishers
Jefferson, North Carolina, and London

Acknowledgments Those covering the Cardinals in 1985 for the *St. Louis Post-Dispatch*—especially John Sonderegger, Cardinals' beat writer Rick Hummel, and sports editor Kevin Horrigan—chronicled the team with great precision and flair. My thanks to them for giving colorful game accounts and behind-the-scenes stories, which added greatly to this book.

Library of Congress Cataloguing-in-Publication Data

Feldmann, Doug, 1970–
    Fleeter than birds : the 1985 St. Louis Cardinals and small ball's last hurrah / by Doug Feldmann.
      p.   cm.
    Includes index.
    ISBN 0-7864-1165-1 (softcover : 50# alkaline paper) ∞
    1. St. Louis Cardinals (Baseball team)—History.   I. Title.
GV875.S3F46   2002
796.357'64'0977866—dc21   2001007752

British Library cataloguing data are available

©2002 Doug Feldmann. All rights reserved

No part of this book may be reproduced or transmitted in any form or by any means, electronic or mechanical, including photocopying or recording, or by any information storage and retrieval system, without permission in writing from the publisher.

Front cover: Ozzie Smith after his game-winning home run in Game Five of the 1985 National League Championship Series *(From the collections of the St. Louis Mercantile Library at the University of Missouri–St. Louis)*

Manufactured in the United States of America

McFarland & Company, Inc., Publishers
   Box 611, Jefferson, North Carolina 28640
     www.mcfarlandpub.com

In cherished memory of Jerome

Table of Contents

Foreword (by Rick Horton)	1
Prologue	3
1. "Whiteyball"	5
2. The Rites of Spring: Not-So-Great Expectations	19
3. Out of the Starting Blocks	37
4. Illicit Activity	50
5. Heating Up the Turf	70
6. The Changing of the Guard	84
7. Labor Clashes and the Mid-Summer Classic	103
8. The Clock Strikes Midnight	116
9. It's Up to You, New York	131
10. "How Do You Like Us Now?"	148
11. A Collision on the Interstate	168
Epilogue	187
Appendix A: 1985 Final Standings	191
Appendix B: 1985 St. Louis Cardinals' Batting Statistics	193
Appendix C: 1985 St. Louis Cardinals' Pitching Statistics	194
Appendix D: 1985 St. Louis Cardinals' World Series Statistics	195
Appendix E: 1985 Kansas City Royals' World Series Statistics	197
Index	199

Foreword (by Rick Horton)

As spring training 2001 came to a close, I could sense the excitement about the upcoming season. Who will have breakout years? How will players respond from off-season operations? Most importantly to me, how will my beloved Cardinals fare in this new season? This excitement takes me back sixteen years ago to another spring filled with questions and uncertainties.

My experience with the 1985 Major League Baseball season is best summed up by Whitey Herzog's five-minute team meeting on Day One of spring training. After repeating his two very simple rules for the benefit of the new players, "Don't ever be late, and hustle at all times," the White Rat stated very directly that we were going to go to the World Series in 1985. He believed this in spite of the last-place predictions for the Redbirds by most sports publications. He went on to say that we were going to utilize a "bullpen by committee" to replace Bruce Sutter, who had signed with Atlanta during the off-season. As soon as his short meeting was over, Whitey came straight to me and informed me that I would be one of those relievers. I had been a starter throughout my young baseball life, including my rookie season in St. Louis the year before. I remember his words as if they were yesterday instead of 16 years ago: Whitey told me that by throwing strikes, fielding my position, and holding runners on, I could do a good job pitching regularly out of the bullpen. The best manager in baseball had informed me that we were headed to the World Series and I would play an important role on the team. I believed him. We believed him.

The story of that wonderful summer is chronicled in *Fleeter Than Birds*. Doug Feldmann's book captures the feel of the pennant race as it unfolded throughout the summer months of 1985, complete with player personalities, sportswriter's insights and fan excitement. As I read more and more, I remembered the great fever that swept St. Louis. Fans were wearing red everywhere; "What did the Mets do last night?"... "Coleman stole two more today!"... I will never forget the building murmur in the stands when Vince and Willie led off from first and second base. The nervous, unsettled pitcher, teammates on the edge of their seats, young fans itching to see yet another double steal. The running Redbirds have since been dethroned by the power Redbirds with a man named McGwire serving as king, but Cardinal fans of the 80s style of baseball can relive the great thrills of 1985 with Feldmann's work.

Reading the book was a great personal journey for me. It brought back the emotions of a memorable time in my life, and teammates and coaches who came together in a special way to do something great. The book offers a look into the life of our team leaders: Herr, McGee, Clark, Smith, and Forsch.

In this book, you can rediscover the excitement of big hits by Pendleton, Clark and Smith; the solid pitching of Tudor, Andujar and Cox; the genius of Herzog at filling in the pieces along the way. Reading about my great friends and Sunday night bridge partners Van Slyke, Dayley, Lawless, and Worrell brought me back to the original ties that bind.

Specific games and even pitches reminded me of the people I shared those moments with; reliving the ending of the '85 World Series was somewhat of a catharsis for me. As any Cardinal fan can tell you, we did not win the World Series in 1985, but I thank Doug for reminding me that it was indeed a magnificent run.

Prologue

I was a 15-year-old camper at the Mickey Owen Baseball School in Miller, Missouri, in the summer of 1985 when news broke of a possible strike by the Major League Baseball Players' Union. I had barely recovered from the lengthy stoppage in play from 1981, and I could not believe that it was happening again. There were two things I could always look forward to on my calendar: seeing my friends at the start of school in September, and seeing baseball return the following April. Major League Baseball had indeed *begun* its season in April 1985, but the thought of the schedule's being interrupted again was almost too much to bear. I commiserated with my fellow campers, including my closest buddies there — one from Tyler, Texas, one from Neosho, Missouri, and one from Chicago — about how there might be no more baseball on TV for the rest of the summer. We began our typical morning practice with an extra-long speech from the wise camp instructors, explaining to us that it was simply the state of the game in 1985 — that its very essence was changing right before our eyes. Afterwards, we got right to work with our morning jog and stretching exercises, while along the way we heard the coaches yell from a distance, "Always respect the game...."

Fifteen years later, after becoming a college coach and professional scout myself, I sometimes don't know what to tell young people about the *essence* of the game. Certainly, I tell them that it is a great game; the greatest of all. It rewards hard work. It blends teamwork with individual talent. It has a history that is rich and colorful. But as money continues to change the game — apparently for the worse — it seems, for some intangible reason, to have less purity about it that I can convey to younger players.

In a feeling shared by many my age and older, it breaks my heart to drive by the ball field of my hometown and see it empty on a perfect summer's day. After getting home from a couple of weeks at Mickey Owen, I couldn't wait to show my family and friends the new skills I had picked up, and I headed right to that ball field — which was *never* empty on a perfect summer's day.

Somewhere, I had lost part of the romantic quality of baseball with which I fell in love. Why was 15 such a pivotal moment in my baseball thinking? I believe it was a point at which I was teetering between childhood and adulthood, at least as far as baseball was concerned. I knew, back then, that I respected the game; 15 years later, I'm not sure that I *appreciated* it like I do now. While growing older has increased my bitterness about players' salaries, skyrocketing ticket prices, and prima donna superstars, it makes me love watching the intricacies of the game all the more. For as Branch Rickey once observed, "Man may penetrate the outer reaches of the universe, but for me, the ultimate human experience is to witness the flawless execution of the hit-and-run."

At 15, on the fence from the side of childhood and waiting to jump over to adulthood, I still saw good things from both angles. That summer of 1985, I particularly took note of a group of players from St. Louis. Not only were their skills exciting for a child to watch, but their appreciation of and respect for the game was something of which an adult could be proud. They exceeded everyone's expectations, and made the best out of what could have been a catastrophic summer for baseball.

Thinking about those players from St. Louis, I finished my morning jog at Mickey Owen, started stretching, and smiled to myself, knowing that everything was going to be okay.

Doug Feldmann

1

"Whiteyball"

When beer magnate August A. Busch, Jr., bought the St. Louis Cardinals in 1953, he possessed many of the same characteristics as his fellow owners in professional baseball. He had made his fortune in a business other than sports; he also called most of the people who worked for him by their last names. However, he also carried some of the newfound "personable" characteristics that some other owners had, such as Horace Stoneham of the Giants and Walter O'Malley of the Dodgers. He liked to mingle with the players and keep close track of the on-field happenings of the club. He knew in the back of his mind that baseball, and the Cardinals in particular, provided an outstanding market for his beer product. But he also became a true fan of the game, and with his money secure in other areas he did not fret about the bottom line that his ball club brought at the end of the season. He would host lots of parties for the club, with plenty of Budweiser and fun to go around.

What he could not buy, however, were players—and his fellow owners informed him of this fact as Busch thought he was going to purchase an instant winner in St. Louis. O'Malley initially wanted $600,000 to move Gil Hodges from the Dodgers to the Cardinals, and then backed off the deal anyway. A similar situation arose a few years later, when Busch thought that half a million dollars would get Ernie Banks away from the Chicago Cubs. "No sale," said Chicago owner Phil Wrigley.

Busch knew that a fine stadium would help propel the team to greater heights, and he went to work on that job shortly after he gained control. It is often left untold that the lowly Browns were the owners of the Sportsman's Park property, and the Cardinals were the renters. With the club drawing less than 100,000 during some seasons (particularly during the Great Depression), the Browns were often barely able to make payroll. As for the home field, Sportsman's Park was the only pasture in the big leagues on which two teams played, and the constant use wore out the field and the facilities twice as fast. The Browns never had much revenue from ticket sales, to be sure. At a Browns reunion dinner in 2000, former pitcher Ned Garver laughed when he noted, "Nice to see that there are about 150 people here at the dinner tonight. Too bad we couldn't have gotten 150 people to go to one of our games."

Though the Browns held the deed to old Sportsman's Park, their own lease on life was running out. The attraction of a new stadium in Baltimore was too appealing, and the Brownies left town as the club was sold to a syndicate on the East Coast. Baltimore was getting its first major league team since 1902, when the local franchise packed up and headed for New York. At that time, a seven-year-old by the name of George Herman Ruth was terrorizing the Baltimore streets.

Busch seized the opportunity, and purchased Sportsman's Park after the Browns vacated. He then pumped money into renovations that the Browns' owners could never afford, primarily seeking to shore up the decrepit locker rooms and to enhance the grandstand areas. He was denied by major league executives in his attempt to rename the place "Budweiser Park," for an alcoholic product in the title appeared uncouth to the league officers. Thus, Busch resigned to his own surname for the park, and the structure became known as "Busch Stadium" for the last 13 years of its existence.

Even with this major facelift for Sportsman's, Busch had his eye on the horizon — which included his vision of a glistening new downtown stadium to shine brightly in the distance. The Cardinals continued to labor through a fruitless decade in the '50s, with a high-water mark of second place under Fred Hutchinson in 1957 being the anomaly among mostly losing records.

Improvements to the on-field display were gradually made as well, and ground had already been broken on the new stadium when the Cards and Yankees were battling for baseball supremacy in the fall of 1964 at the former Sportsman's Park. Since 1946, fans in St. Louis were wondering if they would ever see another pennant in the Grand Dame of Grand Avenue, and their prayers were answered as the Cards nudged out the Phillies for the league crown, and then the Yankees in the World Series. While the Cardinals were capturing their last championship in the old ballpark, a public referendum had already been passed for the clearing of 30 acres of land by the downtown riverfront at the corner of Seventh and Spruce streets, and the historic First Shoveling took place on May 24, 1964. The huge, circular structure began to change the view around the Mississippi River bridges along with its sibling — the Gateway Arch — which went up simultaneously. They served as beacons of civic progress for those passing the downtown area.

It was a cold night two years later, when on May 12, 1966, the first game was played at the new palace. Home plate had been unearthed at the old Busch Stadium four days earlier by longtime head groundskeeper Bill Stockslek after the final game at Grand and Dodier, loaded into the cargo bin of a waiting helicopter behind second base, and transferred to the new ballpark. Those arriving at the new Busch Stadium received a commemorative "First Nighter" certificate and enjoyed a comeback victory by the Cardinals, overcoming a 3–2 deficit in the ninth inning and winning in the 12th on a single by Lou Brock.

The city of St. Louis was proud to show off its new riverside area to the rest of the nation, and of course Busch Stadium and the Arch were the jewels. As a fitting tribute to the revival, Busch was awarded the 1966 All-Star Game. With the exception of the Yankees in the 1964 World Series, American Leaguers had not ventured into St. Louis since the Browns left town before the 1954 season, and those in the Junior Circuit were re-introduced to the unique heat-and-humidity combination to be found only in St. Louis in July. As the first pitch was thrown at the '66 Mid-Summer Classic, the mercury had reached 115 degrees. Casey Stengel was serving as an honorary coach for the event, and of course everyone was interested in his thoughts on the new ballpark. After pausing to think a moment, Casey uttered, "Well, it sure holds the heat well."

Busch's love for his Cardinals was no more apparent than in the team's pennant-clinching contest at the end of the 1964 season. Announcer Harry Caray had left the broadcast booth to report the final inning from behind the Cardinal dugout. "Gussie" could be heard yelling behind Harry's shoulder, "Let's go! Get him out!" as the final putout was made.

Unfortunately, the labor strife that was beginning to develop in baseball started to wear on Busch. His love for the game and his team remained, but some bitter contract disputes — particularly with Steve Carlton and Curt Flood into the 1970s — caused Busch to begin to lose his original passion for the game and start applying his cold business tactics to the sport out of necessity. As the 1980s rolled around, he began to focus more on the balance sheet, while still seeking a knowledgeable baseball man to bring the Cardinals back to prominence. He found the sharp, down-to-earth mind that he wanted in Whitey Herzog.

Herzog had an uncommon respect for old-time baseball. He fondly recalled his school days in which he would skip lessons to play in a ballgame — or just see one. "The principal used to scold me for cutting class," it occurred to him, "but then he'd ask me the score and the details. I think he recognized a scholastic failure when he saw one." Growing up in nearby New Athens, Illinois, the route that Herzog took to the ballpark in St. Louis as a youngster was traced by legendary St. Louis sportswriter Bob Broeg.

"From New Athens, he'd coax rides to Belleville with coal-truck drivers. Next, he'd take an Edgewater Hills bus into St. Louis at the foot of the Eads Bridge for 15 cents. For another dime, he'd bus up Washington to Grand, then transfer north to Grand and Dodier."

Herzog was playfully loafing in the Ozarks, fishing and golfing, when he got the call from Busch in June of 1980. He was recently let go by the Kansas City Royals—basically for his inability to beat the New York Yankees in the American League playoffs. Herzog was replacing Cardinal icon Ken Boyer with St. Louis, and he relieved him in the middle of a doubleheader in Montreal.

Herzog had begun his coaching career with the Kansas City A's in 1965, and then moved on to the New York Mets the following season. After eight years, he joined the California Angels' staff for a couple of seasons before getting his first manager's job with the Texas Rangers in 1973. He was also named Manager of the Year in 1976 for leading the Royals to a first-place finish in the American League West with a 90–72 record.

Never before had Busch had a manager who was as frank with him as Whitey was; over a few Budweisers, Herzog was more than willing to point out what he felt to be the problems of the Cardinals, and what should be done to fix them. Oftentimes, heated words were exchanged between the two strong-willed men, but the honesty was beneficial while it was brutal, and Busch knew it. Red Schoendienst was elevated on August 28, with Herzog's consent, to finish out the 1980 season as field manager, allowing Whitey the flexibility to see other clubs and formulate possible trades in his other role as general manager. One of the reasons that Busch was advised to hire Herzog was because of the diversity of his experience; Whitey had worked as coach, minor league director of development, and other front office jobs for a variety of organizations. Herzog was comfortable making decisions to which he alone would have to answer.

"The only thing Gussie Busch asked of me," he recollected, "was that he be informed of deals before they hit the newspapers. That was it; nothing more. I had free reign to build the club as I saw fit. And if a player didn't want to do it the way I wanted him to, I'd just trade him." He began his employment by mounting his personal caricature of Stengel in his office, the same picture that hung where he worked in Kansas City. The flurry of moves then became so turbulent that Cardinal fans had to almost daily check the "Transaction" section of the sports page just to keep up.

1. "Whiteyball"

Nothing short of immediately, Herzog began to mold the team that he wanted. Schoendienst remembered that, within a week's time, Herzog had unloaded 13 players and acquired nine new ones. Red also did his part in setting the framework for the '80s, bringing up a little-known infielder named Tommy Herr to play shortstop. "I told Whitey I knew he was not a shortstop and was a second baseman," Schoendienst said, "but this way I could get him some playing time and see what he could do. Whitey was all in favor of the idea." Herr was considered a top basketball prospect coming out of high school, averaging 23 points per game in his senior season. He had been offered a basketball scholarship to Duke University, but the offer was pulled when the Blue Devils changed coaches. It was speculated that Herr was by-passed in the baseball draft because most teams thought that he would pursue basketball in college. He signed as a free agent with the Cardinals for $10,000.

In the winter meetings before the 1981 season, Herzog traded veteran third baseman Ken Reitz to the Chicago Cubs along with first baseman Leon Durham and third baseman Ty Waller for star reliever Bruce Sutter. Schoendienst pointed out that the Cubs wanted Herr instead of Reitz, but Herzog held firm and wouldn't make a deal involving Herr. It was thought that Sutter was going to pair with Rollie Fingers in the bullpen, as the veteran had just been acquired from the Padres. In a flash, however, Herzog packaged Fingers and long-time catcher Ted Simmons (whom Whitey wanted to move to first base under Simmons' protest) to Milwaukee. Simmons, Fingers, and pitcher Pete Vuckovich went to the Brewers for pitchers Dave Lapoint and "One-R" Lary Sorenson, along with outfielders Sixto Lezcano and David Green. Green was the raw talent that Herzog really wanted, and he envisioned the Nicaraguan as a future star.

Next, he added a couple of castoffs in catcher Darrell Porter from the Royals and pitcher Joaquin Andujar from the Houston Astros. Andujar, who was acquired for outfielder Tony Scott, announced to the press in St. Louis when he arrived in June of 1981 that the Cardinals had gotten "one tough Dominican." He finished the '81 season by making eight starts for the Cardinals, resulting in an impressive 6–1 record in St. Louis. The front office was surprised that the club could get Andujar, a promising young pitcher, so easily.

In another deal that Herzog considered a "steal," the Cardinals sent unspectacular pitchers Sorensen and Silvio Martinez to the Phillies for outfielder Lonnie Smith, who by 1980 after three years in the big leagues had finally allowed his incredible talents to take over. He had warp-zone speed and was an immediate fit in Herzog's plan for a cinder-tracked outfield. Offense was definitely the one-sided aspect to Smith's game, however, as noted by Porter. "You kind of held your breath when the ball went out there," Porter remembered about balls hit in Smith's direction. "He might fall on his face, or he might make a great play." Nonetheless, the Cardinals thought that the gifted Smith could improve defensively with time.

Then came the biggest move of all, as the flamboyant Garry Templeton was sent packing to the San Diego Padres for fellow shortstop Ozzie Smith. Herzog knew that Smith had the lesser offensive talent of the two, as Templeton was the first switch-hitter to get 100 hits from both sides of the plate in the same season. But Herzog believed that, along with being better defensively, Smith had better "make-up" than Templeton. He knew that Smith, who had a great work ethic, would play that style of ball that Whitey wanted. Templeton had first rubbed Herzog the wrong way by telling him that he didn't want to play day games after night games. Upon hearing this, Herzog wanted (at least privately) to get rid of Templeton immediately. He almost struck a deal with the Cubs, which would have sent Templeton to Chicago for shortstop Ivan DeJesus. Instead, DeJesus would be later shipped to Philadelphia for Larry Bowa and Ryne Sandberg, a deal that would improve the Cubs' fortunes later in the decade.

Jack Buck, the legendary radio announcer for the Cardinals, recalled the circumstances surrounding the Smith-Templeton swap. "It took him [Herzog] about three months to work the deal, and how he talked the Padres into it, I'll never know. Smith's agent had upset the Padres with some of his statements and actions, and the Padres thought a change of scenery would help Templeton become the player that everyone thought he should be. Luckily for the Cardinals, Smith was on a team owned by Ray Kroc, the founder of McDonald's, who knew how to make hamburgers and millions of dollars, but didn't know a lot about baseball.

"When Herzog pulled off the Templeton-for-Smith trade, I wonder if he knew he was getting a Hall of Fame player and the greatest defensive shortstop of all time. He was looking at the trade as more of addition by subtraction because he wanted to get rid of Templeton."

The new man in town was born Osborne Earl Smith on the day after Christmas, 1954, in Mobile, Alabama. He later found himself in California, playing his collegiate ball at Cal Poly–San Luis Obispo. Smith was selected in the fourth round by the Padres in the 1977 draft, and he immediately paid dividends as the runner-up for the 1978 National League Rookie of the Year Award to Bob Horner of the Atlanta Braves.

The Cardinals' final record of 59–43 in 1981 was the second-best mark in the National League that season, next to the Cincinnati Reds' ledger of 66–42, but ironically, both teams were excluded from postseason play because of the split-season emerging from the players' strike. As it turned

1. "Whiteyball"

out, it was a sum total of four second-place finishes for the two clubs. Nonetheless, it was obvious that the Busch-approved tinkering with the ball club by Herzog had begun to work, and with the '81 season in the books for St. Louis, Whitey hit the road to do more.

By 1982, the shift from power to speed in baseball was becoming all too apparent — and not just in St. Louis. Royals catcher John Wathan had set a major league record for catchers with 36 stolen bases. And coming off his sensational rookie campaign in 1981, outfielder Tim Raines of the Montreal Expos dispelled any notion of a sophomore jinx by swiping 78 bags. The Cardinals participated in this running frenzy, too, but Herzog wanted to start concentrating on his on-field duties and stop making deals. He turned over the job of general manager to Joe McDonald on April 10, 1982.

The 1982 season also saw the arrival of a new star on the north side of Chicago. Sandberg, thought to be a throw-in in the Bowa deal and seemingly destined for the minor leagues as Bowa's understudy, won the third base job and played sparkling defense in April despite enduring an 0-for-27 slump to start his tenure in a Cubs uniform. He broke out with two homers in one game and finished his rookie year with a respectable .271 average while also contributing 33 doubles and 32 stolen bases. With the acquisition of Ron Cey in 1983, Sandberg was asked to make the move to second base. That year, he became the first player in history to win a Gold Glove in his first season at the position. He followed up the feat in 1984 with not only a Gold Glove, but the National League Most Valuable Player Award as well, as the Cubs reached the postseason for the first time since the end of World War Two.

The Grand Plan for Busch's organization appeared to be ahead of schedule, as the Cardinals emerged out of a series at Philadelphia in September of '82 with the division lead. From there, they won eight in a row, which included five straight against the Mets at Shea Stadium in New York. The "Runnin' Redbirds" motored their way to St. Louis's first playoff appearance in 14 years.

The Milwaukee Brewers had beaten out the Baltimore Orioles in a tight 1982 American League race, and then disposed of the Angels in the American League Championship Series. Cecil Cooper singled home the tying and winning runs in the seventh inning of Game Three to complete a three-game sweep. Shortstop Robin Yount had been mired in relative obscurity in Milwaukee before his MVP season of 1982. Known as a quality player within the Wisconsin region, he finally gained overdue national prominence as the main cog in "Harvey's Wallbangers," the nickname given to the club led by manager Harvey Kuenn. It was also the season of his first Gold Glove award, as he was beginning to gain recognition for his fielding ability as well. The Brewers had brought Milwaukee the city's first pennant since the Braves' flag in 1958. They had pounded out 216 home runs, led by Gorman Thomas's 39 (which was the league high, shared by Reggie Jackson of the Angels). The offense was sparked by a young Paul Molitor, who in batting .302 for the year earned the nickname "Ignitor" for his penchant for starting rallies. He was driven around the bases by his mates to score a franchise-record 136 runs. The powerful Cooper added a .313 average, 32 home runs, and 121 runs batted in to the attack.

The Cardinals met the Braves in the National League Championship Series. Atlanta had begun the year with a record 13–0 start, led by a catcher-turned-centerfielder, Dale Murphy. Murphy won the National League MVP award by hitting .281 with 36 home runs and 109 RBIs. Despite the newfound celebrity status for Murphy, however, he denied most offers for product endorsements. He did agree to sponsor milk, however, because he said that it is "one thing that I actually use. I didn't want to put my name on stuff that wasn't in my house." Despite the prowess of Murphy, the Cardinals beat out Atlanta to bring a thirteenth pennant to the Gateway City. They then capped Herzog's magnificent ascension by beating the Brewers in seven games in the World Series, ending with Sutter's dramatic strike out of Thomas at Busch Stadium as St. Louisans rushed the field in a frenzy.

Herzog was not about to rest on the laurels of a championship; instead, he sought to make his club even better. Just when everyone thought he might have swiped the last stroke on his *Mona Lisa*, he made another move — and it rocked the Cardinal world. On June 15, 1983, he persuaded McDonald to unload popular first baseman Keith Hernandez to the Mets for pitchers Neil Allen and Rick Ownbey. It was obvious that Herzog was not afraid to ride the trade winds.

Countering this personality somewhat on the field, his greatest "smarts" perhaps came in knowing not to be too smart and make too many strategic moves. "Whitey had been in the game long enough to know that being a manager wasn't exactly brain surgery," Schoendienst once noted. "There were certain points in a game where decisions had to be made, but managing a club was kind of like cooking a steak. If you have good enough players, you won't be able to screw it up too easily. If you have a good enough piece of meat, you can hardly ruin the thing unless you burn it up."

Much like Schoendienst had been in his full-time stint as the Cardinals' manager in the late 1960s and 1970s, Herzog approached his job with a *laissez faire* policy towards his players. He allowed the team to discipline itself—after he had placed people on the roster that he felt capable of accomplishing that. The "kangaroo court" of his peers was the place where a player would have to answer charges, be it an unsuccessful sacrifice bunt or being late for the team bus to the airport. Herzog demanded only two things of his players: that they show up on time, and hustle all the time. He was, in a way, a shining reflection of Stengel, one of his teachers, for whom he coached while with the Mets in the 1960s. Like Stengel, Herzog looked to beat his opponents with daring and guile rather than with brute force.

Herzog knew that there were many ways to be successful in this complicated sport. "Hitting a baseball is a funny thing," he once observed. "If you can stand on your head and hit, that's the way to do it." Stan Musial, as an example, was ordered off-limits to Cardinal coaches by guru Branch Rickey when he came to the club in 1941. "He hits the ball hard—that's the bottom line—and he has his own style," Rickey said. "I don't want any coach fooling with that." The same "hands-off" theory can apply to pitchers, too, and Herzog knew that every trip to the mound involved taking a risk. "When the relief pitchers do the job, the manager is a smart son of a gun," he said. "When they don't, he's the dumbest guy in the world."

Buck noted that another impressive thing about Herzog was his ability to predict what would happen in a game three, four, or five innings in advance. "You have to be a step ahead of the game," one of Herzog's players said anonymously. "He knows what it takes to win. Some managers don't know that." Broeg, who has nearly seen it all with the Cardinals, was most impressed with Herzog. "Over the years, I thought the smartest, most articulate manager with whom I ever traveled was Eddie Stanky," Broeg would write during the 1985 season. "Whitey Herzog has the same smarts, and even better recall."

The team found some hard times again in '83 and '84, as the Phillies and Cubs won the division. Herzog was still looking for just the right mix.

As he built the club piece by piece, Herzog made sure that he had quality assistants alongside him. On the bench coaching with him in 1985 would be Schoendienst, Nick Leyva, Dave Ricketts, Johnny Lewis, Hal Lanier, and Mike Roarke. A backup catcher in the major leagues, Roarke had been the pitching coach at Pawtucket, the Triple-A affiliate of the Boston Red Sox in the International League, for the previous three seasons. From the start, he had a special sense in working with his charges. Pitchers sometimes do not like former catchers as their pitching coaches; it is believed by some that, to really know the feeling of being out on the mound, one needs to have experienced it himself.

But with Roarke, the Cardinals pitching staff found a former backstop that truly did understand all facets of the craft, the emotional and psychological as well as the physical. "The biggest thing about Mike," one of the Cardinal hurlers noticed, "is that he's able to adapt his philosophy to different pitchers." Others on the staff saw similar qualities. "Mike talks to you as a human being and a person, to start with," said one. "Once he is able to communicate and relate, he has the ability to understand that everyone throws differently. He's able to pick out two or three checkpoints with each pitcher. When he picks up those checkpoints, it keeps you doing the same thing all the time. There's more to pitching than just throwing the ball."

A star in both football and baseball at Boston College, Roarke passed up on an opportunity to play in the NFL. "I didn't want to have all those broken bones," he admitted. Even though Roarke had been a teammate of Herzog's with the Tigers in 1963, it was Roarke's work as the Cubs' pitching coach from 1978 to 1980 that impressed Herzog the most, and prompted Whitey to have him join the St. Louis organization.

When he was hired, Herzog smiled when he saw his new "office" at Busch Stadium, as the dimensions were certainly tailored to the type of game that he wanted to play — one of speed. The spacious park was 414 feet to straightaway center field, 383 feet to the power alleys, and 330 feet down the lines. This newer type of ballpark springing up everywhere was now dictating the type of play seen.

"Because of the Astroturf surfaces," Cubs manager Jim Frey claimed, "you need more outfield speed, and every team has two or three burners in the outfield who can fly. Where you once wanted big power hitters in right and left fields, you now have speedsters. They cut down on run production with their defense and don't provide as much batting punch."

In the early 1980s, a speed assault had indeed overcome the game, leaving behind the ponderous, lumbering, home run–thumping sluggers of the '70s. It was in 1982 that a young Oakland outfielder by the name of Rickey Henderson began an all-out demolition on the bases, stealing an incredible 130 bases and breaking his own American League record of an even 100 two years prior. The emergence of the running game mandated a shift in all facets of the sport; for perhaps the first time, it was no longer a concern that catchers be big-time run producers on offense, so long as they could throw people out on the basepaths. Hence, scouts scoured the amateur ranks looking for gifted receivers. Extra training was given to pitchers, both at the professional and amateur levels, in holding runners on base. Skill and practice in bunting was making its way back, too.

Artificial turf had found its way into many major league parks by the end of the 1970s, and managers were beginning to see the value in organizing their clubs around its use. Despite the fake grass being in great supply, purists in the baseball world hailed these things as a modern victory, a grassroots return to "little ball" where home runs and strikeouts were blasphemous and moving runners along inside the park took precedence. The mavericks who introduced the designated hitter to the American League in 1973 would begin eating crow, the purists predicted, as even the AL teams would be forced to conform to a National League game — one of manufacturing runs, utilizing your bench and bullpen wisely, and going home with wins and losses by the score of 2–1.

At the center of this revolution were Herzog and the Cardinals. He felt more at home in the National League, where Earl Weaver and his three-run homers were not needed to win games. Weaver, the longtime manager of the Orioles and one of the most successful skippers in history, abhorred the sacrifice bunt; he saw it as a "gift out" to the opposition, a wasted opportunity for another hit. Herzog, however, sought to bring the craft with him back to the Cardinals and turn it into a true offensive weapon — the "inside game," as it was called. Not only was he insisting that players up and down the lineup be quality bunters, but he was also seeking players quick enough to steal third on a fake bunt, have the bat control to execute the squeeze play flawlessly, and do whatever else to use his entire arsenal effectively in moving runners around the bases.

Back at the end of the strike-infested 1981 season, Herzog believed he had picked up a player for a cheap price who could do all those things.

On October 22, 1981, lefthanded pitcher Bob Sykes was sent packing to the Yankees. The 26-year-old Sykes had performed relatively well, sporting a 2–0 record for the Cardinals in 22 appearances in 1981. In return from the Yankees, St. Louis received a little-known outfielder named Willie McGee. Although McGee had hit .322 at the Double-A level in the Yankees' farm system the year before, they didn't think enough of him to keep him around after superstar Dave Winfield was locked up under a multi-year contract. "He has a chance to be a good player," Joe McDonald cautiously predicted upon McGee's arrival, using a line that had been uttered a thousand times by front office types in reference to a young player.

At first, it looked as if McGee would become a career bench player in St. Louis as well. Much more regard was given to Green, a 20-year-old who displayed awesome natural ability in all facets of the game and whose style of play was compared by some to Roberto Clemente. Green's misfortune with injury, however, would lead to opportunity for McGee while Green fell into greater personal depths. With an injury to Green in May 1982, the door to centerfield at Busch Stadium was opened to McGee and he charged through it. Green had pulled his hamstring in a 6–3 loss to the

Willie McGee, who in 1985 would emerge as an all-around superstar. *(From the collections of the St. Louis Mercantile Library at the University of Missouri–St. Louis)*

Atlanta Braves, and was only supposed to be out a couple of weeks. He turned out to be the second coming of Wally Pipp, however, as his center field position was lost forever.

McGee responded to the chance with a .296 average (best among National League rookies) with 24 stolen bases in 123 games, along with his show-stealing plays in Game Three of the World Series at Milwaukee. He took an extra-base hit away from Molitor in the first inning with a leaping catch, banged two home runs off Brewers starter Vuckovich, and then capped off the evening by robbing Thomas of a homer in the bottom of the ninth by leaping above the wall in center field at County Stadium. "Nobody ever played a better World Series game than Willie McGee did tonight," Herzog said afterwards. His performance during the regular season was good enough for a third-place finish in the National League Rookie of the Year voting.

"I was very fortunate," McGee recalled of his younger days in the big leagues while giving a magazine interview after his career was over. "Everybody that was before me taught me something. I mean, on our club we had Ozzie Smith, George Hendrick, Bruce Sutter, Bobby Forsch, Gene Tenace. Later, Jack Clark. All those guys were *professionals*. They had one goal and that was to be the best team they could be."

He grew up in the Bay Area of Califonia, born Willie Dean McGee on November 2, 1958, in San Francisco. The son of a Pentecostal church pastor and machinist at the Oakland Naval Yards, Willie grew up in a strict household where ball-playing was forbidden on the Sabbath. "They said it was a sin," McGee remembered of his parents' teachings about baseball played on Sundays. "But I never heard in the Bible where it was a sin." So, he found time to play the other six days of the week, and even sneaked out to the ball field on some Sundays too. He passed on a chance to sign with the Chicago White Sox after finishing high school in 1976, but instead chose to enroll at a local junior college. The Yankees signed him the next year, and he toiled awhile in their minor league system, seemingly stuck behind the outfield likes of Reggie Jackson, Lou Piniella, and Winfield in New York for hopes of a major league job.

He followed up his debut in 1982 with his first Gold Glove award and All-Star Game appearance in 1983. Then, in June of 1984, on a day in Chicago in which Herzog would call Sandberg's performance the "greatest I have ever seen," McGee hit for the cycle. He offensive feat, however, could not overcome Sandberg, as the second baseman hit two homers, the final one beating Sutter and the Cards in extra innings. And although the Cubbies were enjoying one of their few moments in the figurative sun, McGee and the Cardinals were putting the pieces back together for more pennant runs in future years.

The arrival in 1990 of Ray Lankford, a youngster with vast potential, seemed to spell the end for Willie in St. Louis. He was moved to right field to make room for the faster Lankford, and McGee was ultimately dealt to the A's in August of the same year.

His curtain call in the major leagues came on October 3, 1999, in the Cardinals' final regular season game against the Cubs at Busch Stadium. It was two weeks prior to the seventeenth anniversary of his Game Three heroics against the Brewers, and one month before his forty-first birthday. A world of change had happened to McGee and the Cardinals in those 17 years, but one thing remained: McGee's love for the game and dedication to his skills. He was found before the game hammering away at a batting tee beneath the stadium, resembling a rookie with something to prove. He would bat just once in the game, a pinch-hitting appearance in the fourth inning when he grounded into a double play. George Brett, the former Royals star and one of the greatest third basemen ever, once said that even with all his career hits, he wanted to ground out to second base in his final at-bat. Why? Brett wanted to run the play out to first base as hard as he could so that he could show his respect for the game. Willie McGee did the same thing, and the crowd of over 44,000 at Busch Stadium roared — easily the loudest cheer ever for a Cardinal hitting into a double play in the home park.

John Morris, another outfielder who had arrived to the Cardinals' organization from the Royals in May 1985, had developed a pretty accurate re-creation of Willie's batting mannerisms. Speaking at the St. Louis Baseball Forecast Luncheon at the Regal Riverfront Hotel in January 2000, Morris invited the audience to stand up. "Okay," he began, "we're all now going to do an imitation of Willie McGee at the plate, so put down your drinks. First, holding an imaginary bat in one hand, hunch yourself over like an "S" and scrape your feet along the ground — that's Willie walking to the plate. Next, shake your head back and forth by trying to touch each of your ears to your shoulders. Then, you need to take your helmet off, with your head all nice and loose now, and scratch the side of your head vigorously with several strokes. Next, reach down and grab some dirt to run in your hands. Finally, you need bend your knees way low and wiggle your butt like this...."

Morris had the crowd in stitches, but it wasn't necessarily fictional humor — rather, a fairly accurate characterization of his old friend. McGee certainly did have an unorthodox playing style. As he "scraped" his feet to the plate to take his turn at bat, many compared him to former outfielder Mickey Rivers, who nearly hobbled like an old man as he approached the batters' box. Once contact was made with the ball, however, the hobbling stopped, and McGee shot like a startled hare towards first, the rest of his body barely keeping up with his lightning feet. Although he handled the bat successfully, McGee prompted Herzog to say lovingly that "he hit more five-hoppers and rug-burners with that goofball swing than anybody I ever saw."

McGee's whole physiology was something of an enigma. Despite being a right-handed thrower of a baseball, he wrote with his left hand — much to the curiosity of the thousands of autograph hounds he obliged over the years. "He was very strong in the hands," recalled Herzog much later, showing his knack for noticing the most minute qualities in a ballplayer. "Very strong hand power. Even to this day, if he had learned the strike zone a little better, and only swung at strikes, Willie might have hit .400."

Hub Kittle, a coach with the Cardinals in the early 1980s, summed it up. "If I ever had to pick a big-league ballplayer and say, 'This is what they should be,' it's Willie McGee."

"He's everything that's good about baseball," added his impersonator, John Morris.

2

The Rites of Spring: Not-So-Great Expectations

When the 1985 preseason baseball publications hit the newsstands, most expected the Cardinals to make hardly any noise at all. Both *Sport* magazine and *The Sporting News* picked the Redbirds to finish last in the National League East, as many national writers believed that the Cardinals had not yet completely re-tooled from the hangover of their '82 World Series winner. In the Herzog spirit, more moves had been made during the off-season, but the consensus was that Cardinals were only treading water. Herzog was somewhat bothered by the fact that Fred Kuhlmann, the executive vice president of the ball club, and Lou Susman, a member of the board of directors, had been given more authority by Busch to make deals. When Kuhlmann was given his position on November 5, 1984, some thought it marked another turning point in the comprehensive, overall shaping of the ball club. Kuhlmann, a graduate of the Washington University School of Law in St. Louis (as well as the Columbia University School of Law), served as general counsel for the Anheuser-Busch Brewery before joining the Cardinals' board of directors in 1967.

One deal made before the 1985 season, in fact, did not seem to have the Herzog stamp on it. It was made by general manager Dal Maxvill— who had replaced Joe McDonald in that role on February 25 — but it nonetheless filled a gaping hole that the team had been lacking for some time. The 46-year-old Maxvill was a native of Granite City, Illinois, just across the river from St. Louis. He had enjoyed a 14-year major league career as a player, 11 of which were spent with the Cardinals. After retiring, he spent a few years in private business before joining the coaching staff of the Mets in 1978. He then spent a few years with the Cardinals before becoming third base coach with the Braves in their division-winning year of 1982. Over on the West Coast was a power hitter that Maxvill liked, and he got him.

Newly-acquired first baseman Jack Clark predicted that he should be able to "drive in 130 runs and score 100 runs this year" for the Cardinals. A knee injury had limited him to only 203 at-bats with the Giants in '84, but he did manage to hit .320 and sock 11 home runs. He was most happy to leave San Francisco for St. Louis.

"The Giants never seemed to know what direction they were going in," he revealed as preliminary workouts in February 1985 got going. "It got to the point where you were almost playing for yourself. 'We're not going to win anyway,' you'd say. The lack of winning made it all not exactly worthless, but the competitiveness wasn't there, the drive wasn't there to win." As the 1985 season would unfold, things would get progressively worse for the Giants, including a legal dispute with the City of San Francisco over the failure of the team to pay the utility bills at Candlestick Park. Despite the Giants' denial, the city claimed that the club was in arrears of more than $100,000 on interest due for the charges.

Clark was also fighting his way out of bankruptcy, a total of $800,000 that he was in debt because of poor investment advice from others. "I learned the hard way," Clark admitted. "Players don't know. These agents talk so fast and they have all these deals that are guaranteed to do this and that and it's just not so." He was content to have two fresh starts for his life in St. Louis—one in baseball, and one in his financial portfolio.

In getting Clark, the Cardinals had sent Gary Rajsich, Jose Uribe, Green, and LaPoint to the Giants. The Cards had discovered that Green was not going to be effective at first base, despite his offensive capabilities, and San Francisco was ready to take a chance on his troubled past. Green had been battling alcohol problems, but was nonetheless regarded as a great talent—even still by Herzog. "I used to think Tempy (Garry Templeton), when I first got here, was the best," Whitey mentioned in recalling his most gifted players. "But David Green had the most all-around talent."

It was clear that Clark was not going to miss the Giants, but were the Giants going to miss Clark? Not particularly, according to San Francisco manager Jim Davenport. "Jack Clark's an outstanding ballplayer, no question about it," he said. "But we did not trade one-for-one. We got four boys who can help us now and for years to come."

Clark was a very important piece to the puzzle. He provided a power source in the middle of the order that, otherwise, would have been noticeably absent. "Even if the goal of your team is speed and defense," Schoendienst said, "you have to have a guy who is capable of hitting home runs.

2. The Rites of Spring: Not-So-Great Expectations

Jack Clark looks forward to a big year with the Cardinals in spring training, 1985. Behind him is Ozzie Smith. *(From the collections of the St. Louis Mercantile Library at the University of Missouri–St. Louis)*

It may not be 'sit on your heels and wait for a three-run homer' kind of offense, but still your lineup needs to have a power threat in it, and the Cardinals finally got that with Clark." He was bringing a career average of .277, along with 163 homers and 595 RBIs into his first season in St. Louis. Few around baseball, however, seemed to pay much attention to the trade.

Nor was much racket made when the Cards acquired a left-handed pitcher from Pittsburgh on December 12, 1984. In exchange for outfielder George Hendrick, who had been one of the few power sources left in the lineup before the Clark deal was done, the Cardinals received pitcher John Tudor and utility man Brian Harper. Herzog was confident that Tudor would be a very effective pitcher in the National League, especially with the improved defense that he would have behind him at shortstop, second base, and center field.

"When I saw Tudor pitch last year," Herzog noted, "I was very impressed with the way he could change speeds. That was the first time I had seen him pitch. He pitched in Fenway Park, which is a tough place for left-handers. He won with losing clubs and learned how to pitch in a park like Boston's. Right now, I consider him the best left-hander in baseball." Tudor was born in Schenectady, New York, but grew up outside of Boston in the town of Peabody, Massachusetts. After playing at a junior college, he finished his collegiate career at Georgia Southern while earning a degree in criminal justice.

In training camp with the Cardinals in 1985 was a speedy young outfielder named Vince Coleman, who two years before had shattered Henderson's modern professional baseball record with 145 stolen bases at Class-A Macon of the South Atlantic League. The Jacksonville, Florida, native was originally drafted by the Philadelphia Phillies in the 20th round in 1981, but he wanted to return for his final year of college to play football and pursue his dream of playing in the NFL. "If they had given me the amount of money I wanted, I would have signed," Coleman said in looking back. "But I wanted no less than $50,000." As turned out, he inked with the Cardinals for only $5,000 as a tenth-round pick in '82, after a tryout with the Washington Redskins fell through. He had been a star runner and receiver at Florida A&M University, where he broke his cousin Greg Coleman's kicking records — the same cousin Greg who was the punter for the Minnesota Vikings.

As the first couple of weeks of spring training got going, fans were peeking to see signs of the old Cardinal toughness. From Rogers Hornsby in the twenties through the Gas House Gang in the thirties, through Stan Musial, Mike Shannon, Lou Brock, and into the seventies and eighties, the Cardinals were rarely out-hustled, and rarer yet were they intimidated by umpires. In this sentiment, no one ever questioned if Lonnie Smith was a competitor. He lit the fires of the Cardinals' offensive outbursts necessary to claim the '82 World Championship, and no one ever tried to quell that energy. However, that energy got him into trouble on March 21.

American League umpire Larry Young was working the Cardinals' game with the Red Sox that day, and he enraged the St. Louis outfielder when he claimed Lonnie trapped a ball that Smith believed he caught. It occurred in the seventh inning, and for the remaining frames, Smith and Young jawed at each other every time Smith would take and leave the field. Finally, as Smith assumed his position in the bottom of the ninth, he went over to Young again, now more infuriated than ever. "He laughed at me and tried to intimidate me," Smith claimed after the game. "I said, 'Don't bother me — and take this with you,'" as he described himself offering Young one of the fingers on his hand. Sensing violence, home plate umpire

2. The Rites of Spring: Not-So-Great Expectations 23

Dave Pallone restrained Smith, upon which the latter wrestled Pallone to the ground. Other players finally intervened, and the matter was left for the commissioner's office to decide the penalties. When the statements were filed, and all parties had a chance to have their say, Smith was distraught again. "Only Bob Davidson's report [another umpire on the job that day] was true. The other guys [Young and Pallone] are lying through their teeth. I think they [the commissioner's office] are trying to get everyone's side of the story. Maybe they want to see if guys change their stories."

It was a promising spring, like spring was every year for baseball fans. As poet Donald Hall had put it, "Spring, with all things green, was the hope of the earth; and baseball has that same hope." Furthermore, baseball seemed to be undergoing a renaissance in the mid–1980s, with a lot of young stars such as Dwight Gooden, Kirby Puckett, and Wade Boggs arriving on the scene. Crowds at big league ball parks were growing, and larger television contracts appeared to be spreading plenty of money around for everyone to share.

But just as the nightmares of the 1981 strike appeared to be well behind the baseball world, a chilling storm lurked on the horizon. There was no new labor agreement, and work stoppage threatened to occur at some point during the 1985 season. Most people in the game, though, appeared unconcerned. "Alarm at this point would be premature," Cardinals' player representative Tommy Herr said on March 23rd. "That being said, there is still not a whole lot of progress so far. Progress could be compared to an anthill."

Part of the dispute between the players and owners was the distribution of the newfound wealth in television revenue, which would approach nearly $225 million for the 1985 season. Another topic on the table was players' union proposal of upping the minimum major league salary to $70,000 from the existing $40,000. "The only thing that bothers me is that the players are always regarded as the bad guys," Herr continued. "That's a calculated thing on [the] ownership's part. I think that if people had a true picture, they would think different. The assertions that the owners are losing all of that money and forecasting losses of $150 million are not true. There's all kinds of ways to show a paper loss, but it's not really a cash loss."

After the owners hired New York University accounting professor George Sorter to tap out the numbers, the actual deficit was officially listed at $31 million. Then, the players hired their own economist to examine the books—Stanford University professor Roger Noll. In reality, it was certainly worse for the smaller-market teams, such as Kansas City. "We're hopeful," said Royals co-owner Ewing Kauffman. "If we draw 1.8 million, we'll only lose $1.5 million."

Meanwhile, the Cardinals attempted to stay focused on the business of getting better as a ball club, as they beat the Royals 5–3. A certain outfielder was the hitting star, with a double and a single, as "Lonnie Smith made news with his bat Friday [March 23rd] and not with his mouth," according to *St. Louis Post-Dispatch* writer Rick Hummel.

The following day, catcher Mike Lavalliere became the first roster casualty of the spring as he was re-assigned to the Cardinals' minor league camp. He had broken in with the Phillies in 1984 and was struggling with his defensive work behind the plate. He had a knee problem that forced his release from Philadelphia, but made a mark for a possible future return to the Cardinals. "I just wanted a place where I'd have a chance to play," Lavalliere noted. "The Phillies figured me as a backup at every level." He added one compliment to the Cardinals' professionalism displayed at their training camp. "There's a different kind of atmosphere here than in Philly. It's like there are more underdogs here. Nobody acts like a star, and they make you feel comfortable."

The day after Lavalliere's release, the Cardinals let go of another catcher — Glenn Brummer. Brummer was best known for his steal of home off the Giants' Gary Lavelle to win a game at Busch Stadium on August 22, 1982 (a quintessential Herzog moment ... the steal of home by a back-up catcher to win a game in extra innings). Now, just over two years later, it appeared that the Cardinals were going to go with Porter and youngster Tom Nieto behind the plate, the latter showing promise by hitting .279 in 33 games as a rookie in 1984. Some viewed these moves as risky, with Porter only batting .188 when Lavalliere and Brummer were let go. Brummer was understanding, although disappointed, about his release. "I've taken it pretty well," he said. "There's nothing I can do.... It's one part of baseball you don't like to talk about. It happens every day to other people."

Even though there was tough news for some people behind the plate, good tidings came from out on the pitching mound. Veteran Bob Forsch was able to throw without pain in his right elbow for the first time the next day. He had been working on a forkball to diversify his attack, and was looking for a level of consistency with all his pitches that because of injury was slow in coming. Forsch was the ultimate team player on the Cardinals, and he believed, even after a seasoned 11-year career, that he didn't have his job made. "I'll probably have to pitch better than I've pitched so far to be on the team," he imagined. Herzog was predicting — even with Forsch's sore arm — that this was the best starting pitching staff he had to date in his tenure with the Cardinals. "If he comes back," Herzog speculated,

2. The Rites of Spring: Not-So-Great Expectations

"Forschie will be our number five starter. Every other year here, he was always our number one or number two."

Forsch had been the mainstay of the Cardinals' staff for many years. He had been selected in the 38th round of the June 1968 draft by St. Louis, and then broke into the big leagues as a 24-year-old rookie in 1974. He went on to do something no other Cardinal pitcher has ever done — throw two no-hitters in his career, which came in 1978 and 1983. His brother, Ken, added another "no-no" to the family's total in 1979 against the Braves as a member of the Houston Astros. Bob took over as the Cardinals' ace his second year, beginning a ledger of pitching endurance that few have matched in St. Louis lore. He threw 215 or more innings in every season from 1975 through 1982 with the exception of two — one being the strike-shortened season of 1981.

The decision on how many pitchers to keep on the roster — 10 or 11 — was becoming increasingly difficult for Herzog. This was mainly because the Lonnie Smith/Larry Young situation had yet to be resolved, and Herzog didn't know if Smith would be available on Opening Day. Inconsistency in the bullpen during spring training had not made his decisions any easier; he was particularly disappointed in the performance of Ownbey, who was nursing a sore hamstring for the second spring in a row. And as in the previous March, Ownbey was sent back to the minors. After two so-so years with the Mets in 1982 and 1983, Ownbey appeared in only four games for the Cardinals in 1984, all of them starts — and three of them losses.

From the beginning, pitcher Danny Cox was able to list some notable moments on his resume. In his very first major league start in 1983, he was matched up against the legendary Steve Carlton of the Phillies. He dueled with the great lefthander for ten shutout innings before leaving the game. In addition, it was Pete Rose who earlier in the year had nicked Cox for the first major league hit he allowed. His stellar performance in that game gave the Cardinal organization a taste of his potential. Later that season, he would get his first big league win against another legend, Nolan Ryan.

Unfortunately, a sore shoulder would cause the record for his rookie year to finish at a disappointing 3–6, and he was sent to Louisville to begin the 1984 season. "He wasn't mature enough to remember that he had three pitches," Herzog said when the demotion took place. He was referring to Cox's tendency to rely mostly on his fastball. After a 4–1 start in Triple-A, he returned to the Cardinals to make 13 starts and go 6–3 for the parent club in 1984. With such a strong second year, he looked to join the starting rotation on a permanent basis in 1985.

Danny Cox. *(From the collections of the St. Louis Mercantile Library at the University of Missouri–St. Louis)*

Cox issued an imposing stance on the mound, with a 6' 4" frame carrying 230 pounds. He was a "military brat," visiting nearly the entire world during his childhood. His father was an Air Force master sergeant, and the family stops had included Germany, England, Texas, Washington, Georgia, and Colorado, among others. He and Kurt Kepshire, another young pitcher seeking to crack the starting staff, had gained the nickname of the "Possum Brothers" by team trainer Gene Gieselmann because of their nocturnal lifestyles. Kepshire soon became a fishing buddy of Cox, and the pair often rented a private lake near Union, Missouri, to relax and catch some bass. To relax further, they sometimes cleaned, cooked, and ate the bass on location as well.

The bullpen had seemed to come crashing down the previous December, when Sutter, who may have been the first true "closer" in history, signed a six-year, $10 million free agent contract with the Atlanta Braves. The previous season, he had tied the major league record for saves in a season with 45, and logged an impressive 1.54 ERA. "I'd like to get 300 [career] saves and get into another World Series," Sutter said when he joined his new club. "Definitely, I'm with a team that has a chance to do that."

In revealing other factors involved in the situation, Sutter eventually came clean. "The money's there," he said wryly. "I'd be a fool not to take it."

After the Sutter bombshell was dropped, Maxvill, Kuhlmann, Herzog, and others scrambled to assemble new parts in the bullpen. "My whole

2. The Rites of Spring: Not-So-Great Expectations 27

team was the preliminary act to Bruce Sutter's show stopper, and the whole world knew it," Herzog admitted. Jeff Lahti was having upper body problems, fighting a stiff neck and shoulder which hampered his delivery well into March. Lahti, a hard-throwing right-hander, was acquired on April 1, 1982, from Cincinnati in one of Herzog's last moves as general manager. It was hoped that Allen would also emerge as a force in relief. Contributions were sought from left-handers Ken Dayley and Rick Horton, too. Dayley was acquired along with first baseman Mike Jorgensen in June of '84 for third baseman Ken Oberkfell. Dayley had been the number-one draft pick of the Braves back in 1980, but never seemed to be able to find a home in Atlanta as he spent the majority of his time at their Class AAA team at Richmond. Horton was a fourth-round pick of the Cardinals in 1980, and 1985 would be his second big league season.

Interestingly, Dayley and Lahti had played against one another in high school and college while in Oregon, with Dayley hailing from Dalles and the University of Portland, and Lahti from Hood River and Portland State University. "It's a little bit of home away from home," Lahti said about having Dayley around. "It's really fun."

Jorgensen's career had a tough detour left in its wake, as he was hit on the head by a pitch from Andy Hassler while playing for the Texas Rangers in 1979. Three days after the incident, doctors found a blood clot on his brain. "My wife thought I was dead," Jorgensen remembered. "I knew it was bad when I tried driving home and it felt like the wheels were falling off." The incident almost ended his playing days, but he found the courage and strength to come back.

To help handle the pitchers, a new catching prospect had arrived on the scene in the 24-year-old Nieto. With his experience as

Ken Dayley shows the form that made him a force out of the Cardinals' bullpen. *(From the collections of the St. Louis Mercantile Library at the University of Missouri–St. Louis)*

a back-up in 1984 with the Cardinals, he seemed poised now to challenge for more playing time. When the Cardinals signed him, they knew that they were getting a solid defensive man behind the plate; his improving bat had been the biggest surprise in recent seasons, though, as he posted two .270-plus seasons at Louisville in '83 and part of '84. "You've got to give him credit," Herzog said. "He's worked like hell and improved with the bat over the years. I know Tommy can do the job defensively." And Nieto was indeed grateful to be with the Cardinals. "I have a lot of fun playing baseball, and it's a lot more fun playing in St. Louis than anywhere in the minor leagues." And although the plan was for Nieto to play against the left-handed pitchers and Porter the righties, it was the consensus of the Cardinals' brass that Nieto would be the everyday catcher at some point.

Meanwhile, the Mets and their newfound star, Gooden, looked like they had no pitching problems whatsoever. On March 26, Gooden fired five dominating innings against the Red Sox, striking out nine (including the first five hitters he faced) and allowing only three hits. In just his second season, the young man who would not turn 21 until after the 1985 season was already hailed as an early favorite for the Cy Young award.

Where was the toughest place to play in the National League, at least for the Mets? That was easy—according to New York pitcher Ron Darling. It was the Cubs' home park. "It's ten times tougher for us to play in Wrigley Field," he revealed. "The fans there are very hostile. In what other stadium do fans yell, 'Throw it back,' when an opposing player hits it out during batting practice? In other places, like San Diego, they say, 'Oh, can't we have a ball, please?' In Montreal, they all yell things you can't understand. In Chicago, they throw frisbees at our heads when we're running in the outfield."

Added utility player Danny Heep, "One of them told me that my family had been abducted by the Shi'ites."

And the gritty little Lenny Dykstra, who truly could look the part, said that "They kept asking me if I was on a high school field trip." Finally, Clint Hurdle revealed that he got the most biting blurb of all. "Hey Hurdle," he repeated, "your wife had the baby. It's a boy and he's a bum, too."

Elsewhere, the other news in the National League East was the fight over the shortstop position in Chicago. Bowa was the incumbent, and despite his holding the career record for fielding percentage by a shortstop, was viewed as the weak link in the Cubs' offensive chain. He was being challenged by young Shawon Dunston, an exciting, free-swinging, strong-armed player who supposedly had hit .790 his senior year at Jefferson High School in New York City (this figure was listed, although most high school

2. The Rites of Spring: Not-So-Great Expectations

sports statistics, especially batting averages in baseball, are often unreliable *and* misleading). Dunston was 22 years old and Bowa was 39, so it appeared to the Cubs management to be the right time for a change. "I think Dunston can be an outstanding player," predicted Frey, "because he's a hitter at a defensive position." He had hit only .233 at Triple-A Iowa in 1984, however, and this caused some concern for the Cubs. And during spring training of '85, he was struggling to make the .200 mark. But the skills that made him the number-one overall pick in the 1982 amateur draft were apparent, and it was equally apparent as time wore on that Bowa was on his way out. Toward the end of March, the Cubs called the Angels and offered Bowa for another veteran, left-handed pitcher Tommy John. The Angels refused the deal.

It was nearly the end of March before the Cardinals were able to kick their vaunted running game into high gear. After stealing just nine bases in the previous 11 exhibition games, the Redbirds stole five on March 27, four of them on double-steals. "That was exciting today," Ozzie Smith admitted. "That's the way we're going to have to play if we're going to win." And Coleman, opening more eyes every day, scored from first on a hit-and-run single off the bat of Andy Van Slyke. Herzog already had a good reference on Coleman from a learned Cardinal family member: "George Kissell [player development coordinator for the Cardinals] has helped with most of the young Cardinal players for over 40 years, and he said that Coleman works harder than any player he has handled. Now, that's a great compliment."

A disappointment in the spring had been the play of Terry Pendleton — a disappointment to himself, if nobody else. "You're my third baseman even if you hit .220. Stop worrying," Herzog told him. The problem was that Pendleton wasn't hitting even half that by the end of March; he had a paltry .107 mark. He had been a seventh-round draft pick by the Cardinals in 1982 from Oxnard, California. He rose through the system quickly, reaching the big leagues in just two-and-a-half years. When he was called up to the Cardinals in mid-summer 1984, he soon earned a National League Player of the Week award in early August by hitting .444.

Meanwhile, Herzog was pondering another decision — where to bat Tommy Herr in the lineup. Herzog issued a challenge to Herr, saying that if he could prove that he could steal bases consistently, that Herzog would bat him second. "Second is my best spot," Herr concurred, "but we've got about six lead-off hitters here." With a three-steal performance (including one of third base), and a three-hit performance as well (to raise his spring training average to .351) on March 28, a deal appeared to have been struck between the two men. However, unforeseen changes in the roster would alter the strategy in the coming weeks, and Herr would be moved to yet another spot in the lineup.

There had been talk over the winter of trading Herr, who had become disgruntled in his contract negotiations with the club. The most intriguing call to the Cardinals came from the Orioles, from whom the Cardinals wanted left-handed pitcher Mike Flanagan. Baltimore did not want to make the move, however. The Orioles' pitching staff was being held together by Flanagan and right-hander Dennis Martinez, the latter of whom was trying to hold his own life together. "I can't help rooting for him after all he's been through, and I just don't mean the drinking," his pitching coach Ray Miller admired. "He was trying to pitch here with a civil war going on in his country (Nicaragua). His father died in an automobile accident, the rest of his family had to go to war, and he was trying to keep his mind on pitching in Baltimore."

Roster judgments to be made about reserve players were gradually becoming clearer as March neared its end. Tito Landrum, who led Cardinal pinch-hitters with a .391 average in 1984, was rewarded with a three-year contract to cement his spot. Between Landrum and Steve Braun, St. Louis looked like they would have a solid right-handed/left-handed combination of bats off the bench, with Landrum also facing a good share of the left-handed pitching if Van Slyke was moved permanently to the outfield from third base, which looked more probable each day. Landrum had signed with the Cardinals in 1972 after playing at Eastern Oklahoma State Junior College. He was born in Joplin, Missouri, but spent time in New Mexico and other places due to being in a military family, like Cox. He was traded to the Orioles in 1983, and then went back to the Cardinals the following year — both times for the same player, Floyd Rayford. In late 1983, his home run in extra innings against the Chicago White Sox won Game Four of the American League Championship Series, and sent the Orioles into the World Series.

Then there was a cruel joke, Cardinals fans thought, when on April Fools' Day newspapers reported that the club was considering the possibility of trading Ozzie Smith. There was nothing funny about it, however, as contract negotiations between Smith and Kuhlmann and Susman had broken down. "I think obviously if we can't sign him, that there's got to be some thought about trading him," conceded Kuhlmann. A couple of days later, it was confirmed that the club had received offers for Smith from other teams. When asked by reporters how many inquiries there actually were, Maxvill responded by saying, "More than two, and less than 25."

Fears around Cardinal territory increased the following day when

2. The Rites of Spring: Not-So-Great Expectations 31

Maxvill made a move in acquiring infield prospect Jose Oquendo from the Mets, along with pitcher Mark Davis, for pitcher John Young and infielder Argenis Salazar. Oquendo had always been highly regarded by Maxvill and Herzog, despite performing unspectacularly in his first two seasons in New York. He had not hit above .222 in the big leagues, but Herzog wasn't concerned. "I'm sure you know we didn't get him for his bat," Whitey quickly pointed out after the deal. "I haven't seen him play any play badly in the field." Reports quickly surfaced that the Cardinals and Smith were at least $800,000 apart in a variety of money issues (Smith was currently under a three-year deal worth $3.6 million), and dealing the "Wizard" now looked imminent. The primary suitors appeared to be the Yankees, Mets, Pittsburgh Pirates, and the Los Angeles Dodgers. "I read in the paper that they might trade Ozzie Smith," Oquendo said when arriving at the Cardinals' camp. "I hope this means I get a chance."

Over at the Reds' training camp in Tampa, there was concern about another legendary player. Pete Rose, the Cincinnati player-manager who was closing in on Ty Cobb's all-time hit record, had hardly penciled himself in the lineup at all during the spring. He brushed off questions about his health by claiming that he simply wanted time to observe other players, particularly the rookies. "What's wrong? Do I look bad at the plate?" Rose challenged the writers who asked his reasons for not playing much. "Yeah, I'm ready. I'm going to play every day this week." Rose, who would turn 44 in April, was only 94 hits away from Cobb's magical mark, as soothsayers around the country began predicting the date during the summer that it would happen. "I'm not going to worry about the record until I'm close enough that I can break it that day," the man they called "Charlie Hustle" pointed out. "No one has ever gone 95-for-95 in a game."

Rose also claimed that his newfound role of player-manager with the Reds wouldn't affect his game, as it was the writers—not him—who were making a daily issue of the mark. "I get accused of talking about records," he continued. "But it's the guys who interview me who ask about them. They also say ball players don't have as much fun as they used to 25 years ago. I do.

"I don't find it tough doing anything, playing or managing. I just try to keep it as simple as I can. I get to the ball park early, just as I did when I was just playing. In spring training, I always had breakfast at a quarter to eight, and then went to work. When we have a night game, I'm in the ball park at two o'clock in the afternoon. It's fun. You're in trouble if you don't like going to the ball park."

Reds' catcher Alan Knicely was honored to have him around. "The whole attitude of the team is Pete Rose," Knicely asserted. "For me to see him playing in the field and give his all and also managing is an inspiration." Added veteran Dave Parker, "Pete Rose is a walking ball of enthusiasm. Everybody wants to play for him."

What was the driving force for Rose, now in his 23rd major league season? A friend asked that question while riding in a car with him. "Pride," Rose simply responded, as the friend waited for an elaboration on the response. None came.

Another Pete Rose was in camp with the Reds, too—15-year-old Pete Jr., who was starting to play the game at Oak Hills High School in Cincinnati. Manager Dad allowed the boy to take some intra-squad game swings with the major leaguers. "He stands almost five-feet-eleven and weighs a nickel over 150, but there's no pending sense of great growth or bulging muscles, no sign of tremendous speed," the Associated Press noticed.

Reds owner Marge Schott was making her expectations clear for new Executive Vice President Bill Bergesch. "If it goes wrong, he'll be the one to blame," she told a Cincinnati writer. "He promised me a World Series ring. You know how women react when they don't get what they want."

Another place where rumors were flying was the Phillies' camp in Clearwater, where the whispers had star third baseman Mike Schmidt headed to the Dodgers for possibly seven players, including their hard-throwing new reliever, Tom Niedenfuer. Schmidt, however, said that no such deal would occur. How much would it take to get him to the West Coast? "Some Dodger-blue sweatbands, about $40 million or $50 million and a backup role in a Clint Eastwood movie," the slugger said.

And over in Lakeland at the Tigers' camp, leg spasms were causing manager Sparky Anderson so much pain that he was afraid he would miss his first Opening Day since 1970. That was about all that was concerning Detroit, however, as the defending champion Tigers looked like the team to beat again in '85. They had gotten off to a torrid 35–5 start in 1984, which included a no-hitter by Jack Morris the first week of the season against the Chicago White Sox. The Tigers never looked back, as they became only the fourth team in baseball history to start the season in first place and remain there every day of the year, ultimately winning the American League East by 15 games. They finished the campaign by demolishing the Royals and Padres in the postseason. The Royals missed their top star, Brett, for part of the '84 season with an injury. They were looking forward to his making more of a difference in 1985, and make a difference he would.

Before heading north, Herzog was contemplating a position switch with Clark and Van Slyke, with Clark going to first base despite not having much experience at the position. Herzog finally decided that Van Slyke and Landrum would form a nice platoon in right field. Above all else, Her-

2. The Rites of Spring: Not-So-Great Expectations

zog said, he wanted to keep from shifting Clark from the outfield to first base and back to the outfield again — that, with a fixed position in the field, he could be counted on for better offensive numbers. Clark was welcome to the idea of moving to first base. "I think I'll be in the game more all-around," he figured. "In the outfield, you have a tendency to wander a little bit. You're pretty much involved in each play that happens in the infield." While in San Francisco, Clark had received some first base tips from Willie McCovey, the slugger nicknamed "Stretch" for his flexibility in handling throws from the infield.

Van Slyke, meanwhile, was all but resigned to returning to the outfield — especially after a particularly bad showing at third base in one game. "Even my one-and-a-half-year-old son doesn't want me at third," he claimed. Van Slyke, while dealing with his shuttle between the infield and outfield, was also trying to find himself at the plate, batting .176 as the exhibition season neared its end. The Cardinals had loved his strong arm, running speed, and pop from his left-handed bat since he came to the majors, and were now looking to find a good place for him in the field.

As the exhibition schedule was starting to wrap up, Herzog commenced his final experiment by putting Herr in the third spot of the batting order. Herr hadn't been placed there much before, but Whitey put the issue in another perspective. "Listen," Herzog told him. "It's going to take a while to learn to hit third, but remember, Jack Clark is hitting behind you. On 2–0, 3–1, you're going to see fast balls that you can hit."

And with still no answer from the commissioner's office on the Lonnie Smith situation, Herzog was finding it hard to piece together the team that would begin the season, let alone the batting order. "You'd think they'd do *something*. Does it take that long to make a decision? I've got to get my roster set."

He did decide that, against right-handed pitchers, Porter was going to bat in the fifth spot behind Clark in the lineup. He had wanted Pendleton to assume a more prominent role in the order, but his poor spring suggested that Terry still had things to prove to Herzog. "I really wanted to hit McGee fifth, but with the way Pendleton is hitting, I can't hit him third." So, it was decided that McGee would take the two slot, in front of Herr, with Pendleton dropping down to sixth and Van Slyke and Landrum seventh, against right- and left-handers, respectively. At the outset, however, Herzog was willing to try just about anything — mostly stemming from a .231 team batting average at the close of spring training.

Herzog also announced that Andujar would be his opening day starter in New York against the Mets on April 9, the first time in his big league career that he would start the season's first game. It would be Gooden, the sophomore dynamo, facing him. "After you pitch the first game, you have to pitch the second, the third, and the fourth," Andujar said, trying to put things in perspective for the entire year. "It's going to be a long road. If we [the team] do the job were capable of, we'll be all right." Meanwhile, *Sport* magazine added another prognostication in predicting that Herzog would be the first manager fired in 1985.

An edict finally came from the commissioner's office on April 4 about Lonnie Smith. Baseball czar Peter Ueberroth suspended him for the next three exhibition games and fined him $1,000, a sentence that appeared light to some. Smith admitted that "It could have been a lot worse," but also was quoted as saying that "I don't think anything I did was wrong, other than bumping the umpire." When asked if he was surprised at the light penance, umpires' union chief Richie Phillips gave no comment, due to the fact that no videotape was available from the incident. "It's difficult for me to be super-critical of what happened," Phillips pointed out, "where I have never seen what happened."

With the dilemma finally resolved, the Cardinals sent Coleman back to the Triple-A farm team at Louisville. It was revealed that the plan all along had been to send him back to the minors. "I don't think he's ready yet," Herzog said a couple of days before Coleman was re-assigned. "He struck out 112 times last year. He's got a lot of learning to do. But he should get better." Then, with a twinkle in his sharp eye, Herzog added, "You might see him up here before the year's over." With Coleman going back to the minors, the Cardinals broke camp as the only National League team in 1985 not to have a rookie on their initial roster.

A few days later, Ueberroth handed down another decree concerning veteran pitcher Vida Blue of the San Francisco Giants. The 35-year-old Blue, who earned fame as one of baseball's best left-handers in the early 1970s with the Oakland A's, was seeking the opportunity to pitch in the majors once again. He had been suspended for the entire 1984 season by then-Commissioner Bowie Kuhn for a drug possession conviction in 1983. Before Blue could be considered for reinstatement for the '85 season, he was given several conditions by Kuhn. Blue had to prove he was no longer involved in drugs, in addition to consistently attending treatment for his addiction. Ueberroth believed that these conditions had been met, and Blue was allowed to join the Giants on their Opening Day roster.

Just as the fans in St. Louis got themselves ready for another exciting summer of baseball in the Gateway City, trouble was brewing in another sport. The football Cardinals, who had arrived from Chicago in 1960, looked like they might be flying the coop. "Are the football Cardinals leaving St. Louis for Phoenix?" the *Post-Dispatch* wondered. "Conflicting

2. The Rites of Spring: Not-So-Great Expectations 35

smoke signals were sighted — and being promoted — all day Wednesday and Thursday [April 3 and 4] here and in Phoenix ... [football] Cardinals' owner Bill Bidwell has said only that he expects to reach a decision by April 15." Bidwell had longed for a city that was football-first, and some believed that he would now be finding his chance out in the Southwest. However, the following day it was announced that there would indeed be professional football in St. Louis in 1985 after all. "As of today," Bidwell confidently told the press, "we are suspending all activities involved in any possibility of playing in any other location."

In return for Bidwell's sign of good faith, city leaders promised to look further into the construction of a new domed stadium for the football Cardinals. Some other local officials, however, were not so convinced of Bidwell's agenda. "The gun has merely been put back in the holster," warned U.S. Senator Thomas Eagleton, a Democrat from St. Louis. "But the gun is still loaded and in the holster." Eagleton and others feared that the one-year reprieve was an underhanded effort on the part of Bidwell to assure speedy ground-breaking for a football stadium in St. Louis.

But business in baseball went on as usual, and the Cubs got ready to defend their 1984 National League Eastern Division title by beating the Cleveland Indians, 6–3, in their final exhibition game on April 5. Left-handed pitcher Steve Trout picked up his second win of the spring as Bob Dernier and Leon Durham each went 3-for-4. The Cubbies finished preseason play with a 17–13 record, good enough not to cause worry for Chicago fans, and they headed north with "unfinished business" after losing to the Padres in the National League Championship Series the previous October.

There was also a lot of talk around Chicago concerning the fate of the Cubs' ball park — on two fronts. On the one hand, there was the ever-present discussion of the possibility of adding lights to Wrigley Field. The pressure from residents around the ballpark, fearing the God-knows-what that would be going on in their front yards and backyards after games, always seemed to fight off such rumors. A more pressing issue arose — the unconscionable act of *replacing* the park. Ueberroth gave his support for renovation of the existing stadium. "I think baseball ought to be played at Wrigley Field for the long term," he said in support of the venerable building. "I'm concerned that Wrigley Field stay as a major league ballpark." Ueberroth also supported the idea of night baseball for playoff games at the park, which was becoming a hot issue for TV networks, as the networks did not want to continue broadcasting postseason baseball in the daytime with lower viewership.

Despite a lack of respect from the baseball forecasters around the country, Herzog knew the parts were in place for what he wanted to accomplish in 1985. He now had the players he wanted, a team that would run the opposition into submission. He would later remember, "These were bright ballplayers, guys with an *idea*—Ozzie, Herr, McGee, Pendleton, the whole group. They saw the big picture and, as far as stealing went, they figured out more on their own than my coaches or I ever taught them.

"If I have a motto, it sure as hell ain't '*Whiteyball*,'" he informed the skeptical media. "My motto is, '*Run, boys, run.*'"

3

Out of the Starting Blocks

As the beginning of the regular season approached, it appeared that a trade involving Ozzie Smith was inevitable. "We aren't anxious to trade him, but we have to listen," Maxvill carefully told the press. "When you're caught in a situation like this, when negotiations are in progress and not going very well, you have to cover yourself a little bit." The Cardinals were most afraid of losing Smith to free agency, thereby receiving nothing in return. So they continued to listen to offers, while not initiating any of their own. Herzog said in a pained voice, "I'd say there's a reason we're collecting shortstops."

The latest addition was Ivan DeJesus, who came from the Phillies along with reliever Bill Campbell on April 6 for left-handed pitcher Dave Rucker. DeJesus, who was thought to be a rising star with the Cubs in the late 1970s, had recently slipped from the starting shortstop position in Philadelphia, relinquishing the role to Steve Jeltz. He had started in the Dodgers organization, and had been part of a 1977 trade that brought Bill Buckner to the Cubs in exchange for Rick Monday. Campbell was bringing with him 119 career saves (including an American League–high 31 in 1977) and an experienced arm to the bullpen — something Herzog desperately wanted before the season began. And Campbell, despite being 36 years old, had shown great endurance in relief. As recently as 1983 with the Cubs, he had posted 123 innings in 83 appearances.

Neither side in the Ozzie situation appeared to be backing down, but there at least seemed to be some mutual respect. "Lou Susman is a tough negotiator," admitted Ed Gottlieb, Smith's agent. "Any time you deal with Lou Susman, you're dealing with a big leaguer. At the same time, he's fair. He's also very careful, and I have to be very careful. I'm dealing with the future of a man's life." All in all, Gottlieb was confident that a deal would get done. "The Cardinals haven't told us that they weren't going to trade him, but they said they were not going to let him get away. They said that if this went to free agency, they'd outbid the other guy."

Most around the city were preparing for the worst—even Broeg, the seasoned dean of St. Louis sportswriters. "If the Cardinals lose their shortstop, Ozzie Smith, they'll lose not only the finest-fielding infielder these four eyes have ever seen," Broeg warned, "but also one of the finest fellas—particularly noteworthy in an era in which ballplayers are more independent than ever, for reasons even more obvious than the size of their paychecks."

Smith himself wasn't sure what was going to happen. "I'm playing Tuesday. But beyond Tuesday, I don't know." The Cardinals were in the process of finishing their exhibition schedule on April 7, posting a 6–1 victory over the Mets as Pendleton, Herr, and Landrum each collected two hits. That same day, another big-name star was getting the deal he wanted. Nolan Ryan, who the previous April had broken Walter Johnson's career strikeout record, got a two-year contract extension from the Astros. It was also announced that the 38-year-old would be their Opening Day starter against Fernando Valenzuela and the Dodgers.

The Cards were still planning on going with Joaquin Andujar on Opening Day in New York. People often had difficulty understanding what Andujar was trying to say—not so much because of his Spanish accent, but because he would make up his own rules for grammar. He once said that life in the big leagues could be summed up in one word: "yaneverknow." He would also talk about himself a lot, but sometimes, he would do it in the third person—and then jump back to the second person at the end of the sentence. "For Joaquin Andujar to play, I have to fool around a lot before the game," as he described his pre-game rituals. "It's not only the St. Louis club but too many players in baseball are too serious. You have to enjoy yourself, you know what I mean?" Despite his strange ways, he was one of Herzog's favorites. Whitey himself suggested that Andujar work for the Cardinals in some other capacity when his playing days were over. "I'd like to be an instructor, like Hub Kittle," he thought out loud one day in spring training, staring up into the sky while sitting in the dugout.

The only major injury the Cardinals had heading into Opening Day was Lahti, still smarting from muscle spasms in his neck and upper back. To avoid creating a problem on the roster, Lahti agreed to go on the disabled list and be activated on April 18 as the Cards headed to Shea Stadium.

After losing the National League East title to the Cubs by six-and-a-

3. Out of the Starting Blocks

half games in '84, the Mets were looking for a final piece to the puzzle to put them over the top in 1985. They believed that they had found that piece in catcher Gary Carter. Stuck in obscurity playing for the Expos in Montreal, Carter was pictured by the New Yorkers as not only a good power hitter and defensive catcher, but a vocal leader on the field and in the clubhouse as well. The Mets had sent a good amount to Montreal to get him, including infielder Hubie Brooks, catcher Mike Fitzgerald, outfielder Herm Winningham, and pitcher Floyd Youmans.

Carter was a baseball fan among baseball players. He had perhaps the most extensive baseball card collection among his peers, signed more autographs than anyone else, and generally had a great time being a major leaguer.

Joaquin Andujar frustrated reporters, but also did the same with hitters. He said that life in the big leagues could be summed up with one word: "Yaneverknow." *(From the collections of the St. Louis Mercantile Library at the University of Missouri–St. Louis)*

Unfairly, a few in the press found him to be too fond of the limelight, but he never refused to sign his name for a wide-eyed kid. He also always seemed to have a smile on his face — part of the reason that reporters and autograph-seekers sought him out. Davey Johnson, his new manager with the Mets, knew the truth about him.

"Gary Carter takes time with the media," Johnson explained. "And when you go out of your way to sign all the autographs, and take time to do a personalized picture when you'd rather relax on the bus.... If that's gonna cause jealousy or pettiness among the other players, then the other 24 are wrong." Herzog echoed Johnson's sentiment. "I've been here five years, and he's never missed a game. He hustles. He plays more than any catcher I've ever seen. I can't see anything wrong with him."

Carter would catch and bat fourth in his first game with the Mets, as they heaped a $2-million-dollar salary on him to help bring home a pennant. Was Herzog worried about the home run power that the Mets and other teams in the National League East seemed to have so much of, and the Cardinals so little? "We don't need to hit home runs," Whitey said confidently. "With our speed, I think we can win with ten singles."

As was tradition, the Reds played the first game of the season, beating the Expos 4–1 in the middle of a Cincinnati spring snowstorm braved by 52,000 souls. Rose immediately resumed his assault on Cobb, picking up two hits and three RBIs. Luminaries Ueberroth and Schott were seen scurrying for cover when the snow came in the fifth inning, causing a 21-minute delay in the game.

In New York the next day, the temperature for the Cardinals and Mets was not much warmer. It was listed at 45 degrees at game time, and dropped steadily as the day went on. A fine total of 46,781 was on hand to witness the event in spite of the blustery conditions. The Cardinals were literally left out in the cold — at least temporarily. As the team bus pulled into the stadium several hours before game time, they were forced to wait several minutes, as the result of the simultaneous arrival of Vice President George Bush's motorcade.

Gooden, the confident youngster, strode to the hill as his emergence from the dugout was greeted by a roar from the crowd. He sent Lonnie Smith, Herr, and Pendleton down in order in the first, and then his mates came to bat. Andujar struggled with his control in the first frame, as the Mets parlayed walks to Daryl Strawberry and Howard Johnson, a hit-by-pitch of Carter, and a couple of hits into a 2–0 lead. Jack Clark paid immediate dividends leading off the second, however, as he nailed an 0–2 pitch over the wall in left to pull the Cardinals within one run. The teams traded blows from then on, knotted at ties of 2–2 and 5–5, with the game heading into extra innings. After the Cardinals went down in order in the tenth, Cards' reliever Neil Allen, who had pitched effectively in the ninth, struck out Keith Hernandez looking (the man for whom he had been traded). Carter then came to the plate.

"I threw the ball down and away," Allen said of his first offering to the newest Met. "That's what the scouting reports said to do. It appears the scouting reports were wrong."

Allen threw a low-and-away curve ball — "The best curve ball I'd thrown all day," he said — and Carter planted it in the Cardinals' bullpen in left, over the outstretched leap of Lonnie Smith, giving New York a 6–5 win. Smith turned himself around twice in pursuit of the fly ball, and admitted after the game that a better route to the ball would have given him a greater chance for a catch. After circling the bases, Carter shared

3. Out of the Starting Blocks

his elation about his opening act. "I feel wonderful, enthusiastic, excited, every kind of adjective you could think of," he said in giving his team a win on the first day. "If I were to have a fantasy, it couldn't have been written any better than this."

In addition to Clark, the batting stars for the Cardinals were Herr and Ozzie Smith, with three and two hits, respectively. Pendleton sat dejectedly in the dugout after the game, the result of an 0-for-5 performance at the plate in a carry-over of his struggles from the spring. Andujar, who was subsequently relieved by Dayley, Campbell, Andy Hassler and Allen, suffered a bruise on the index finger of his pitching hand as he tried to stop a smash off the bat of Hernandez in the first inning. Campbell in particular was a bright spot on the staff, striking out the first three New York batters he faced.

Elsewhere around the league, Vida Blue showed that he was indeed back, picking up a victory in relief in the Giants' win over the Padres. Blue was happy to be back, but knew the road of recovery in front of him was still long. "After all, I only threw two pitches and got one out," he said in gaining his first win since 1982. "I'm just trying to keep this in perspective ... maybe my higher power is looking out for me." Also, two-time former National League MVP Dale Murphy had two hits and two RBIs in Atlanta's 6–0 shutout of the Phillies, and Ryan struck out four batters in his 2–1 win over the Dodgers. Interestingly, Carlton was on Ryan's tail on the strikeout list, as "Lefty" got three Ks of his own in Philadelphia's loss. Yet another veteran pitcher, 40-year-old Tom Seaver, got his 289th career win in the White Sox's 4–2 triumph over the Brewers in Milwaukee. And yet another pitching record fell, as Seaver made his 15th Opening Day start, surpassing Walter Johnson's standard.

The Cubs picked up where they left off, as they and their ace pitcher, Rick Sutcliffe, beat the Pirates 2–1 in Wrigley Field—the same team they beat to clinch the division title in 1984, sending them to their first postseason appearance in 39 years. It was the fifteenth straight regular season victory for Sutcliffe, who produced a sparkling 16–1 ledger for the Cubs in '84 after coming over in a June trade from the Cleveland Indians.

For the Cardinals, John Tudor, the benefactor of an unseemly 36 hits for the opposition in just 23 innings of spring training work, would get the ball from Herzog for game number two.

It was suggested by Hummel that some of the team members should have been looking forward to the next destination on the road trip. "Ordinarily, Pittsburgh is not the garden spot among cities that National League baseball players visit," Hummel pointed out after the St. Louis encore to the '85 opener. "But for the Cardinals' Neil Allen and Terry Pendleton, it might as well be the Bahamas." Despite getting his first hit of the season, Pendleton made two errors; and Allen, although not being charged with the loss this time, was in the game once again as the Cardinals dropped another extra-inning contest, 2–1. The Mets had loaded the bases in the bottom of the eleventh when Allen allowed a walk to pinch-hitter Danny Heep. Pendleton's first error allowed the Mets to tie the game in the fourth at 1–1, spoiling a masterful pitching performance by Tudor. The left-hander allowed only three hits in nine innings, with just the one unearned run, before giving way to Hassler. Ron Darling was equally tough on the mound for New York, however, also allowing a sole run in seven innings of work. Roger McDowell came on in the tenth to get the win, and St. Louis was still searching for its first victory.

Despite Allen's struggles the first two days, his teammates had support for him — especially Ozzie Smith. "These are tough times," he admitted. "It's tough for him to pitch in this place. All he can do in that situation is mess up. If he gets them out, he's just doing what he's supposed to do." Added Darrell Porter, "He worked so blasted hard in the spring ... then he starts off like this. It's really disheartening." Added Roarke, "He could easily say, 'Oh geez, what's gonna happen next?' But it's a situation where he wants to go back and show what he can do. He's a competitor, and he's going to stay that way."

What was probably more disheartening for Porter was the news he received the next day: a foul tip that caught him on the big toe of his left foot had broken the bone, and he was placed on the 15-day disabled list. As the Cardinals made their way to Pittsburgh, Mike Lavalliere was recalled from Louisville and given the nod to start the first game against the Pirates. "I was kind of shocked," was Porter's reaction to the diagnosis, since he was able to play after the toe was hurt. "I suppose x-rays don't lie." Clark was also smarting, nursing a sore shoulder that was the product of a collision with Mets' shortstop Rafael Santana.

In the opener in the Steel City, starting pitcher Kurt Kepshire lasted only three innings — including a four-run first — as Pittsburgh belted its way to a 6–4 win, the Cardinals' third loss in a row. At least another bright spot shone in the bullpen, as left-hander Rick Horton shut down the Pirates in the seventh, eighth, and ninth, allowing the Cardinals to climb back into contention. A rally fell short in the final frame, however, as Pendleton hit into a double play that plated the final St. Louis run, and McGee was then retired to end the threat. Meanwhile, the Mets advanced to 3–0 on another game-winning home run by Carter, the lone run in a 1–0 shutout of Pete Rose's Reds, mostly authored by sharp starter Bruce Berenyi.

Even by chance, things did not improve the next night. Allen was once again the foil, allowing a hit to former Cardinal George Hendrick in the eighth inning and a subsequent sacrifice fly by Tony Pena to give the Bucs a 4–3 win. Danny Cox had given the Redbirds a decent six-inning effort, but it was not enough. The 0–4 start marked the worst beginning of a St. Louis season since the 1973 edition began 0–5.

The goose egg was removed the following day; good thing, said a relieved Herzog. "I was going [home] to Kansas City if we didn't win this one. It's amazing to start a season losing that many games. It gets to be a monkey on your back."

Andujar found a groove in the series finale at Pittsburgh, permitting one run over seven innings and winning behind Clark's second home run, 10–4. Joaquin also contributed two hits to the Cardinals' offensive attack, as did Pendleton, McGee, and Clark. There was still some concern about Andujar's pitching hand. The same one that had been hit by Hernandez's drive in New York was jammed while running the bases, and he had to be removed from the game. Landrum was also hurt in pre-game practice, adding to the Cardinals' injury list as the team looked forward to its home opener the following night back in St. Louis.

Montreal was coming to town, and was sending right-hander Bill Gullickson to the mound. Gullickson, the Joliet, Illinois, native who had struck out 19 Cubs in his rookie season of 1980, had become a mainstay of the Expos' staff. Long-time St. Louis favorite Bob Forsch was the choice for the Cardinals, but all of the attention in town was focused on the Ozzie Smith deal — or lack of one. News on the topic had been scant for the past couple of days, so much speculation spread that something big was about to happen — either a trade or a long-term deal with the Redbirds, it was assumed. Fortunately, it turned out to be the latter.

Smith and his agent Gottlieb agreed to a five-year, $8.7 million deal for the Wizard to stay in St. Louis. Part of the deal included partial ownership in a wholesale distributorship of the Anheuser-Busch Company. It had been a priority for Susman, who all along had remained the Cardinals' chief negotiator in the talks, to get the deal done before the Cardinals had their home opener. And despite his willingness to entertain trade offers, Smith was happy to stay in town. "I believe it's better for Ozzie to be here," said Gottlieb. "It's better for him to play where he enjoys himself. He enjoys Anheuser-Busch, and he'll be working with those people the rest of his life." Added a grateful but uncertain Andy Van Slyke, "I hope the Good Lord has a plan for me to play here with him for four more years. He's going to be here, but I might not. And if the Good Lord wants to bless me financially, I'll take that too."

The agreement immediately paid off for the Cardinals. Smith equaled his home run total from 1984 with one swing of the bat in the sixth inning off of Dan Schatzeder, who had followed Gullickson in relief. The blast — like his '84 home run, coming in the Cardinals' first home game of the year — was part of a St. Louis offensive attack that netted 11 hits as the home team was victorious, 6–1. And Forsch was masterful, going the entire way while allowing only one run, no walks, and scattering eight hits. It was Forsch's first complete game in two years, going back to when he had no-hit the Expos. Three of the Cardinals' knocks came off the bat of Pendleton, who was showing signs of life at the plate.

They blew a great outing once again by Tudor the next night, however, as the offense produced one run on four hits. Slick rookie left-hander Joe Hesketh of Montreal toyed with the Cardinal batters all night, as a gathering of 20,145 — less than half as many as attended the opening night home game — had hardly blinked before the two-hour game was over. The Cardinals were dropping in the standings, while in Chicago, the Cubs were off to a 7–1 start. Herzog knew that something needed to be done. Something different, something exciting, something to give the team a jolt.

With McGee nursing a sore leg, and Landrum now placed on the 21-day disabled list, Coleman got the call to be promoted from Triple-A. He was in Nashville, Tennessee, where the Louisville club was playing. "Hey, they've got TWA flights from Nashville," Herzog suggested. "We better get him up here."

Upon his arrival in St. Louis, Coleman was called in by Maxvill for a private meeting. "Look, Vince," he began, "You've had a nice spring [despite the fact he had batted under .200], but I want you to realize, right now, that you're only going to be with us for about a week, and then you'll be sent to Louisville."

Coleman politely nodded, and responded. "Yes, Mr. Maxvill, I understand. But I want you to know that I'm going to be here the whole year."

Maxvill smiled and said, "That's great, Vince. I want you to have all the confidence in the world. But you have to understand that once McGee is healthy, you'll be sent back down to Louisville."

Once again, Coleman affirmed the denial. "Yes, Mr. Maxvill, I understand. But I want you to know that I'm going to be here the whole year."

Coleman had been off to a slow start for Louisville, batting .136 in their first five games. It was Herzog's original plan not to give Coleman a starting position, but rather insert Brian Harper into right field and move Van Slyke to center in McGee's absence. No need to worry about that switch, Whitey assured everyone. "He's [Van Slyke] a Gold Glove candidate anywhere you put him in the outfield. I think Willie McGee is the best center fielder in the league, but Andy is just as good." But, as Herzog's

3. Out of the Starting Blocks

pre-game intuition would tell him to do, Coleman was placed in center field for his major league debut on April 18, while Van Slyke stood in his customary right field position. Not wasting any time, Herzog also inserted Coleman into the lead-off spot against the Expos' veteran right-hander Steve Rogers.

If it were not for Coleman, Rogers would have left town with a shutout in his pocket. In the third inning, with the Cardinals already down 2–0, Ozzie Smith reached second after singling and being sacrificed over by Kepshire, the St. Louis starter. Next up was the 23-year-old Coleman (who later admitted being terribly nervous in his first at-bat, in which he grounded out to short), and he promptly laced a single into left, putting Smith at third. Tommy Herr later hit a sacrifice fly to score Ozzie, and that was the Cardinal offense for the night as Montreal won, 7–1. Rogers was a native Missourian, and had once pitched against former Cardinal Jerry Reuss, a product of Ritenour High School in St. Louis, in a high school state championship game. Rogers hadn't been overly impressed with Coleman. "He'll get picked off a lot until he's been up for a while," Rogers said, citing the rookie's youthful recklessness. "We picked him off a lot when I was with Indianapolis [the Expos AAA club]." Nevertheless, Coleman was able to show off his lightning speed, swiping two bases in his debut. He would make his greatest impression, however, just 24 hours later.

"How 'ya gonna keep him down on the farm?" was the response by Hummel after Coleman's encore on April 19. He led off the Cardinals' game against Pittsburgh in the home half of the first with a single, added another RBI single in the third, and scored after doubling in the fifth. His real gem came in the eighth inning, however, as he lined a low-and-away fastball from Pirates veteran left-hander John Candelaria down the right field line for a triple.

Jack Buck's call of the play on KMOX radio set the tone for what would be heard the rest of the summer. "Now, Coleman at the plate ... swing and a drive into the right field corner — base hit! Cardinals take the lead! Coleman goes for second ... Coleman flies for third! Coleman is safe with his fourth hit of the night!"

To be sure, this was the beginning of the electricity that fans across the Midwest, sitting on the back porches of their houses, would get from Coleman, McGee, Van Slyke and the others via the microphones of Buck and his partner Mike Shannon during the summer of 1985.

Coleman's three-bagger had scored DeJesus and put St. Louis ahead, 5–4. And, seemingly energized by the rookie's effort, Allen found his old stuff and shut down Pittsburgh in the ninth for his first save, rescuing a strong eight-inning effort by Andujar and Horton. McGee, perhaps buoyed

Vince Coleman moves toward first on a bunt attempt. *(From the collections of the St. Louis Mercantile Library at the University of Missouri–St. Louis)*

by Coleman's show as well, noted that his aching leg had gotten considerably better in the past day. Also contributing to the victory was Herr, who added a strong 2-for-4 outing with three RBIs, and Lonnie Smith and Tom Nieto also chipped in with a couple of hits.

Although Coleman's trademark — the stolen base — was denied in his only attempt of the evening in the first inning, he showed that he was capable of bringing other talents to the offensive table as well. Broeg wrote that Herzog told him, from what he had seen, that Coleman "has a chance to break Hall of Famer Lou Brock's stolen base record in eight or nine years." Immediately, people in the game wanted to know his base-stealing secrets. "You have to know that you're going to steal a base," Coleman advised about the art. "Not think, but know. Once I get on base, there has never been a time when I didn't think of stealing a base."

Allen was strong the next night, too, as he came to the aid of Cox — this time, for a two-inning stint — as the Birds beat Pittsburgh again, 4–3. Herzog did slip McGee into the game defensively in the eighth inning, but the manager wasn't pleased with how McGee looked at the plate, noticing that his thigh problem still hadn't completely healed. The Cards pieced together their runs, assuming their final lead in the sixth when Clark walked, Van Slyke was hit by a pitch, and the Pirates made a couple of errors that resulted in a 4–1 St. Louis lead, which stood up. Coleman meanwhile, understandably showing all the signs of an on-again, off-again rookie, endured a hitless night. In all fairness, he had been hit on the foot by a line drive in batting practice off the bat of Lonnie Smith, and Cardinal trainers were afraid that the foot was broken. He was later given the go-ahead to play after the diagnosis was negative, and he made himself available for the contest.

3. Out of the Starting Blocks

The game also ended the career in Pittsburgh for Kent Tekulve, who was the embodiment of the word "lanky." The 38-year-old reliever was dealt after the game to the Philadelphia Phillies for fellow bullpen man Al Holland and a minor leaguer. Tekulve, whose rubber arm was always on call for managers Chuck Tanner and Danny Murtaugh over the years, resembled something of a bespectacled silkworm with a nasty sidearm delivery that baffled hitters. He had been with the Pirates organization since 1969, including a magnificent 1979 season in which he led the National League with 94 appearances in helping Willie Stargell and the Bucs win the World Series over the Orioles.

The Cardinals completed a three-game sweep of the Pirates on Sunday the 21st, powered by a grand slam off the bat of Pendleton which brought home a 6–0 victory. It was another strong outing for Forsch, as he (throwing a minuscule 47 pitches in six innings), Hassler, and Campbell combined to blank Pittsburgh on six hits. The bullpen got another boost as Lahti was reactivated from the disabled list, finally having recovered from his sore back. To make room for the fireballing right-hander, backup infielder Art Howe was put on waivers. Coleman resumed his show on the bases, swiping three bags and being caught twice more. The Cards were still below the .500 mark with a record of 5–6 after the victory, trailing the first-place Cubs and Mets, who both owned 8–3 marks. The Cubs pitching staff was looking particularly impressive, as Dennis Eckersley had just authored his second straight shutout in his 4–0 blanking of the Expos, the first time a Cubs pitcher had thrown back-to-back shutouts in eight years.

Still in the offing were the labor problems that baseball possessed, and it was reported the following day that talks between the owners and the players' union might be put off for as long as two months while the players studied the financial status of all the clubs. Players' union representative Donald Fehr still did not rule out the possibility of a strike at some point, and stated that only bold moves by the players, such as setting a strike deadline date, seemed to get the owners' attention. "Nothing happens from their [the owners] side," Fehr complained, "because they're unwilling or unable to do it until some sort of deadline is set." In response Lee MacPhail, head of the owners' negotiating team, suggested that their side was willing to talk at any time. "I don't see any reason why we couldn't start talking about why we think we have these problems and what we might be able to do about them," he said. "We'd be prepared to do that."

All the while, those who truly loved the sport were looking forward to the pitching matchup set for Busch Stadium on the afternoon of Wednesday, April 24, between Gooden and Andujar. The Mets were in town, and the two teams had split the opening games of the series. Gooden had stormed on the scene in 1984, running away with the Rookie of the Year award behind his 17–9 record and 276 strikeouts. Still, people knew relatively little about the teenage phenomenon. When he arrived in big league cities, members of the press were anxious to learn all they could about him. He generally remained quiet, and let his actions on the mound do the talking. Andujar, on the other hand, left little to be wondered about.

A considerable daytime crowd of over 29,000 convened at the park to watch the battle. What was expected came to pass, as the moundsmen twirled shutouts into the seventh inning. It was at that point when Herr, Clark, and Van Slyke strung together some hits and walks to score two runs off "Doctor K," and Gooden soon left the game. The Cardinals added three more runs in the eighth off McDowell, as Andujar allowed a lone run in the ninth for a 5–1 complete-game win. Andujar used the occasion of his success to air his frustration at the papers.

"They [the sportswriters] just want to write my name and make me look like a stupid clown," he chirped. "I don't give a [bleep] anymore. I've never been on the front page of the *Sporting News*, and I've been playing for ten years."

As much as Andujar's talking got him into trouble, he didn't find himself in near as much trouble on this day as another pitcher, former big leaguer Denny McLain. The ex–Detroit Tiger, who in 1968 became the first 30-game winner in the majors since Dizzy Dean with the Cardinals in 1934 (and last since '68), was sentenced on April 24 to 23 years in prison for his part in racketeering, extortion, and drug dealing. The majority of McLain's sentence came from his role in transporting three kilograms of cocaine three years prior. Although not completely contrite, he did seek a better future for himself. "The lessons I've learned in the last 13 months have prepared me for the rest of my life…. I've gone through a lot of shame and disgrace." He also admitted that his gambling problem, which caused a pair of suspensions from the baseball commissioner's office in the early 1970s, continued to haunt him. The judge involved in the case noted that McLain's perceived lack of remorse was a major determinant in the sentence that she imposed.

The Cardinals unfortunately could not carry on the momentum from the strong effort by Andujar. The Montreal Expos visited again the following day and promptly took four straight from St. Louis in a series sweep. Everything had faltered—the hitting, the pitching, and even the defense. The Cards then had an off-day April 30 in preparation of the Dodgers' arrival, as the National League standings looked like this heading into the month of May:

3. Out of the Starting Blocks

Eastern Division	W	L	Pct.	GB
Chicago	11	6	.647	—
New York	11	6	.647	—
Montreal	12	7	.632	—
St. Louis	7	11	.389	4½
Philadelphia	7	11	.389	4½
Pittsburgh	5	12	.294	6

Western Division	W	L	Pct.	GB
San Diego	10	8	.556	—
Los Angeles	11	9	.550	—
Cincinnati	10	9	.526	½
Houston	10	9	.526	½
Atlanta	8	10	.444	2
San Francisco	7	11	.389	3

For the Cardinals, it wasn't the start that they had hoped for, but it was also somewhat better than what others had expected. "I've been saying that we could finish anywhere from first to last," Herzog said. "But now I'll tell you one thing — we *won't* finish last."

4

Illicit Activity

The big story in the National League for the month of April had been the Braves' Murphy. Like the Cardinals, Atlanta had been struggling to get to the .500 mark. But their performance was due in no part to their center fielder, who was returning to his MVP form of two years prior. On the last day of April, he slapped a two-run double into the gap at Cincinnati's Riverfront Stadium to help the Braves to a 8–4 triumph over the Reds. With the hit, Murphy tied the opening-month record for runs batted in with 29, a figure also reached by Ron Cey of the Dodgers in 1977. "I can't hit like I have in the month of April for the rest of the year," Murphy admitted, "but hopefully I can build on this. Right now, everyone is asking me to project what I can do if I stay consistent. I really don't know." Murphy's production had dropped a bit in '84, as the normally fast-starting hitter was batting only .274 at the All-Star Break. He did catch fire soon enough to wind up at .290 for the year. The Braves as a team were also looking to return to playoff form, trying to make the postseason for the first time since 1982, when the Cardinals swept them in the National League Championship Series. A week after Murphy tied the RBI record, Braves pitcher Rick Mahler won again to lift his record to be a sparkling 7–0. The rest of the Atlanta starters: 0–9, with a 4.77 ERA.

The Cards began their two-game meeting with the Dodgers with an impressive 6–1 win. Andujar was "on" once again, out-dueling Reuss to snap the team's four-game losing streak. Andujar logged a complete game, scattering seven hits and walking only one. In their typical character, the Cardinals produced five of their first seven hits off Reuss through the infield variety. "That's our game," Herzog said afterwards. "We don't want to hit 'em too far." And Coleman, who had recently taken over the league lead in stolen bases, notched his twelfth of the year, which kept him two ahead of teammate Lonnie Smith in pacing the circuit. Excitement had hit the right field bleachers *before* the game, too, as a swarm of bees descended upon a spot where a queen bee had affixed herself. That area of the stands was closed for the evening.

Word was starting to spread around the American League about Coleman's feats, mostly about his raw speed. Was stolen-base king Rickey Henderson concerned about competition from the newcomer? "I'm not worried about Vince Coleman," he said, shaking his head. "Until someone steals 100 bases, I'm not concerned, and I haven't seen anybody do that yet."

A heartbreaker came the next day, an afternoon tilt in the second and final contest of the series. Cox, Horton, and Allen had stymied the Dodgers for 12 innings, allowing only one run. The Cardinals, however, could only manage a single tally against Orel Hershiser and Ken Howell in the same period. Both teams' runs came in the very first frame, in fact, with the Cardinals' score resulting from a Coleman triple and Herr single. In the Los Angeles twelfth, Ken Landreaux doubled and was moved to third on a groundout by Bill Russell. Then Allen, who was working feverishly to get out of his third inning of relief work, was called for a balk by third base umpire John McSherry. McSherry had ruled that, in coming to his set position in the stretch, Allen had raised his hands and set them a second time. Allen raced over to McSherry, who was buffeted by third baseman Pendleton, and then was joined at the scene by Herzog. Their appeals, of course, fell on deaf ears. It was only the second balk called on Allen in his major league career, and his first in two years.

The contention by the Cardinals after the game was not so much that a balk occurred, but rather that it was called for the wrong reason. "It wasn't a common sense call," Herzog fumed in the post-game press conference. "Allen wasn't trying to deceive the base runner. I could see it if the runner was breaking from third." Herzog also noted that, earlier in the game, Cox had balked and nothing was called; in addition, he felt that Hershiser had quick-pitched four times on the afternoon.

After an off day on May 2, the Cards next welcomed the San Francisco Giants to town, their first meeting since the Clark trade in the off-season. The David Green Plan had not worked out for the Giants, as the former Cardinals prospect was batting a miserable 3-for-39 (.077), with all three hits being singles. In addition, there had been speculation that he had experienced a relapse with his drinking problem that had plagued him while with the St. Louis organization. Giants manager Jim Davenport was very concerned about Green's situation. "I told him [Green] that he's not going to be able to play if he doesn't take care of himself at night.... I don't know how bad his problems were here [in St. Louis] with alcohol." Despite having dealt him away, Herzog still maintained some faith in Green's ability that was wasting away. "If David would wake up one morning and say, 'I'm going to do it,' there's no telling what he could do."

Richard Justice of the *Baltimore Sun* had another idea. "It was bad enough that the Giants traded Jack Clark to St. Louis and made the Cardinals instant contenders, but one of the players they got in return was Green, whom they thought was 24. He turned out to be 31." By mid–May, Clark had homered in all of the first eight ball parks in which the Cardinals played.

In addition to the meager return on the Green investment for San Francisco, Gary Rajsich was hitless in eight at-bats, and Jose Uribe was batting an unimposing .244. Dave LaPoint, the fourth player acquired for Clark, had an 0–4 record on the mound but was maintaining a fine ERA of 2.22. Coming into the series with the Cardinals, the Giants were hitting a weak .206 as a team, as LaPoint and the other pitchers on the San Francisco staff were struggling to get wins. The left-hander was optimistic about the future, however. "These are probably the best four games I've ever pitched in my life," LaPoint said in a positive tone. "We're too good of a team to get down and start pointing fingers. We have a lot of talent, a lot of new players, and new management." Herzog had praise for his former pitcher. "David is going to win some games," Whitey predicted. "He's one of the better pitchers in the league. But when you're gonna get a Jack Clark, you've got to give something up."

Also struggling to get into the victory column was Cardinals left-hander John Tudor, the one for whom Herzog expected great things in spring training. By May 3, he found his record at 0–3, and he got the ball for the first game in the Giants series. The deal that got Tudor from the Pirates had been criticized by some, for there were those who felt the bat of Hendrick could not be replaced in the lineup. With the Giants' poor offense, perhaps there was no better club with which Tudor could right himself than San Francisco, and he took advantage of the opportunity. Tudor scattered five hits, walked no one, and struck out five in going the distance for an easy 8–1 win over Mike Krukow.

The Giants' struggling hitters had produced only seven runs in its past five games, and were shut out by Tudor until Dan Gladden tripled and Chili Davis singled in the ninth. The hitting stars for the Cardinals included the previously struggling Porter, who in going 2-for-3 had yanked his first home run of the year, and Clark who hit his fourth dinger among the three hits he had against his former club. And Coleman continued to leave vapor trails on the base paths, doubling and stealing third in the first inning, and beating out an infield hit (followed by another stolen base) in the seventh, both times leading to Cardinal runs. The Giants were only getting a preview, however, of the speed show to take place the following night.

"They ran the Kentucky Derby in Louisville without the best thoroughbred to hit the town the past year," Tom Wheatley of the *Post-Dispatch* wrote.

Coleman had followed up his introduction to the Giants by swiping three more bases—bringing his league-leading total to 17—in guiding the Cards to 6–4 win in front of a large crowd of over 41,000. Coleman was one of only five Cardinals to get two hits on the night (along with Ozzie Smith, McGee, Pendleton, and Clark), but there was no question that the rookie outfielder was stealing the show.

"I think he's here to stay," admitted Ozzie after the game.

Herzog, nonetheless, had every intention of putting Landrum back on the roster when he became healthy, so a decision had to come soon. With Coleman surfacing so unexpectedly, it was quickly becoming crowded in the St. Louis outfield. Lonnie Smith had been playing well, and so had McGee since coming back from his leg injury. That left Andy Van Slyke on the bench, but Herzog did not want to rid himself of Van Slyke, either, because of his talent and versatility. There was more thought of moving Van Slyke back to third, as Pendleton continued to struggle with the bat and glove. Pendleton was hitting just .222 (18-for-81), and with the Cardinals relying so much on speed rather than pop, it was believed that more slug was needed out of the third base position.

To finish off the Giants' series, the 0–4 LaPoint took on the 4–0 Andujar, and the Law of Averages finally tilted in the favor of the fun-loving left-hander. The hefty LaPoint "mowed down his former teammates quicker than you can say, 'Double double cheese cheese burger, burger, please, please,'" reported one paper, in reference to a recent advertisement for a fast-food chain. LaPoint, who guessed his weight to be in the "240- to 250-pound range," silenced the St. Louis sticks with a 5–0 whitewash. It was the second shutout of his career, matching the six-hit blanking he had fired at the Mets as a member of the Cardinals the previous June.

During the Giants' series, Ozzie Smith made his first error of the year after a month of play.

The Padres were next in town, and all was not well with the defending National League champions. After bowing to the mighty Tigers in the 1984 World Series, the Friars were off to a mediocre 12–10 start as they came to St. Louis, which was still good enough for a second-place standing and one game behind the Dodgers. The team was dealing with a good deal of internal strife as well, most of which was stemming from the season-long suspension of Alan Wiggins, their young second baseman who in '84 had stolen 70 bases. The suspension was handed down by the Padres' front office on Sunday, May 5, as the team was finishing up a series in Chicago against the Cubs and preparing to head south to St. Louis. Wiggins had been admitted to a drug and alcohol rehabilitation center at the end of April, his second run-in with such problems that dated back to 1982.

The Wiggins case was the tip of the iceberg, however, in what some felt would ultimately be an apocalyptic problem in the sport. For while the Padres were dealing with the Wiggins situation as an internal matter, the *New York Daily News* was simultaneously looking to break a story that would implicate a number of big league players—among them, several stars—in a federal drug-trafficking charge. Several players had already been called to testify to a grand jury in the case, including Keith Hernandez, Lonnie Smith, and Tim Raines. Furthermore, a television station in Pittsburgh reported that the main traffickers entangled in the case, for some reason, had open access to the Pirates locker room in Three Rivers Stadium, and that several of the Pittsburgh players were involved as well.

Then, on May 8, a stunning announcement was made. Ueberroth mandated that all people employed in professional baseball—from players to office staff—were to be tested for drugs. "We will include everyone from the owners on down," he stated. "This means that it will include the more than 3,000 minor league players, the American and National League offices, scouts, the major league front office personnel ... everyone." Texas Rangers president Mike Stone smartly said, "This is one test that I won't have to study for." The issue of testing centered itself in the on-going labor dispute, and could be traced back to January 25, 1985, when the Dodgers deleted a drug-testing clause from the contract of outfielder Mike Marshall. Mandatory drug testing had been forever opposed by the players' union, and the topic was now piled on the existing matters that had to be resolved between the players and the owners. Someone perhaps should have tested the Montreal Expos' pitching staff for everything, as on May 13 they fired their *fourth* consecutive shutout, a 4–0 blanking of the Braves in Montreal behind starter David Palmer and Jeff Reardon.

While no timetable for the testing plan was immediately released by Ueberroth, he did say that the details of the plan would be announced in the "very near future." The following day, Maxvill received a call from the Federal Bureau of Investigation, in which an agent told him that no inquiry was planned into the Cardinals or the City of St. Louis for having a role in the case—for the time being.

Lonnie Smith had an easy solution to getting drugs. "We Federal Expressed it back and forth," the *New York Times* reported him as saying.

"I Federal Expressed him the money, he [the dealer] Federal Expressed the stuff. He would use a phony address for his address. I thought it was kind of creative in a way. He'd send me newspapers from Philadelphia and tape the stuff inside the papers." Herzog estimated that, when he took over as the Cardinals' manager in the middle of the 1980 season, about two-fifths of the club was using cocaine. How did it affect their play, he was asked? "We were dead last when I got here," he answered. He also suggested that drug abuse may have been part of the downfall for the Cardinals in 1983, as they failed to defend their championship. "I don't know how you want to say this, or if I should say it," Herzog phrased carefully, "but the reason we didn't win might be that we had three or four guys messed up."

Lonnie Smith told stories of how he would hide drugs when going on the road, usually by rolling them up in seven or eight pairs of pants or in invisible pockets on the sides of socks that he owned. Dave Parker readily admitted selling drugs "directly and frequently" in front of Three Rivers Stadium in Pittsburgh while playing for the Pirates. No player of any age or reputation was beyond suspicion, as former Mets' outfielder John Milner claimed that Willie Mays' locker was a source of amphetamines before games at Shea Stadium. "You went into Willie Mays' locker and got it? Willie Mays?" he was asked by stunned reporters. "The great one, yes," Milner responded. "I never seen him take it. It was there."

Perhaps the saddest stories of all came from Raines, who admitted that he carried small vials of cocaine in his uniform pockets, and would use the drugs in between innings in the dugout or clubhouse restroom. And in many situations, Raines allocated, he would slide headfirst into a base to avoid ruining the stash of cocaine he had in his back pocket. The Expos' president, John McHale, thought that the team's drug problem was the reason they could not catch the Cardinals for the 1982 division title, but Raines disagreed. "That's his opinion. Mine is that there are 26 teams, and certainly the Expos aren't the only team where players were using drugs."

Joel Youngblood of the Giants thought that a lot of players picked up their drug habits playing in the winter leagues in Latin America. "I think a lot of it starts in winter ball in Venezuela; you are right next to Colombia," Youngblood explained. "If you don't speak the language, what else is there to do except to play ball and hang out by the pool? A lot of players were exposed to it, and it was cheaper." As part of his crusade, Ueberroth sought to test players going to, and coming from, the winter leagues. "If we are going to shut down drugs in baseball," he announced, "we are going to have to shut them down everywhere…. I'm going to go outside the United States and Canada. There are places where players play where people look the other way."

Not too many people denied that the problem was escalating, and most hoped that things would get better before real tragedy struck. "The image is a frightening one," wrote George Vecsey of the *New York Times*, in painting a disturbing hypothetical scene about the effect of drugs in the game. "A pitcher, zonked out from something he inhaled between innings, decides he can blow the batter away with an inside pitch. The batter, zonked out from something he inhaled between innings, decides he is immortal and leans into the pitch."

The Cardinals remained one of the few teams that mandated drug testing for their minor league teams. "It's a step in the right direction," Tommy Herr believed. "If you don't get started down there, you won't get started up here, either."

Back at Busch Stadium, the Cards split their two games with the Padres and hit the road for the West Coast. When their team bus pulled into their hotel in Los Angeles in preparation for a series with the Dodgers, a camera crew from NBC news wanted to know which Cardinals were involved in the drug case. Somewhat surprised by the sneak attack, Fred Kuhlmann and Lou Susman repeated the FBI assertion that no St. Louis player had ties to the ring.

In the midst of the off-field problems in baseball, the standings on the morning of May 16 looked like this:

Eastern Division	W	L	Pct.	GB
New York	21	9	.700	—
Chicago	18	11	.621	2½
Montreal	19	13	.594	3
St. Louis	14	17	.452	7½
Philadelphia	11	20	.355	10½
Pittsburgh	10	21	.323	11½
Western Division	W	L	Pct.	GB
San Diego	18	12	.600	—
Houston	17	15	.531	2
Los Angeles	17	16	.515	2½
Cincinnati	16	16	.500	3
Atlanta	13	18	.419	5½
San Francisco	13	19	.406	6

While hoping to defend their division championship from the threatening Mets, the Cubs' experiment with rookie dazzler Dunston at shortstop seemed to be fading. Through 23 games, he was hitting only .194 and

4. Illicit Activity

had made nine errors. So, on May 16, the Cubs decided to send him down to Triple-A Iowa. "I just want to make sure that the pressure Shawon puts on himself doesn't start to affect the team," general manager Dallas Green said. "He's going to be a fine player, and he's down on himself."

Larry Bowa, the veteran whose job had been taken by Dunston in spring training, was now in a battle for the starting spot with a third contestant, Chris Speier. Bowa, however, let his frustration with the situation be known from the start. "I feel like the twenty-sixth player on a 25-man roster," he said, as his playing time dwindled through the first month of the season. Frey, however, didn't care for any dramatics on his ballclub. "This is worse than *General Hospital*," he replied. "If he [Bowa] ever gets to manage and is still young enough to play, he can write his own name into the lineup."

As it would turn out, the Cubs would win nine out of their next 12 games with Bowa starting at shortstop. And with Bowa back at the helm, Dunston now became the bitter one. "When you get a position, you'd think they'd at least stay with you for two months," he wondered as he packed his bags for Des Moines.

The Cardinals took four wins in seven games on a swing through L.A., San Francisco, and back down to San Diego. Tommy Herr had ascended to lead the National League in batting at .368 (39-for-106), although he had been a career .276 hitter before the 1985 season. He was starting to eyeball a possible trip to the All-Star Game in Minneapolis in July. "I'd like to play in it," Herr noted humbly. "Everyone who has played in it has said how great it is." Danny Cox, meanwhile, was among the league's pitching leaders with an even 2.00 ERA.

It seemed as if some people were waiting for Coleman to falter, so that decisions on playing time in the outfield would be made easier; but as it turned out, Vince would complicate matters by continuing his solid hitting (.284 by mid–May) and sizzling base running. And, with each passing day cementing Coleman's permanent spot — not only one on the roster, but also in the daily starting lineup — it became apparent that a trade involving one of the outfielders was going to occur. The two obvious candidates for a deal were Van Slyke and Lonnie Smith.

Previously, it looked as if Van Slyke would be the choice to go, as he had been squeezed out of playing time for the most part of April. However, a recent surge at the plate had Van Slyke over the .300 mark, and he was once again showing his great skill on defense at several positions. To make things more difficult, Smith's guaranteed salary of $1.6 million over two years was harder to pawn off on other clubs than Van Slyke's less imposing figure. But when all factors were weighed, the final attention was turned to Lonnie, and a taker was found in the Kansas City Royals, a club desperately looking to inject life into a lethargic offense and running game. The only other speedster the Royals had was center fielder Willie Wilson, but he too had an unstable past, as he was convicted on drug charges after the 1983 season. Maxvill and the Royals' general manager, John Schuerholz, held several talks about Smith as the Cardinals continued their western trip.

A deal was finally struck on May 17, as Smith was sent to Kansas City for John Morris, a 23-year-old outfielder from North Elmore, New York, who had been the Royals' number-one draft pick in 1982 out of Seton Hall University. Morris's best season to date in the Royals' system had been at Class AA Jacksonville in 1983. That year, he hit .287 with 23 home runs and 91 runs batted in, in addition to stealing 30 bases and being named the MVP of the Southern League. The rumors about a trade had maligned Smith more than anyone thought it would. "I had thought about quitting very seriously," he mentioned after reporting to the Royals. "I had thought about it for the last three weeks. I had told some of my teammates, but I'm not sure they believed me." As for the Cardinals' end of the deal, they were very pleased. "John Morris is the top prospect in their organization," Maxvill announced. "We've all checked with tons of people to find out about this young man, and all the reports are excellent."

There was speculation in both cities that Smith had been dealt out of fear of a relapse into his drug and alcohol battles. "I'm not concerned about what people think of my problem," he retorted. "My doctor, my counselor, and my wife know I'm clean. I don't want to look behind me. I want to look ahead." Despite his assurances, some found it interesting that his stock had dropped so low. It was indeed surprising to many that Morris—although a potential superstar in his own right—was all that could be had for Smith, a former National League MVP runner-up (in 1982). In fact, Morris himself was flattered and surprised to be the only player leaving Kansas City in the deal. "When I was traded, I was asking who the other three guys were who were traded with me," he joked.

Herzog offered a parting comment that suggested Smith would definitely be an asset for the Royals. "Lonnie and I have been pretty tight, and he's been an awfully good ball player for us. He's always been a catalyst for us. But he's always been the type of player that didn't want to sit on the bench. I'll say one thing—if we had the DH [designated hitter] in the National League, he would have died a Cardinal."

Suddenly, left field in St. Louis belonged to young Vince Coleman all by himself.

Another roster move was made by the Cardinals on May 17, as speedy

4. Illicit Activity

infielder Tom Lawless jumped into the spot vacated by Smith's departure. Lawless had started the year in Triple-A after being picked up from the Expos for pitcher Mickey Mahler back on March 25. The Cardinals did not lose any speed by including Lawless in their plans; he had been successful on 21 of 23 stolen base attempts in his major league career, and in five minor league seasons, he had swiped 293 bags. (In an answer to a baseball trivia question, Lawless earlier in the year had become the first man ever traded for Pete Rose — part of a deal between Montreal and Cincinnati after Vern Rapp was fired as the Reds' manager in August of 1984.) The Cards were happy to have one more runner in the bunch. "So he is another rabbit," the *Post-Dispatch* would announce on May 24, "and he fits in fine on the club that leads the National League in stolen bases." In the ultimate compliment to pay to a Cardinals utility player, St. Louis writer Dave Luecking described him as "Mike Ramsey perfected," in reference to the Cardinals' "Supersub" from 1980 to 1984.

"He knows how to play aggressive baseball," Herzog added. "He's a throwback to the old cornfield players. There are certain guys like that. Hard-nosed kids who know what it's all about. He fits all the bills — he's a better offensive player than Ramsey."

Lawless discovered that he would not have a chance to play regularly in Montreal. "When you have nine infielders with some good contracts [in camp with the Expos], you can see the writing on the wall," he resolved. "You have to figure it out and go in nicely and ask them to make a deal. They did that for me, and I was lucky enough to come to St. Louis."

It was the time of year (mid–May) when strange and sometimes unpleasant things usually start coming in bunches in the baseball season. On the 17th, Doug Rader of the Texas Rangers became the first managerial casualty of the season, being fired by the club after a 9–22 start in the American League West. And in Pittsburgh, Pirates general manager Pete Peterson was dismissed after working for more than 30 years in the organization. The Pirates were 12–25, solidly entrenched in the cellar of the National League East. Down the turnpike, Mike Schmidt was booed loudly by the home fans in Philadelphia — something nobody thought would ever be heard, even from the coarse Phillies followers — after his batting average had sunk to the .189 mark.

There was no discussion as to the job security of Herzog, despite the Cardinals' sub–.500 beginning to the season. The disappointment was not laid at the feet of the on-field or off-field management, but rather at those of a few key players who had not been contributing as expected. Porter had been one of these, as the 1982 World Series MVP struggled to find his form. He was batting .149 by mid–May, but in a statistic even more startling — if that's possible — all 17 base runners that had attempted to steal on him to that point had been successful. "He was credited with one caught stealing, however," Rick Hummel granted, "when the Montreal Expos messed up a suicide squeeze and a runner was flagged down between third and home."

Nieto, the right-handed-hitting catcher who had been used almost exclusively against lefties to this point, was promised more playing time by Herzog against right-handers. Other than Porter and Ozzie Smith (.211), no Cardinals regular was below the .260 mark, as the team batting average of the same figure ranked third in the league behind Montreal and Atlanta. On the mound, though, the performances of Allen (5.56 ERA) and Kepshire (5.61), two individuals counted on to fill large voids, had not been satisfactory to that point. It was obvious that Herzog's confidence, particularly in Allen, had begun to wane. "I've given him an opportunity to do the job, and he hasn't done it," the manager noted plainly. "It's not that he hasn't tried, but he's not making enough good pitches where I can put him under fire."

After leaving California, the Cardinals headed to Houston to commence a three-game series at the Astrodome. Despite Cox's being knocked out in the second inning of the opener on eight hits, the visitors hung on in a tough battle to emerge on the victorious end of an 8–6 score. Houston starter Bob Knepper did not fare much better than Cox, as the lefty was eradicated by the St. Louis bats after giving up nine hits in three innings of work. Rick Horton pitched 4⅔ strong innings of relief for the Redbirds, and Ken Dayley logged his second save in securing the win. A tall order, however, was in store for the next day.

The Cards had yet to face Nolan Ryan on the year, who in the previous season had shattered the career strikeout record. The "Ryan Express" was still one of the most dominating forces in the game at age 38, more physically fit and stronger than most of the 25-year-old pitchers with whom he competed. His off-season workout regimen and diet were legendary, and it seemed like he would be able to strike hitters out forever. He had an easy look of confidence and power in his eyes on the mound, as his fastball — once said to be clocked at over 100 miles per hour — still turned bats into sawdust.

Going into the May 18 contest with the Cardinals, Ryan had been hitless for the 1985 season in 20 at-bats. Nonetheless, he displayed his penchant for delivering in the clutch with a two-run a single in the eighth inning off Allen to lead the Astros past the Cards 6–5, although he got relief help in the ninth from Mark Ross. Following his recent strategy, Herzog sought to put Allen in a situation where success was probable — and

4. Illicit Activity

it did seem probable against the light-swinging Ryan. The great Texan was able to line a single over Clark's head at first, however, and it proved to be the difference in the game. Ryan struck out six in 8⅔ innings, while Ross was credited with his first big league save in getting the final St. Louis out in the ninth. And according to radar guns in operation at the Astrodome, Ryan threw 17 pitches over 97 miles per hour in the first three innings, and closed out by touching 96 while facing his last batter. On the Cardinals' side, it was another so-so start for Kepshire, who gave up four runs in five innings of work.

It wasn't a typical outing for Ryan versus the Cardinals, however. His career mark against St. Louis after the win stood only at 8–11.

A frightening (but ultimately harmless) injury hit

Rick Horton, one of the dependable arms out of the Cardinals bullpen. *(From the collections of the St. Louis Mercantile Library at the University of Missouri–St. Louis)*

Ryan a month later, as he was bitten by a coyote he was chasing off his land near Alvin, Texas. Even before the results of the rabies test on the coyote had come back, Ryan did not appear to be worried about the situation. "I'm not foaming at the mouth," he reported. Nonetheless, he did acknowledge that it was somewhat painful for the veteran rancher. "I thought I'd stuck my hand in an alligator's mouth," he said.

The *Post-Dispatch* decided on May 20th that "so far, the George Hendrick–John Tudor trade has been a wash." This was in reference to the fact that Hendrick had only one homer and a .210 batting average for the last-place Pirates, and Tudor was trying to reverse the direction of his 1–6 record, made worse by his 7–3 loss to the Astros in the final game of the series the previous day. His ERA was still a very respectable 3.44, but as Herzog put it, "All I know is he's 1–6. That's really all that matters." The skipper, though, knew that his only left-handed starter had the ability to turn things around. His allowance of five runs in six innings made the possibility of a comeback victory difficult for relievers Lahti and Allen, as Houston rookie starter Ron Mathis (a St. Louis native) logged the same amount of time but yielded only three runs. Van Slyke nailed his seventh home run, but the six other Cardinal hits were not enough.

The White Sox were now inquiring with Pittsburgh about Hendrick, as the South Siders were looking to rebound from their collapse in 1984, which had followed an American League Western Division championship the season before. Injuries to Ron Kittle and the lack of an adequate in-house replacement for him in left field led to Chicago's making the call to the Pirates, but no deal was struck as the Sox feared that Hendrick's 35-year-old body might be damaged goods.

Up on the North Side of the Windy City, the first major blow was struck to the Cubs' empire. While losing to the Braves 3–0 in Atlanta, their ace Sutcliffe pulled up lame with a torn hamstring and went on the 15-game disabled list. While running out a ground ball, he had lunged with a long stride for the base and felt his leg pop. Not long afterwards Trout, the left-hander who was the Cubs' number-two starter in 1984, would also go on the DL, as the Cubs suddenly had to scramble to find immediate pitching help.

When the Cards returned home the next day to open a stint with the Braves, there was an old familiar face in town—Bruce Sutter, who laid the crowning jewel in the Cardinals' 1982 world championship with his strike-out of Gorman Thomas. Did he think that the people of St. Louis were disappointed in him for leaving for more money? "I think I gave the people an honest effort while I was here," Sutter reconciled with the local press. "They've got true fans and they can appreciate what I've done."

Sutter's new club was not greeted nicely by the St. Louisans, however. Andujar won a rain-delayed opener easily by a 14–0 score, as the Dominican shut out Atlanta on six hits to run his record to a strong 7–1 before 34,754 who braved the intermittent storms. Coleman swiped two more bags to run his league-leading total to 28. His offensive assault on the Braves was aided by three hits and five RBIs off the bat of McGee.

The two outfielders reversed their roles the next day. Coleman got his first major league homer—fittingly, of the inside-the-park variety—and McGee stole three bases to up his ledger to 14 for the season. Horton gave the Cards over three innings of strong relief in securing a win for Cox, 6–3. In spite of Allen's troubles, the "Gang of Four," as the other pitchers had been named by Mike Roarke (Campbell, Dayley, Horton, and Lahti, the latter just beginning to find his groove), had ably combined to fill the

4. Illicit Activity

absence of Sutter, a person who everyone thought was irreplaceable. "The Cardinals lived with Bruce Sutter," *Post-Dispatch* scribe Bernie Miklasz acknowledged, "but they're not dying without him."

On a down note, league-leading batter Tommy Herr (.377) did not start the game because of a sore hamstring, the first time in 37 games that the infield of Clark, Herr, Smith, and Pendleton did not begin the game together, as Lawless got the nod instead. Tommy was available for pinch-hitting duty later in the game, however, and responded with a single. Clark also kept up his hot hitting, batting for a .533 clip in the previous two weeks. The big bat of the day belonged to Atlanta third baseman Bob Horner, though, as the slugger launched two home runs into the left-field bleachers—the second a prodigious blast beyond the first section of seats.

Forsch relieved an ineffective Kepshire in the first inning of the last game of the series, and pitched a stellar 6⅓ innings with 87 pitches in getting a 5–3 victory to complete the sweep, as Dayley picked up his third save of the year. Forsch also homered, a shot into the stands with two out in the fifth off Braves starter Mahler, who was looking to become the National League's first nine-game winner on the year. Though he was not in his familiar role as a starter, Forsch understood his current spot. "Any time you can pick up a win, you have to be happy about it," he said after his big day. "My job is long relief now, and I went in there and everything seemed to work out just right today." The Cardinals were now at the .500 mark (with a record of 19–19) for the first time since April 24.

More good news came for the Cardinals off the field as well. It appeared that the club was close to signing its number-one draft pick, 20-year-old pitcher Todd Stottlemyre out of Yakima Valley Community College and son of the former major league hurler Mel Stottlemyre. At that time, there were two professional baseball drafts during the year (winter and summer), and Stottlemyre was the club's first-round pick from the previous off-season session. After a year at the University of Nevada–Las Vegas, he transferred to Yakima Valley and posted a dominant year in leading the school to the national junior college championships. Stottlemyre noted that he was "anxious to sign, but it's going to have to be a fair contract," he revealed. "I'd rather sign than go back to school, but school is an option for me."

As it turned out, Stottlemyre did not sign with the Cardinals, and returned to school to play his final collegiate season. He was then chosen by the Toronto Blue Jays in the first round of the June selections—officially known as the "Secondary Phase" of the draft. The Cardinals took their chances with another pitcher on their first pick, left-hander Joe Magrane out of the University of Arizona.

University of Auburn junior Bo Jackson, the early favorite for the 1985 Heisman Trophy as a running back in football, was being wooed by the California Angels to sign a baseball contract. In addition to being an All-American on the football field, Jackson was also a first-rate prospect on the diamond, and rumors around the Auburn campus circulated that he had even beaten UA's number-one singles player in a tennis match — a sport Jackson had never played before in his life.

Later on draft day, Toronto came back to use its 36th pick on pitcher Jim Abbott of Flint, Michigan. Abbott had been born with only one arm (his left), and he pitched with his glove tucked under his right shoulder. He hoped to become the first one-armed player in the major leagues since outfielder Pete Gray of the St. Louis Browns in 1945. Abbott did not sign, but rather opted for a baseball scholarship at the University of Michigan.

And as for short-term help on the mound, the Cardinals did not express any interest in picking up Steve Rogers, the veteran of the Expos' staff who had just been released by Montreal. It was reported that the Angels, Astros, Cubs, and Yankees were the teams most interested in him. No one would bite, though, and the right-hander finished his 13-year big league career — all in Montreal — with 158 wins, over 1,600 strikeouts, and 37 shutouts. Rogers himself was in disbelief about the move. "When I was the opening-day pitcher, I thought I was preparing for 35 starts — not five," he mentioned. "I was living a month-long lie."

Also off the field, talk of a players' strike to occur sometime during the summer never seemed to go away. Both sides were holding fast to their positions, with apparently little room for movement. The owners projected that they would lose approximately $155 million by 1988 if they gave in to the players' demands. After calling a meeting of the team representatives, players' rep Donald Fehr announced on May 25 that no strike would take place before July, but that a work stoppage was a grave possibility with the owners' rejection of the players' most recent proposal. Specifically, Fehr's and the players' latest accusation involved the owners' trying to destroy free agency with the "Payroll Plan," a method in which each team would have a salary cap in congruence with its payroll figures. Fehr demonized the proposal by calling it an attempt by the owners to "turn back the clock to a bygone era."

Herr was sounding even more pessimistic. "My gut feeling is that it's [a strike] a definite possibility.... I would say the view of the Players' Association is such that if we're forced to, we're not afraid to go again. Nobody wants to. But it seems like every time we negotiate, it's an 11th-hour negotiation and we're backed against the wall every time."

The next stop for the Cardinals was Cincinnati, where Andujar upped

4. Illicit Activity

his record to 8–1 with a 6–4 win that was saved by Dayley. The left-hander got the powerful Parker to fly out with the tying runs on base with two out in the ninth to secure the win. The Redbirds caught Rose in the midst of his career-hit chase, and they slowed things down a bit for the Reds' leader as Andujar plunked him in the leg in the first inning. "I said, 'Thank you,'" Rose debriefed to reporters after the game. "When you're 1–2 in the count, you don't mind getting hit. Especially when it's twilight and you can't see a thing." Rose did get two hits closer to Cobb later in the game with a pair of singles.

After taking the next game from the Reds as well (a 7–2 triumph, with Herr raising his average to .385 and now tied for the league lead in RBIs with 35), the Cardinals made a stop in Louisville, Kentucky, to visit their Triple-A farm team and play an exhibition game. The Cardinals' executives that made the trip (especially Maxvill) were most interested in seeing the progress of John Morris, who after being acquired in the Lonnie Smith deal was looking to help the big club in St. Louis. The Louisville Redbirds and the Cardinals were to play their exhibition game after Louisville completed its regularly scheduled American Association game against Iowa, the Cubs' Triple-A affiliate. Morris doubled in both of the Redbirds' runs in a 2–0 blanking of Iowa, but then went 0-for-3 as the Redbirds beat the parent-club Cardinals 6–3 in a game that was shortened to $6^2/_3$ innings because of rain. Louisville third baseman Bill Lyons hit a three-run homer off Kepshire as part of a five-run second inning. As for a couple of players from the Cardinals that continued to struggle, Rick Hummel reported that "both Porter and Allen received a smattering of boos here, indicating that Louisville fans are not much different from their peers in St. Louis."

In addition to Porter and Allen, it had been a difficult start to the season for reserve outfielder Tito Landrum. Hampered by injuries since spring training, his physical condition never offered him a chance to pursue more playing time. By the time the Cardinals arrived in Atlanta at the end of May to begin a series with the Braves, Landrum had been to the plate only six times on the season, the result of a strained abdominal muscle that was taking a long time to heal. He was needed in the first game in Atlanta, however, because Van Slyke had pulled a muscle in his calf, and the wet field conditions at Fulton County Stadium made Herzog decide to bring Landrum in for Van Slyke in the fourth inning. Herzog did not want to risk further injury to Van Slyke, as he felt that Landrum was well enough to play. He certainly was well enough — he responded with two hits in an eight-run Cardinal fourth inning, the first of which was his initial home run of the year that drove home Clark and paved the way for a 9–3 St. Louis win.

It was the fourth win in a row for the Cardinals over the Braves, and the second time that Forsch had beaten them in the past week. Steady Bob had run his record to 4–2, while Lahti pitched three scoreless innings for his third save since returning from his back problems. Forsch also proved that he was still a battler, getting warned for two pitches near the head of Braves outfielder Terry Harper after Murphy homered for Atlanta's first run. And still looking to beef up the pitching staff, Maxvill reported after the game that he was negotiating with veteran left-hander Larry Gura to possibly join the club. The Cubs, however, would beat the Cards to the punch and sign the lefty to replace Trout in the starting rotation, with Trout still on the disabled list battling an inflamed elbow.

Sutter got some revenge on his former team the next day, pitching two shutout innings to save the win for Steve Bedrosian, 5–3, as Tudor suffered his seventh loss of the season against only one victory. The Cardinals were even worse in all the games he had started, with the lone win in ten total tries.

"Strange things happen when he pitches," said Herzog.

On the bright side, the Cards hit three home runs—something they had not done since the end of the 1983 season—as Landrum left the park for the second night in a row, joined by Herr and Van Slyke. And Allen, who relieved Tudor in the seventh, showed some promise with two innings of scoreless work. The team finished the road trip on a strong note as Andujar got his ninth victory the next night as the Cards shut out the Braves 6–0. It was a pyrrhic victory, however, as the right-hander had to leave the game after five innings with soreness in his shoulder. It was something that had bothered him in his previous outing as well, but both he and Herzog did not think it was serious. It was Campbell who came to the rescue in this contest, throwing four stellar frames without allowing a hit for a lengthy save, his second on the campaign. Clark also nailed his ninth homer of the season, doing so in his ninth different ball park on the year.

The Cards were due to return home on Friday, May 31, to open a home stand with the Cincinnati Reds in Busch Stadium. There was still a lot of non–baseball business to be attended to, however. There were a good deal of grumblings coming from Commissioner Ueberroth's office about his across-the-board, mandatory drug testing program—grumblings that actually originated in his office. "There has been an overwhelmingly negative reaction," the *New York Times* quoted one of the office employees as saying. "A feeling of suspicion has been created. We feel like we're all guilty and we feel that if we speak out, our jobs will be in jeopardy." The issue developed into an on-going debate in regard to personal privacy, and there was speculation that the presence of a Constitutional violation and the involvement of the U.S. Supreme Court was a possibility.

In the other related legal matter that was continuing, seven individuals were indicted by a grand jury in Pittsburgh for a drug racket that involved over 100 counts of wrongdoing (in the end, the number of counts would total 165) with each count punishable with a maximum 15 years in prison and a $25,000 fine. A total of 11 players had testified to the grand jury to this point since the spring of 1984, with each player given immunity for his testimony. Six of the alleged drug traffickers were from Pittsburgh; the other was a food caterer from Philadelphia named Curtis Strong, who through his attorney claimed he was innocent and was being used as a scapegoat to protect the players who had been involved in the drug transactions. Strong originally became a suspect because his catering business served the Phillies' clubhouse. He was dismissed by the club after the Phillies' first five home games of 1985, a club spokesman said, because he charged too much for his services.

Back in St. Louis, meanwhile, Donald Fehr was at the ballpark to meet with Cardinals' and Reds' player representatives to discuss the possibility of a strike, with a vote from the players likely to be taken before he left town. Herr announced that a strike vote among the Cardinal players was almost assured to be unanimous. "He [Fehr] needed to come here and say it," Herr informed the press, "because most of what we read in the papers is all one-sided in favor of the owners." During his meeting with the Cardinals players, Fehr was not given immediate permission to set a strike date, but it was expected to be granted in the coming days.

The Reds players gave Fehr their immediate support, including Rose. "My vote is like every other player's vote should be — to honor the players' association ... it's not a matter of sympathy with the players' association, but a matter of doing the right thing," Rose explained. His decision did not sit well with Marge Schott, who was said to be "bothered and disappointed" with Rose's decision to side with the players' union. Such a move would mean that Rose, a player-manager, would be the only manager in the major leagues not to be paid if a strike occurred. There was also talk of a possible players' boycott of the All-Star Game in Minneapolis on July 16. "We've discussed all the options," said Fehr. "That's one of them. We haven't foreclosed any of the options."

Herr tried to remain optimistic. "Nobody wants a strike. Those of us who went through it before know how terrible it was. It's a last resort. We were backed against a wall before [in 1981]. The owners had that strike insurance, but we [the players] stuck together. This time around, you would think that they would have learned their lesson." In some places, however, the fans didn't seem to care. A sign that read "PLEASE STRIKE" was seen posted outside Veterans' Stadium, home of the Phillies and their 18–30 record.

But there was also good news in the papers on June 1. Herr continued to lead the National League in hitting with a .376 average (59-for-157) and was tied with teammate Clark for the circuit lead in RBIs (36). "Pitchers haven't been able to solve this mysterious transformation of Tom Herr," Miklasz marveled, "a lifetime .276 hitter who is now Ted Williams ... with two jackrabbits [Coleman and McGee] batting in front of him and a jackhammer [Clark] in back of him, Herr is getting fat on a lot of nervous pitches."

In addition, Coleman was running away with the stolen base lead (29) in front of teammate McGee and Bob Dernier of the Cubs (17 each). The improved Cards found themselves only four-and-a-half games out in the National League Eastern Division standings:

Eastern Division	W	L	Pct.	GB
New York	27	15	.643	—
Chicago	26	17	.605	1½
Montreal	27	19	.587	2
St. Louis	24	21	.533	4½
Philadelphia	17	27	.386	11
Pittsburgh	15	29	.341	13

Western Division	W	L	Pct.	GB
San Diego	26	17	.605	—
Cincinnati	24	22	.522	3½
Houston	24	22	.522	3½
Los Angeles	22	24	.478	5½
Atlanta	19	26	.422	8
San Francisco	16	28	.364	10½

Out of Atlanta, the news remained temporarily favorable. Despite the Braves' poor start, owner Ted Turner gave manager Eddie Haas "a vote of confidence" after a meeting with team officials. In doing so, Turner assured Haas that his job was safe — at least for now. Haas gained the nickname of "Mr. Mute" by the Braves players because of his solitary, hours-on-end sittings in the dugout before games. The team's poor start sparked some wry humor on Peachtree Street. "If this is America's Team," writer Dave Kindred wondered about the moniker, "America should sue for slander."

While there was speculation with strike talk that no postseason would be played at all, contingencies were necessary because of the Cubs' long-sought success in 1984. Due to money lost from daytime playoff games in '84, the Cubs were presented with an ultimatum from the ABC television network. ABC, who held the broadcasting rights for the World Series in 1985, decided that all Series games would be played at night. With Wrigley Field still without lights, this forced the Cubs to consider using Comiskey Park, the home of the White Sox, as their home field if they made it to the postseason. "ABC has a right to do that under the contract," affirmed Ueberroth. The parks in Atlanta and Los Angeles—two places that had grass fields, à la Wrigley, and suited to the Cubs liking—were also being considered.

"We're just hamstrung trying to get lights installed," moaned general manager Dallas Green. "The law's got us, the legislature's got us, and the city council's got us." The talk also heated up about the construction of a new stadium in the Chicago suburb of Schaumburg, an area rich in development and with interstate access. "If we get beat in the legislature and we get beat in the courts," Green warned, "we have to look at alternatives. One of the alternatives we mentioned was one in Schaumburg." Chicago mayor Harold Washington proposed looking into a new domed stadium for the city (to perhaps house the Chicago Bears of the National Football League as well), but no interest was gleaned from the idea.

But despite the prospect of no lights in, and no replacement for, Wrigley Field in the foreseeable future, things were still happy on the North Side. With Sutcliffe and Trout starting to become healthy, and with their veteran shortstop back in place, the Cubs looked like they were ready to make another playoff run.

5

Heating Up the Turf

The game on June 2 brought more bad news for Darrell Porter, as he broke the index finder on his left hand on a play at the plate. Porter, who only recently had fully recovered from his broken toe suffered earlier in the season, was hitting just .125 at the time of the injury. To take his place, the Cardinals promoted catcher Randy Hunt from Triple-A Louisville, his first trip to the major leagues.

The Cardinals began play back at home in sparkling fashion. Danny Cox came within four outs of a perfect game, and Coleman and McGee each stole two bases as St. Louis ran away from the Reds in the first game at Busch, 5–0. (A couple of days earlier, Coleman had set a Cardinals' rookie record with his 31st steal, breaking the mark of 30 achieved by Bake McBride in 1974.) Veteran shortstop Dave Concepcion singled with two out in the eighth inning to spoil the effort of Cox, who wound up facing two batters over the minimum in allowing two hits and no walks in the complete-game shutout. Former Cardinal John Stuper, who aided the Redbirds' run to the '82 World Series title, was the loser.

Kepshire continued to struggle as he lost the second contest, 9–3, and Jay Tibbs — a high school teammate of Gooden back in Tampa, Florida — shut down the Cards in the finale 8–3 to give the Reds the series. It was a cooling-off for Forsch (4–3), the Cards' starter who was riding a hot streak until he was belted for five runs in $3\frac{1}{3}$ innings on this day. The game started promisingly as Coleman walked and took off for second as McGee shot a ball through Rose's legs at first for an error, followed by a two-run single by Herr to increase his league-leading RBI total to 41. Tibbs settled down thereafter, and went the distance, scattering seven more hits after Herr's blow. McGee had an unusually poor outing in centerfield, letting a few balls drop in front of him and sail over his head.

5. Heating Up the Turf

Rose got two hits on the day, pushing his career total to 4,158, just 54 behind Cobb. And of course, talk of a potential players' strike made fans worry about his ability to break the record in 1985. It was pointed out by one writer that Rose would have gotten at least 60 hits during the time missed from the 1981 work stoppage.

John Tudor was Herzog's choice as the Astros came to town. He was receiving only 3½ runs per game of offensive support in his ten starts on the year, which was part of the reason for his poor record to this point. He calmly shut down the Houston attack, pitching shutout ball through five innings and finally becoming a beneficiary of the Cardinal bats. Coleman re-opened his running game with his 35th and 36th steals — including his first steal of home in the major leagues, which occurred in the very first inning, with Herr simultaneously taking second base — and the Redbirds cruised in to a 9–5 win. The Astros were still without their young shortstop, Dickie Thon, who had been beaned in the head by a Mike Torrez pitch in the first week of the 1984 season. Thon was looking like a budding superstar, but his career was derailed by a pitch that shattered part of his left eye socket. Also missing from the Astros lineup was team leader and long-ago Cardinal farmhand Jose Cruz, who had been shelved for the past two weeks with a broken foot.

On June 4, Coleman turned in his best big-league performance to date. He was a perfect 4-for-4 at the plate, while scoring four runs and stealing three more bases (to up his total to 39) as he helped Andujar reach double figures in wins (10–1) with a 6–1 victory over Houston. The Astros couldn't do anything to keep a winning streak going; it was the ninth time already in 1985 that the club had lost two games in a row. As for the Cardinals, it looked like things were finally starting to fall into place. "It's very exciting to be part of a winning ball club and contributing," Coleman pointed out after the game. "We're hitting and running, and scoring runs. We hope to do that the rest of the season." Also building a stellar season for himself was McGee, as he was impeccable at the plate with a 3-for-3 night, including a double and his twenty-second stolen base of the year. The Cardinals now had 107 steals on the season, far and away the league lead, as Van Slyke added his tenth of the year as well. McGee did not praise himself, however — he saved it for the rookie left fielder.

"He's got a good head on his shoulders," McGee noted of Coleman. "He carries himself well. He's not arrogant. He listens. He's good. He's an inspiration."

There was still some concern about Andujar's sore arm before the game began, but he breezed through the Houston lineup to the tune of a four-hitter with only one walk allowed.

The press began catching on to the possibility of Coleman breaking Brock's National League record of 118 steals set in 1974. In fact, the way that Vince was off and running, it didn't seem inconceivable that he'd even take a crack at Henderson's major-league mark of 130 set in 1982. There was also talk of upping his salary with a revised contract, as his current deal was paying him the major league minimum of $40,000. Even Coleman himself was aware of the changes that he had brought to the game. "They tend to change their pattern of pitching when I get on base," he said of the pitchers that peer nervously over their shoulders at him at first. "They hurry it to the plate so that the catcher has a chance to get me. And they tend not to throw strikes. They throw something good for the catcher to handle." Even so, the media did not go so far as to name the 26–23 Cardinals as a contender yet. "No doubt, they have the most exciting second-division club in baseball," the *Post-Dispatch* reminded readers of the standings.

There seemed to be fighting all around town when it came to St. Louis sports. The football bureaucrats were still fighting to keep the football Cardinals in town; on the night of the final game of the Astros series, St. Louisan Michael Spinks knocked out Jim McDonald in the eighth round to retain his world light-heavyweight boxing title; and the Cardinals were indeed fighting for respect in the crowded National League East, with the Mets having jumped out in front of the incumbent Cubs.

The Astros did take the final game of the series, powered by a home run off the bat of Springfield, Missouri, native Mark Bailey. But spirits in the Cardinals clubhouse remained positive, inspired by all the unexpected forces—Coleman, Dayley, Nieto, Clark, Campbell, Horton, to name a few—that had arrived on the scene.

They had been doing yeoman's work in keeping the Cardinals within striking distance, putting them just close enough to make a move on the teams ahead of them. This was being done by picking up wins against inter-divisional clubs. Their chance to really make some hay—and show that they did belong on the same field as the big boys—came on June 7, as they traveled to Shea Stadium in New York to take on the Mets. As the summer months dawned, the Cards knew that this was a golden opportunity to open some eyes around the league. It was a big four-game tilt, including a doubleheader slated for Sunday, June 9.

To get off to a good start in the series, Kepshire needed to bounce back from several poor outings. He had won the fifth spot in the rotation coming out of spring training, but had mostly been disappointing until now. Herzog, however, still had faith in him, and he gave Kepshire the ball against the tough right-hander Ron Darling in front of 35,000 at Shea.

5. Heating Up the Turf

Kepshire's control had particularly been a problem, as he had walked 19 batters in his last 21 innings. But he started sharp and stayed sharp on this day, permitting only one free pass and three hits into the eighth inning, keeping the score tied at 1–1. He had a hand in the Cards' getting that run, as he lined a double past third and later scored on a McGee single to put St. Louis up 1–0 in the third. Later, he got help from Horton, Lahti, Campbell, and Dayley to send the game into the 13th, when St. Louis exploded on Mets' reliever Doug Sisk for six runs en route to a 7–2 win. Kepshire had been at his wits' end about his struggles, so he decided to go for broke — and it worked. "I had to return to my old game plan," he explained. "I'm going to give them hell, and to hell with it."

The following day, Tommy Herr hit a solo home run in the ninth inning — his 50th RBI of the year — to account for the only run of the game in a 1–0 shutout for John Tudor. It was the second time in two seasons that Herr had homered off the Mets' Tom Gorman, but this was Herr's first game-winning home run in his life. Gorman had been brought in after Mets starter Ed Lynch had matched goose eggs on the scoreboard with Tudor for eight innings. Tudor permitted the same allowances as Kepshire the day before, in giving up only three hits and one walk. The Cardinals had mustered only three hits off Lynch and Gorman as well, but Herr got the one that really counted. Rick Hummel noted that Herr's batting average (now .371) had been below .300 only twice in the season — once on Opening Day, and then again on April 19. "Right now, he's the best player in baseball," Herzog said simply of his second baseman. Herr echoed the confidence, but described it in terms of the whole unit. "Offensively, we're as good as anybody in our division and maybe the entire league."

The Cards and Mets split the Sunday doubleheader, with Gooden (9–3) beating Forsch (6–4) in the opener, 6–1, while Andujar got win number 11 in the nightcap against Calvin Schiraldi, 8–2. Andujar was getting twice as many runs per game from his offense (7.2) as Tudor, and his record showed it. The right-hander had matched the best start (11–1) in the National League since 1959, when Pittsburgh hurler Elroy Face was 17–0 for the Pirates (Andujar's record would be matched shortly by Andy Hawkins of the Padres). The win against the Mets was also the 100th triumph of his career. At the plate, Pendleton had the big highlight with an inside-the-park grand slam in the second game; and McGee had four hits on the day before, having to leave in the fifth inning of Game Two with leg problems. His work had raised his average to .359, with Herr still leading the league at .373. In taking three out of four in New York, the Cardinals' record stood at 29–25, four-and-a-half games behind the first place Cubs, who led the Mets by one-and-a-half and the Expos by a full two.

As the Cardinals were completing their series in New York and getting ready to move on to Pittsburgh to play the Pirates, Rick Sutcliffe sent the Bucs back to Three Rivers by firing a 1–0 shutout in Wrigley Field — his first appearance in three weeks since going on the disabled list. "It was kind of like Opening Day for me again," the tall, bearded thrower said. It was a great symbol of hope for Cubs fans, as their main man looked ready to assume his leadership role again. The Cubs were also yearning for the return of their other leader, outfielder Gary "Sarge" Matthews, who had joined Sutcliffe on the disabled list on May 29. The 34-year-old Matthews, in his 13th major league season, had undergone surgery on his knee to remove torn cartilage. The date for his return was not known. The Cubs knew that his leadership and experience would be missed, and they needed him back as soon as possible. Matthews, however, cautioned fans not to expect too much too soon. "I'm not going to be a messiah or anything," he told the *Chicago Tribune*. "I'm just going to try to come back and do the things I'm capable of doing."

Two days before Sutcliffe's return, it looked as if the other contender, the Expos, had found another arm. Mickey Mahler — making his first major league start since 1979 — threw a one-hitter against the Giants in San Francisco as the Expos won, 6–0. In other recent laurels, Willie McGee had been named the National League's Player of the Week by hitting .556 on 15-of-27 batting with six runs batted in and four stolen bases. The Cardinals as a team continued their hot hitting also, leading the circuit at a .272 clip on June 10, easily outdistancing the Padres who were next in line at only .257.

The Pirates were a franchise in disarray as the Cardinals arrived. The club had been put up for sale by president and majority owner Dan Galbreath, and in Galbreath's original proposal, the new buyer had to be someone who would keep the club in Pittsburgh. As the summer approached and no takers were found, however, he amended his conditions and said he would entertain offers that would take the team elsewhere. The most recent submissions came from Tampa, Denver, Indianapolis, and Newark, with an initial price tag of between $40 million and $45 million, "based on other recent sales," Galbreath said. A new owner would also have to contend with a lease the Pirates had with the City of Pittsburgh, effective through 2011. Joe Brown had recently been brought back for a second stint as general manager after Pete Peterson was let go, and he wasn't happy with the way things were, either. "I didn't come back to be caretaker at a cemetery," he complained. "We've got to make some changes ... if we just let things go as they're going, we'll be up to our rear in crocodiles."

By mid–June, the Pirates had been in last place of the National League

East for all but one day of the 1985 season, and the club reported that it had lost over $6 million in 1984, with larger losses coming over the current campaign. In a desperate effort, several of the city's radio stations and newspapers urged fans to attend the June 25 game against the Cubs at Three Rivers Stadium as a "finger on the pulse" for the fans' true support of the team. Home attendance for the Pirates in 1984 was 773,500, the lowest in the league; numbers for the 1985 season had been averaging only 11,000 per game to date, and if a similar figure was seen on the "Ballot-by-Ball Park" game — as it was dubbed by most in the press— then a case could be made for the team moving to another city. "If they can't fill the stadium for one game when you have a combination of an outstanding attraction, a concerted effort by the media, business community and civic organizations," projected Bob Keldan, sports editor of the *Pittsburgh Post-Gazette*, "then you would have to question whether the people of the city feel that retaining a major league franchise is a priority."

Others, however, weren't so sure that a one-day reprieve would solve anything. It would be "a commendable response to a grave situation," acknowledged another local writer, Bob Smizek, "but the turnout will prove little. Not even if 50,000 attend will the problem be solved.... [The problem] will not go away with one-day promotions and on-again, off-again intervention by politicians and businessmen."

"It's a farce," added Pirates' first baseman Jason Thompson of the one-day reading of public support. "It proves absolutely nothing. We'll come back from New York on Thursday and there will be 5,000." When the Dodgers came to town with the larger-than-life Valenzuela pitching, the gala spectacle drew only 6,500, which left Dodgers manager Tommy Lasorda scratching his head. "Fernando draws that many off the side streets in Los Angeles. He draws that many who don't even want to come to the ball game."

Third baseman Jim Morrison, called "normally easygoing and non-controversial" by Pittsburgh baseball writer Alan Robinson, summed up his feeling of the local sentiment. "This is a miserable environment to play baseball. There were 31,000 here today [in the most recent game with Chicago], and 26,000 were rooting for the Cubs and 5,000 were cheering for us. My opinion is that it's time for the team to move." In another example of the local apathy with baseball, Rick Hummel pointed out that 35,000 advance tickets had been sold for an upcoming tractor pull at Three Rivers Stadium.

Veteran pitcher John Candelaria, who had experienced championship seasons in the Steel City, had his own barometer on the clubhouse. "There are a lot of guys who'd like to get out, but they won't say so. If you asked,

I'll bet that half the people here would say they want out." Candelaria himself had been seeking a trade since spring training.

And behind it all was the ongoing drug trafficking controversy, which was said to involve several Pittsburgh players. The Pirates were one of the oldest teams in the league, having begun play in 1887.

Cox started off the set in fine fashion, tossing a complete-game four-hitter in beating the Pirates for his seventh win, 6–1. Cox also had two hits and two RBIs at the plate — the latter statistic matching his career total coming into the game. In an effort by Herzog to give him more of a chance to prove himself on the mound, Neil Allen got the start for the second game against the Pirates. Despite better numbers in recent weeks, he still hadn't been able to be consistent with his pitches. It was his first start of the year, matching the lone start he had made for all of the 1984 season. It was understood by all parties that trade advertisement was part of the reason for the start; Maxvill wanted to expose Allen to the other clubs to develop some interest in him. "I feel like I'm in a grocery store, like I'm on the shelf," Allen said of his situation. The talk was that the Yankees might have interest, and they wanted to send either Dale Berra or Omar Moreno to St. Louis in return. The Cardinals did not have much interest in either of those two players, but the talks continued about other scenarios.

The stuff on the grocery store shelf, unfortunately, was still not of good quality. Allen only lasted until the third inning after allowing six runs on eight hits. Horton, his successor, endured a rare rough outing for him, giving up an additional four runs in 1⅔ frames to send Pittsburgh off to a 13–2 victory. Rick Reuschel, the sideways-slinging right-hander who won 20 games for the Cubs in 1977, went seven strong innings for the win. "I feel sorry for Ricky and Ken Dayley [who followed Horton to the mound]," an ever-despondent Allen said in the locker room afterwards. "I set the stage for them, like an actor. It was like a Broadway play."

He then started talking about himself in the third person, as if he had joined the pack of sportswriters that were questioning him. "How can a guy come off spring training, when he gave up one run in 15 innings and all of a sudden this happens?" Meanwhile, in the major local drama that kept unfolding, each of the first two games in the series only drew slightly over 10,000 onlookers.

There was rain the next day, which pushed Tudor's start against Larry McWilliams to Thursday, June 13, which was originally scheduled as a travel day to Chicago. During the holdover, it had been rumored that the Cardinals were trying to acquire veteran hurler Bert Blyleven, a 34-year-old who some thought was on the last legs of his career after a 4–6 start to date in '85 with the Cleveland Indians. Maxvill saw something in him

5. Heating Up the Turf

that would help St. Louis, though, and stayed in contact with the Indians' brass. Cleveland was also getting inquiries from the Minnesota Twins, who were offering second baseman Tim Teufel and one of two catchers (Dave Engle or Tim Laudner), as well as from the Toronto Blue Jays and the California Angels. The Cards had wanted to deal Porter and Allen, but there appeared to be no interest — from the Indians or any other club — for their services. It was apparent that Allen's contract in particular, which called for $2.1 million over the next two years, was too much for any team to swallow. Furthermore, his main "audition" in a starting role in Pittsburgh did not help his cause.

Perhaps Allen should have looked to his old team, the Mets, for a job. The New Yorkers were certainly looking for throwers to mop up their June 11 run-in with the Phillies. Philadelphia outfielder Von Hayes tied a record by smacking two home runs in the first inning, and his teammates chipped in with 10 doubles along the way, as the Phillies steamrolled the Mets in Veterans' Stadium, 26–7. The 26 runs were a club record, and they were the most in the National League since the New York Giants walloped the Brooklyn Dodgers, 26–8, at the Polo Grounds in 1944.

While Allen could not find himself, Tudor's rise from the ashes continued. He gained his third win in a row and upped his overall mark to 4–7, as the Redbirds took the final game from Pittsburgh, 2–1, to win the series by the same margin. They had also run their record on the road trip to 5–2, as they prepared to battle the Cubs in Wrigley Field. Part of the credit for Tudor's turnaround was given to his friend and old high school teammate from Falmouth, Massachusetts, Dave Bettencourt, who was currently serving as a high school baseball coach in New Hampshire. Bettencourt had noticed a flaw in Tudor's delivery while watching a game on TV, and telephoned a remedy to the pitcher. "It was like ESP," Tudor said.

Seldom-used (to this point) Jeff Lahti relieved Tudor with two out in the ninth, with former Cardinal and home run threat Hendrick at the plate. Lahti promptly blew two fastballs and a slider past Silent George, and the game was quickly over with the strikeout. "I was a little nervous," Lahti admitted. "I hadn't been out there in a save situation for a while." Herzog, making another one of his brilliant game-saving moves, had a good reason for not letting Tudor finish the game. "I could have slept with it if George had hit one out on Lahti," he explained. "I wouldn't have if John had allowed a homer to him." Tudor, however, smiled as he politely disagreed with the manager. "I knew George wouldn't beat me," he said confidently. The Cards' two runs came from Clark's 13th homer in the second inning and a Landrum double after Herr had walked and stolen second in the seventh. Thompson homered for the Bucs in the bottom half of the seventh to draw Pittsburgh closer, but the scoring ended at that point. A measly gathering of 4,833 Pirates fans again went home disappointed.

The Cubs had posted a 13–5 record against the Cardinals in Chicago's charge to the division title in 1984. It was the renewal of the "I-55 Series" as the Midwestern rivals set to do battle once again. As was usually the case, a strong contingent of Cardinal supporters showed up at Wrigley Field, just as Busch Stadium was always privy to a throng of Cub-clad fans during the summer. "Cardinals–Cubs," Jack Clark mused, then sat and pondered for a moment. "I'm looking forward to getting involved in that." Herzog, focused on his business as was Clark, was not as nostalgic. "It's no life-or-death matter, but it's an important series because that's the team that kicked our butts last year."

"It's very important," offered Andy Van Slyke. "We have to prove to them that we are respectable." The Cards looked at it as an extra-special opportunity, for they would miss the Cubs' two best starting pitchers during the series in Sutcliffe and Trout, even though both had seemed to have recuperated from their injuries and regained their spots in the rotation. The Cubs were dealing with other injuries too, as Matthews wasn't expected back until July and center fielder Dernier — such an integral part of the Cubs' playoff run in '84 — was trying to play with a broken bone in his foot. Reliable fifth starter Scott Sanderson had an aching back, and even star second baseman Ryne Sandberg was hurting, nursing a strained rib cage that continuously nagged him when he swung the bat. Sandberg had sustained the injury on May 26, and had missed seven games thereafter.

As the Cardinals' plane landed in Chicago on June 14, the standings looked like this:

Eastern Division	W	L	Pct.	GB
Chicago	34	22	.607	—
Montreal	35	25	.583	1
New York	32	25	.561	2½
St. Louis	32	26	.552	3
Philadelphia	22	36	.379	13
Pittsburgh	19	37	.339	15
Western Division	W	L	Pct.	GB
San Diego	34	23	.596	—
Houston	31	27	.534	3½
Cincinnati	30	27	.526	4
Los Angeles	29	28	.509	5
Atlanta	25	32	.439	9
San Francisco	21	36	.368	13

5. Heating Up the Turf 79

The contest at Wrigley between the two teams that everyone remembered from 1984 came on June 23 — almost 12 months to the day — and had become known as the "Sandberg Game," when Ryno nailed his two home runs off Sutter, something that had never been done in one game against the great reliever. Sandberg became the new local icon in 1984, forming a triumvirate in Chicago that included the legendary Walter Payton of the Bears and a flashy rookie with the Chicago Bulls named Michael Jordan. But Sandberg had found success hard to come by at the start in '85. In addition to being hampered by his sore ribs, Sandberg had also been trying to recover from a poor April, as his batting average didn't reach .200 until May 5.

The opener of this series was almost as thrilling as that classic game from a year ago, and it foreshadowed great things to come for the rest of the season. It was punctuated by a play that signified the Cardinals were here stay in the National League East race. Going into the battle, Herr still led the league in hitting (.374) with McGee second (.356), while Coleman continued to set the National League pace in stolen bases and runs scored (41 in each category).

The Cards had opened up a 10–4 lead through six innings, at which point it seemed that the hinges would come off like Sutter's 12–11 loss the previous year. A two-run double by catcher Jody Davis sparked a Cubs rally. After St. Louis had picked up an insurance run in the ninth courtesy of a throwing error by pitcher George Frazier, a Davey Lopes home run with Richie Hebner on base had closed the gap to 11–10 in favor of the Cardinals. Sandberg followed with a double off Lahti, and with two out Forsch was brought in to face Keith Moreland. Moreland, a former defensive back for the University of Texas football team, took a hefty swing at a Forsch curve and sailed a fly ball down the right field line. A strong wind had been blowing off Lake Michigan, wreaking havoc on balls in the air all day long. Clark, Herr, and Van Slyke all converged near the Cardinals' bullpen as the ball seemed to drift back and forth between fair and foul territory. Fearing that he would run into Clark or Herr or the old brick wall that surrounded Wrigley Field, Van Slyke slid feet-first as he scooped his glove under the ball for the out, and the game was over. Forsch, who picked up his first save of the year (and only the second in his 11-year career with the Cardinals) remarked, "That was unbelievable."

"He's a Gold-Glover," Herzog added about Van Slyke after the game. "This kid can play with anybody."

The Cubs ruined their chances to win, as they committed five errors, each of which contributed to Cardinal runs. Andujar was a shaky starter for St. Louis, giving up four runs and seven hits in just over five innings before giving way to Campbell. Joaquin did get enough support from his bats and bullpen, however, to raise his record to a stellar 12–1 on the season. Once again, however, he complained of stiffness in his pitching shoulder, a condition that seemed to be more regular — and thus more of a cause for concern. Besides Andujar, there had been another Cardinal casualty in the course of battle at Wrigley. Pendleton, on a play similar to Van Slyke's catch on the other side of the field, pulled a hamstring while chasing a foul fly in the fifth inning. He was expected to go on the disabled list while Lawless took his place at third. Lawless contributed an RBI double in the sixth after Pendleton left the game. Lawless, who had recently gained the nickname of "Smurf" from Tom Nieto, noticed that "a lot of runs are scored a lot of ways in this ball park."

That would have been difficult for Lawless to prove to his teammates the next day, but even more so for the Cubs. Cox, along with Andujar making his own bid for a spot on the National League's All-Star pitching staff for the following month in Minnesota, shut down the Cubbie bats on four hits in posting a 2–0 shutout. The St. Louis tallies came in the first on a Coleman triple over Lopes's head in center field followed by a Herr ground out, and then in the seventh when Clark pounded his fourteenth homer of the year to lead off the inning. Lopes, who had been a second baseman since breaking in with the Dodgers in the early seventies, was getting his first try in center in place of the hurting Dernier, and was having trouble with fly balls hit directly over his head.

The Cardinals had fought their way back to a .500 record on the road (17–17) after beginning the year 1–8 away from home. With Cox's victory, the club also matched their entire win total (two) at Wrigley for the whole 1984 season. More importantly, they were proving to themselves and other teams that they could win on a natural surface. The speculation was, in other cities around the league, that the speed-laden Cardinals would not be as effective on grass as they were on Astroturf. Counting their previous nine games on grass, the Cardinals had stolen only three bases but had improved their record dramatically. It wasn't just their raw speed that was winning games; their execution on the hit-and-run, bunting, playing solid defense, and having an improved pitching staff all combined to give them success.

"Lately, we've just been doing everything, whatever it takes to win," Clark said proudly after the second victory over the Cubs in as many days. "One day it's a squeeze bunt, one day it's a home run, one day it's the bullpen."

"We're on our way," added Herr. "Anyone who doesn't think we're for real had better look again."

5. Heating Up the Turf 81

Meanwhile, the nerves were becoming ragged and tempers short on the defending champions' side. In trying to fend off all their injuries, the Cubs were becoming all the more grumpy in dealing with the pressure of a tightening National League East. It was reported that there was a lot of finger-pointing going on in the Cubs' locker room, but Jim Frey denied any dissension. "All you've got to do is look at who's not on the field," Frey responded to criticism about his piecemeal club in light of all the casualties. "We've come through a tough period here. You don't think we're doing too good, huh? There are 24 [expletive] teams who would like to be where we are right now."

Wherever that was, they retreated back one game closer to the Cards after the series finale, as St. Louis used a strong performance by Kepshire and Campbell finish off the Cubs, 5–2. It was the first sweep for St. Louis at Wrigley in over three years, and it cemented Kepshire's place in the starting rotation with another fine performance in a big game. The trading deadline had just passed on June 15, and he escaped a possible deal that would have sent him to the Indians along with Dayley for Blyleven. He gave way to Campbell in the ninth, as "Soup" picked up his third save. McGee and Herr had two hits each, as the Redbirds jabbed at Chicago starter Eckersley the full nine innings. The Cardinals had knocked the Cubs out of first place, put the Expos there in their stead, and trailed the former by only one game and the latter by two.

Over in the American League, big news had recently been made by former members of the Orioles' coaching staff. Ray Miller, the pitching guru who had helped develop Cy Young winners Mike Cuellar, Jim Palmer, Mike Flanagan, and Steve Stone in Baltimore, had been hired as the new manager of the Minnesota Twins, replacing the fired Billy Gardner. But a louder blast was heard on June 15, when the feisty Earl Weaver was brought back to lead the Orioles. The ownership felt that Joe Altobelli had the team underachieving (even though he owned a winning record of 31–26 at the time of his dismissal), and Weaver got a standing ovation from a crowd of 39,142 at Baltimore's Memorial Stadium when he brought out the lineup card before his first game back.

An off-day was relished by the Cards on Monday, June 17, as was the fact that they would be home most of the way until the All-Star Break that began on July 15. A roster move was also made on the travel day back home, as outfielder Curt Ford was brought up from Louisville to replace Pendleton, who finally had to go on the disabled list with his ailing hamstring. Ford had been batting .280 with 19 stolen bases at Triple-A, and it was reasoned that he would be sent back there when Porter came off the DL in the following week. The exact date for Porter's return, however, was pushed back further when the Cardinals returned; another examination showed very slow healing in his broken finger.

If success for the team was to continue, the new parts like Ford had to fit. Help from Lawless was needed at third, too, and he provided it. Over 44,000 fans welcomed the Cardinals back to Busch, and the Redbirds chased off future Hall-of-Famer Steve Carlton in the fifth inning after five runs had scored. Lawless had laced two hits on the night in place of Pendleton, and the running game kicked back into gear on the home turf. "The Cardinals won in the fashion they win a lot of games," reported Hummel. "Stolen bases [five], squeeze bunts [one], bunt singles (two), the threat to run [constant, oppressive to opponents] and a well-pitched game by a starter [John Tudor]." Tudor continued his rise back towards the .500 mark with another win, yielding to Lahti in a non-save situation in the ninth as St. Louis held on for a 6–2 final. The stolen bases were definitely back, as Coleman (44), McGee (26), and Herr (14) all padded their totals. For Herr, it was also the 57th time he had reached base in the last 60 games.

As the Cards stayed hot, the Cubs were formulating one the greatest falls in their fall-full history. The Mets beat them in New York 5–1 behind a complete-game win by Lynch, which was the seventh straight setback for Chicago. Despite the fact that they were facing Gooden in their next game, a threat of their club-record 13 straight losses (set in 1982 — and it took a 12–11 win over Carlton and the Phillies to end the streak in the 14th game) seemed improbable. "We have too many good players for this to continue," Moreland assured the faithful. "Gooden's not unbeatable. If you get in a slump like this, you have to forget each loss and go at each game with a positive attitude. If not, you'll never get going." As it turned out, Gooden shut out Chicago 1–0, and in doing so raised his major league–best strikeout total to 125 and lowered his major league–best ERA to 1.66. Sid Fernandez beat the Cubs the next day to complete yet another series sweep of the Bruins, and suddenly they had run their downward spiral to nine in a row.

Andujar, who was distantly sparring with Gooden for personal bragging rights in the league, was on the short end of a 1–0 score in St. Louis the day Gooden turned his trick against the Cubs, and the Cardinals' winning streak had been snapped at five. It was only the second loss of the year for the Dominican, as the 42-year-old Jerry Koosman, a veteran of the National League wars, tossed six shutout innings, which were followed by three more from Don Carman. "He threw 90 percent fastballs," Herzog said of Koosman in reflecting on the game. "He doesn't throw that hard, but he moves in and out and throws the pitch he wants."

"I don't care how old he is," answered Herr, who was held hitless for

5. Heating Up the Turf

one of the few times in recent weeks. "He throws hard. Hard enough." Andujar's temper got the better of him in the ninth, as he was working to keep the Cardinals in the game. The previous June, he had a tight-pitch encounter with Phillies catcher Ozzie Virgil which led to a bench-clearing brawl. The tensions between the two surfaced again in this game. As Andujar came close to Virgil's head with a couple of pitches, Virgil took a few steps towards the mound, as the players in both dugouts made their way to the top steps. After some shouting no more became of the incident, however, and Virgil bounced out to Lawless at third on the next pitch.

"Danny Cox didn't exactly blow the Philadelphia Phillies away Thursday night at Busch Stadium," John Sonderegger of the *Post-Dispatch* wrote about the next game, "and his performance won't conjure up images of Dizzy Dean. But Cox got by, with a little help from his friends."

Ozzie Smith (who was on pace to break Bowa's National League record for fewest errors by a regular shortstop in a season) and Herr flopped all over the infield turf the entire game, as they helped Cox run his consecutive scoreless innings streak to 23 in his 5–0 shutout of the Phils. He did scatter nine hits and two walks, but the end result was 10 runners left on base by Philadelphia as Kevin Gross took the loss. McGee and Herr each had two hits on the night, and Willie had actually overtaken Tommy in the league-batting race for a fleeting moment. McGee's two hits came early in the game, while Herr's came in the sixth and the ninth innings. Sonderegger pointed out that no National League teammates had finished 1–2 in the batting race since Willie Mays and Don Mueller of the 1954 New York Giants, and no Cardinals had turned the trick since Joe Medwick and Johnny Mize in 1937. Herr also extended his league lead in RBIs to 54 with his double to the left in the ninth. The 54 driven home for the year was already five more than his career high.

Now the Cubs were coming to town, and the Midwestern Showdown was getting some extra spice this year. The Cards were out to prove that they belonged on top, and the Cubs wanted to show everyone that 1984 wasn't a fluke.

6

The Changing of the Guard

As usual, there was not a seat to be had in Busch Stadium as the rivals took the field. A grand total of 46,005 had jammed the aisles in anticipation. The backdrop could not have been more fitting: the first day of summer, followed by a beautiful Friday night along the Mississippi, with the Cubs and Cardinals battling at seven o'clock in the world's greatest baseball city. The game signified more than just pure baseball, however — it was a shift of some of the power in the National League East, a shift that had been launched by Andy Van Slyke's great catch a week ago in Wrigley Field to preserve victory for St. Louis, and in doing so throwing the initial punch in a flurry that would put the Cubs on the ropes.

The Cubs learned quickly about the new bandit in town. After Kepshire retired Chicago in order in the top of the first, Coleman started the Cardinals' attack by walking off Eckersley, stealing second easily, and then crashing into Cey in a successful steal of third as the crowd exploded. For the season, it was already the fifth time Coleman had stolen multiple bases in one inning, and he now had a sum of 46. Herr then singled him home, and the Birds were off and running, never to look back. The swiped bags were somewhat of a personal matter for Coleman, who had been picked off by Eckersley the previous week in Chicago and would have been a second time if not for an errant throw by the right-hander.

It was Kepshire who got things going in the Cardinals' third, as he doubled off the right field wall. Coleman effectively moved him to third by pulling a ground ball to the right side, and then McGee singled for a 2–0 St. Louis lead. Another was tacked on the following inning, when Van Slyke's triple was followed by Smith's base hit past the drawn-in Speier at short. In the seventh, Cubs closer Lee Smith was brought in by Frey, with the manager thinking that the tide had to be stemmed at this point and

6. The Changing of the Guard

no later. McGee and Herr promptly walked, and Clark added another triple that cleared Coleman, McGee, and Herr off the bases for a 7–2 Cardinal advantage. Kepshire would tire, allowing a home run to Thad Bosley in the Cubs' eighth, but Dayley and Lahti blitzed Chicago in relief—the latter picking up his fifth save—as the Cards sent the Cubs to their tenth loss in a row, 7–5. The Cubs sent two harmless balls off Lahti to McGee in center field in the ninth to seal the deal. The papers pointed out that the Cardinals' "Bullpen by Committee"—six strong—had combined for 17 saves on the year, two more than what Sutter had by himself at the same point in 1984. "How many pitchers did I use in the ninth?" Herzog asked afterwards. "I'm going to have to get a new pair of shoes."

With the victory, Kepshire was now 3–0 on the season against Chicago, and the Cardinals found themselves somewhere they hadn't been since Opening Day of *1984*—in first place, tied with the Mets at 37–27. The Mets' 6–3 win over Montreal in New York—their fifth in a row—had pushed the Expos out of the top spot. No one could seem to put a finger on what was happening to the Cubs. "It's way too early to call the Cubs the Titanic and the Cardinals the Love Boat," snipped the *Post-Dispatch*, "but St. Louis has beaten Chicago four times in four tries this summer." Adding to the Cubs' woes, starting catcher Jody Davis was now on the sick roll, too, after contracting a viral infection and anemia. He was sent back to Chicago for treatment, and it was assumed that he would find himself on the disabled list. Then when it became known that the Cubs were shopping around for catching help, it was rumored that the Cardinals were interested in sending Darrell Porter to Chicago, but that the Cubs declined (which would have been an unusual trade anyway, of the intra divisional variety between contending clubs). In the meantime, Steve Lake took Davis's place in the Cubs' patchwork lineup that still had an absent Dernier and Matthews, and a sore Sandberg.

McGee's two-hit performance pushed him ahead of Herr in the batting race once again, as Willie's mark now stood at .353, one point ahead of his teammate.

The Cubs thought that they could finally right themselves the next day, sending Sutcliffe, the reigning National League Cy Young Award winner, to the mound. Sutcliffe's return from his hamstring injury had provided hope for Chicago, and he had looked strong in his recent starts. He brought in a 6–5 record and a sharp 2.11 ERA into the series with St. Louis. Few pitchers in baseball history could match his pace that had begun 12 months ago. After being picked up in June of '84 by Chicago from Cleveland, he proceeded to win 16 games in 17 decisions.

Sutcliffe knew that the complexion of the division had changed since the Cubs' success in the past year. "Maybe in spring training it was the Mets, but now I'd say our biggest competition is the Cardinals and the Expos," Sutcliffe said. To be sure, the Mets were having some problems of their own. But their manager, Davey Johnson, wasn't overly concerned. He pointed out that their recent four-game winning streak had landed them back in first place again. "Winning four games didn't help us as much as losing four would have hurt," he explained. "If you go to Las Vegas and you win $25,000, it doesn't cover all your debts. But if you go and lose $25,000, you're in deep trouble."

Things were going so badly for the Mets that they were even missing their doctor appointments. Berenyi, who was having elbow problems, made an appointment to meet with surgeon James Andrews in Columbus. Berenyi got off a plane in Columbus, but unfortunately it was Columbus, Ohio—unbeknownst to him, Andrews had his practice in Columbus, Georgia.

It did look like the worm would finally turn for Sutcliffe's Cubs, as he dominated the early part of the game — which included successive strikeouts of three of the Cardinals' big guns in Herr, Clark, and Van Slyke. No St. Louis player reached first base safely until the fourth, in fact, when Coleman and McGee singled to start a potential rally. The Redbirds batted for 20 minutes, but the assault was controlled by Sutcliffe and the game remained scoreless. It stayed that way until the Chicago fifth when Ricky Horton, who was in relief of starter Bob Forsch and hadn't pitched in nearly two weeks, walked Cubs slugger Leon Durham with the bases loaded to force in the game's first run. As usual, however, Horton righted himself and pitched three more strong innings to keep St. Louis in the game. The Cards finally broke through in the seventh on a ground-rule double by Van Slyke and a pinch-hit single off the bat of Steve Braun. It was only the third hit of the year for Braun, but his role would increase and his production improve in the coming weeks.

After Dayley relieved Horton and pitched a scoreless ninth and tenth for the Cards (helped by Coleman's nailing the speedy Lopes in the tenth when he tried to stretch a lead-off single into a double), Curt Ford finally got his chance. Smith led off the St. Louis tenth with a sharp base hit off Lee Smith, who could feel pressure mounting again. Smith subsequently uncorked a wild pitch, sending Ozzie to second. Nieto then struck out, which brought the 24-year-old rookie Ford to the plate. In giving Ford the opportunity, Herzog liked his left-handed bat against Smith, the hard-throwing righty. Ford worked the count on the rattled Smith to a favorable 2–0, when Ozzie broke for third with the next pitch. Ford swung and drove a base hit to right which scored the Wizard, and the Cardinals' bench leapt

6. The Changing of the Guard

Andy Van Slyke (right) is greeted by Vince Coleman and Tom Lawless after hitting a home run at Busch Stadium. *(From the collections of the St. Louis Mercantile Library at the University of Missouri–St. Louis)*

out of the dugout to welcome home the heroes in the 2–1 win. What ruined the Cubs in this game was squandered chances; Forsch was uncharacteristically wild, walking six in his 4⅔ innings of work. Chicago left ten runners on base, however, as for the year Sutcliffe had gotten only ten runs of support in his six losses.

"Tudor Shows Cubs the Door"

The headline of the June 24 edition of the *Post-Dispatch* said it all. The crafty left-hander needed only 82 pitches to dispose of Chicago in one of the finest pitching performances in the league during the year. Tudor (6–7) allowed a scant two hits, walked one, and struck out six in a dominating 7–0 whitewash of the Cubs. He was happy to remain hot. "You feel yourself getting in the groove. Now I just want to stay in it." It capped his "streak within a streak," as he was named the National League Player of the Week for his 17 innings worth of two-run throwing (not to mention his .429 batting average during the seven-day span). He participated in two Cardinal offensive attacks against the Cubs in the second and fifth with two hits and an RBI.

It was the eighth win in the last nine tries for St. Louis, as they stayed a half-game in front of Montreal in the National League East. Little-used Ivan DeJesus, a former Cubs starter, gave Lawless the day off at third and displayed himself as another suitable replacement for Pendleton. He had two doubles, a run scored, and drove home Herr and Clark in the seventh for the Redbirds' final runs. Dick Ruthven was the unlucky pitcher this time for the Cubs, as Trout was unable to make his scheduled start with a sore shoulder. The game was played in less than two hours, and the weekend contests had drawn over 140,000 to the ballpark in St. Louis.

The Cubs looked forward to a travel day on Monday, June 24, to lick their wounds. They had played for 20 straight days, but to call Monday an "off day" was a misnomer — for they had been "off" for two weeks. "There are all kinds of emotions," Frey summated as the team got ready to head to the airport. "You can get upset. You can get mad. You can get angry. You can go sleepless. You have to understand that the ballplayers are undergoing the same emotions. I don't think they like it any better than we [the manager and coaches] do.... It's like you squandered all the good things you've done for two-and-a-half months." The Cubs were now one loss away from tying the club record for consecutive futility. "Nowadays," Tom Wheatley of the *Post-Dispatch* noticed, "Jim Frey is as jolly as an undertaker."

Wheatley continued by adroitly noticing the superb work of Herzog in orchestrating the Cardinals club, and in Maxvill, McDonald, Kuhlmann, Susman, and Herzog in constructing it.

"In Sunday's 7–0 victory over the Cubs, Herzog's lineup featured:

• A rookie left fielder (Vince Coleman) and a rookie catcher (Randy Hunt).

• A shortstop at third base (Ivan DeJesus).

• A right fielder at first base (Jack Clark).

• An erstwhile third baseman / erstwhile first baseman in right field (Andy Van Slyke).

• A pitcher, projected as the staff's number-two starter, who got off to a 1–7 start this season (John Tudor).

"A check of the lineup that finished last season for the Cardinals shows that:

6. The Changing of the Guard

- The number-one reliever is in Atlanta (Bruce Sutter).
- The number-two starter (Dave LaPoint) and the first baseman (David Green) are in San Francisco.
- The left fielder is in Kansas City (Lonnie Smith).
- The right fielder is in Pittsburgh (George Hendrick).
- The catcher (Darrell Porter) and the third baseman (Terry Pendleton), both having sub-par years, are on the disabled list.
- The number-two reliever is in Nowhere Land, although still a Cardinal (Neil Allen).

"But the players Herzog has been sending up can hit the ball and run, which is why he has himself a first-place club."

While the Cards were doing everything right, there truly seemed to be a curse with the Cubs. As the team played the Mets in Chicago on June 25 after leaving St. Louis, Moreland misjudged a fly ball off the bat of Dykstra in the first inning at Wrigley Field. Dykstra, scooting to third on the play, went on to score on a sacrifice fly by Hernandez, and the gift out proved to be the difference in a 3–2 loss for Chicago, tying the club record for defeats in a row at 13. It had been a hard task in any event, as they were facing Gooden and a raucous crowd that booed every inept move the home club made.

On one of the rare occasions at Wrigley where the majority of the people in the stands were actually watching the game (as opposed to the usual sun tanning or talking on mobile phones), every move the Cubs made was scrutinized by the Bleacher Bums. Gooden rode homers by Carter and Howard Johnson on the way to his 11th win.

It looked as if Moreland would help perpetuate the steak the next day, as he missed two bunt attempts in a crucial situation in the sixth inning. On his last strike, however, he turned into the hero as he slammed a three-run homer off McDowell and the Cubs finally found the oasis in a 7–3 triumph. In trying to convey his sense of relief, Frey said, "We've been in labor for two weeks, and we gave birth today." However, Frey couldn't conceal his foul language even in victory, posing the questions for himself that he knew he would get from the reporters. "I'll save you all of asking the same old questions," he continued. "How did it feel today? [Expletive] great. How did it feel before today? [Expletive, expletive]. It's been a pain in the [expletive, expletive]. Did you feel like you had a monkey on your back? Yeah, a [expletive] gorilla was what it was."

As Chicago celebrated a win, a familiar foe for the Cardinals simultaneously cooled them off in Philadelphia. Koosman, coming off his commanding performance in St. Louis the previous week, solved Andujar and the Redbirds once again to the tune of a 3–1 score. After throwing six shutout innings at Busch Stadium in his last effort, Koosman went the distance this time, allowing just one unearned run while striking out eight. "He's one of the best left-handers in baseball today," Andujar (12–3) admitted after the game. "When I am his age, I wish I could pitch like him." What was most troubling for the Cards was Koosman's effective left-handed move to first base, which kept the St. Louis jackrabbits off balance all night.

Coleman got his 48th steal, but the players mentioned that it was their only true chance to run the entire game. They got their lone run through a gift, on a most unusual scene — two errors in one play by one player. Recently, the Phillies had made an unthinkable switch, moving Schmidt over to first base and giving Rick Schu the job at third. Although the move had worked out for the most part, Schu ran into a problem in the second inning in this game. Smith tapped a ball to him, which Schu first kicked and then fired wildly past Schmidt at first, allowing Landrum to cross the plate.

Herzog relayed an interesting story about Koosman from 18 years prior, when Herzog was working for the Mets and Koosman was struggling to hang on with the club.

"He [Koosman] was at Auburn in the New York–Penn League. I was at the Mets' meeting when they were going to release him, but they kept him because he owed Joe McDonald, who was the minor league director, fifty bucks. They were going to keep him until the first payday. But then he pitched two shutouts. They never thought he threw hard enough."

But he did throw hard enough, as Tommy Herr suggested, to hang on through 1985, and end his career with 222 victories and over 2,500 strikeouts.

It had gotten clearer in recent weeks that Schmidt had become disgruntled with the Phillies' front office and fans. He, along with Carlton, had been the bedrock of the club for over a decade; and now, he mentioned that he and his teammates were more comfortable playing on the road instead of before their unforgiving fans at home. "They're beyond help," Schmidt said of the Philadelphia baseball followers while talking to reporters in Montreal. "I'll tell you something about playing in Philadelphia. Whatever I've got in my career now, I would have had a great deal more if I'd played my whole career in Los Angeles or Chicago, you name a town — somewhere where they were just grateful to have me around. Every player on every team has peaks and valleys; Philadelphia is the worst place on earth to be in a valley."

The media weighed the evidence, and sided with the player. "Schmidt has heard the boos throughout his career — in both good and bad times," concluded the Associated Press. "But now he sounds like a bitter man, winding down a brilliant career in a city that demolishes him every time he pops to short."

Schmidt, admittedly, had been dealing with problems at the plate; he was in a homerless streak that reached 94 at-bats, the longest in his career, before he connected against the Pirates on May 27, the 433rd of his career. Meanwhile, over in the American League, California Angels slugger Reggie Jackson launched his 513th career home run off Don Schulze of the Indians, which put Jackson in tenth place on the all-time list. He would finish his career in 1987 with 563 homers, sixth all-time; Schmidt would hang up his spikes two years later with 548, right behind Jackson in seventh place.

Carlton, the other sacred cow, had contrarily become expendable to the local press. "He has become a six-inning pitcher," said one Philadelphia writer, which while meant as a pejorative towards Carlton might be considered a compliment when given to a starting pitcher today.

Cox (9–3) lost his bid to become the next ten-game winner in the league the following night in bowing to John Denny, 6–4. In the loss, Coleman became the quickest rookie to reach 50 steals in a season, as he pilfered two bags off Denny and Virgil. The final game of the series was salvaged by Kepshire (5–5), who although admitting to "hate pitching day games," shut down Shane Rawley in the afternoon get-away tilt on Thursday, June 27. The difference in the 4–3 final score was Ozzie Smith, who hit his third homer of the season, and just the tenth of his eight-year major league career — and all ten had come right-handed.

The Cards went home to prepare for a visit from the Mets, the latter being two-and-a-half games behind the front-running Expos, and just a full two behind St. Louis.

There had been many things to point to in evaluating the Cards' turnaround. The best microcosm, though, had to be Tudor, and he came full circle on June 28. The lefty reached his immediate goal of returning to the .500 mark, as he went 7⅓ innings with strong bullpen help from Lahti and Dayley in outlasting the Mets, 3–2, in front of nearly 46,000 happy fans. He was now 6–0 for the month of June, and had been cruising through six scoreless innings when George Foster touched him for a home run in the seventh, and Mookie Wilson followed with another in the eighth. Tudor showed resiliency in the close game, however, as he fought back and kept the Cards ahead.

"He battled," said his catcher on the day, Tom Nieto. "He knew he didn't have his good stuff and I knew he didn't. But he hung in there." Tudor's composure was evident; his level-headed perspective had shone through back on June 9, after his shutout of the Mets at Shea Stadium had put his record at 3–7. He was anxious to get back to an even record, but he knew that it wouldn't happen overnight. "You can't win games two at a time. You can't get to seven until you get to four." Now, the elusive .500 milepost had been passed.

The Cardinals combined hits by Van Slyke, DeJesus, and Nieto into two runs in the second inning, and Herr followed in the third with his third home run for a 3–0 lead. The Wilson blast wound up the last tally of the game, as Dayley finished off the last four Mets batters in succession for his sixth save. Herr's 3-for-4 performance raised his average to .346, but it still trailed McGee, who was at .350 (despite going 0-for-4 on the day).

Everyone — especially the Mets — were waiting for the Cardinals to fold. "Things change," Howard Johnson told the press when they asked about the young Redbirds' success. They received some more convincing evidence from Andujar, though, as he followed Tudor's win with a dazzling 6–0 shutout. He walked only one and permitted six singles as his mark improved to 13–3.

Rick Aguilera, the Mets' starter, was run off by the Cards in a second-inning onslaught that also featured a 39-minute rain delay. Curt Ford, making his first big league start, singled to get the party going. After he stole second, DeJesus reached on an error which was followed by a Nieto triple. Coleman then singled home Nieto, and started terrorizing Carter by stealing second and going to third on the catcher's errant throw into center field. When Smith singled to score Coleman, St. Louis had a 4–0 lead, and it was more than the Dominican hurler needed.

The party got even better the next day, as Cox powered the team to a 2–1 win in 11 innings over Dwight Gooden. Cox and Gooden didn't figure in the decision, but the three-headed St. Louis bullpen of Horton, Lahti, and Dayley overmatched Mets left-hander Jesse Orosco. Through the ninth, Gooden and Cox had each allowed only one run (Cox's was unearned) in giving way to their respective relievers. It looked like the Cardinals would beat the star right-hander, as Clark hammered a long home run (his fifteenth) to left field in the seventh. After Clark took a curtain call out of the dugout for the St. Louis fans, the Mets came back to manufacture a run in the eighth. After a scoreless ninth, tenth, and top of the eleventh for the Mets, Coleman knocked a hit down the left field line that scored DeJesus, who had just doubled, for the game-winner. Coleman enjoyed the success against a southpaw, which recently had been hard to come by. "I had been struggling a bit from the right side, but that felt very good," he said.

Excitement in the city was starting to build. "If it's too early for pennant fever," announced the *Post-Dispatch*, "it's too late for cold sweats and

6. The Changing of the Guard

Manager Whitey Herzog congratulates pitcher Ken Dayley after a Cardinal win. At left is fellow reliever and boyhood neighbor of Dayley's, Jeff Lahti. *(From the collections of the St. Louis Mercantile Library at the University of Missouri–St. Louis)*

small talk about waiting and seeing what's next." The series with the Mets had even outdrawn the always-popular Cubs series by 128 paying customers, with 141,245 coming to see the Redbirds tangle with the New Yorkers.

As credit for the Cardinals' success was distributed among the players by most in the media, Jack Clark had a different idea. "The big thing is the manager," he said in pointing his praise towards Herzog. "It's nice to come somewhere where someone is in control and everyone knows it. It's not like he's a sergeant. He's one of the boys. But if he says, 'That's enough goofing around, let's do our work,' we do it. When I played against him, I knew that he was one of the best managers in the game."

"Whitey's fun to play for," Herr concurred. "There's no mistaking that he's the boss, but he lets us play. He leaves so much responsibility up to us. He gives the green light [to steal a base] to everybody, even kids who haven't been here that long."

When the dust of their fury had settled, the Cards had streaked to a record of 19–8 for June. As the month of June closed, the National League standings looked this way:

Eastern Division	W	L	Pct.	GB
St. Louis	43	29	.597	—
Montreal	43	32	.573	1½
Chicago	38	33	.535	4½
New York	38	34	.528	5
Philadelphia	32	40	.444	11
Pittsburgh	24	47	.338	18½

Western Division	W	L	Pct.	GB
San Diego	44	30	.595	—
Cincinnati	39	33	.542	4
Los Angeles	38	34	.528	5
Houston	38	37	.507	6½
Atlanta	33	40	.452	10½
San Francisco	27	48	.360	17½

His couple of instances of heroics notwithstanding, Ford was optioned back to Louisville after the Mets series to make room for Pendleton, whose hamstring had healed. And Tudor was rewarded again for his success, as he was named the National League Pitcher of the Month for June.

Pedro Guerrero of the Dodgers, who hit 15 home runs for a new record for June, was the league's Player of the Month. His record would be broken by Sammy Sosa of the Cubs in June 1998, when Sosa had an amazing 20 home runs—the most in any month in history. How did Guerrero stay hot for so long? "He's from the Dominican Republic," explained Lasorda. "I told him that, here in America, the months of April, September, and November have 30 days, and June has 50. He thinks it's June 38." Guerrero had been acquired by the Dodgers from Cleveland in 1974 for pitcher Bruce Ellingsen, who by 1985 was out of baseball and had become a liquor salesman in Los Angeles. Lasorda noted that, by mere chance, he knew Ellingsen's boss. "It was a trade that worked out great for both parties," he said. "We got a great baseball player and Ellingsen's boss says he got a great liquor salesman."

In spite of his award, Tudor did not let the applause go to his head. After Horton lost to the Expos in extra innings on July 1, Tudor (8–7) came back the next day for his seventh win in a row, and it was another shutout—his third in his last six starts—as he blanked Montreal on three hits and no walks, 4–0. The Cards gave him all the support he needed in a three-run first inning, as Coleman ignited things yet again with a single, stolen base, and run scored on a hit by McGee. Clark and Pendleton added hits to allow Herr (who had walked) and McGee to score. The stolen bases on

6. The Changing of the Guard

the night by Coleman (his 54th), Pendleton (7), and two by McGee (31) had chased the club total to 149 on the year.

In Philadelphia, the Phillies blasted out the lights on Sutcliffe and the Cubs, 11–2. Back in Spingfield, Illinois, the Illinois General Assembly left the lights out on the Wrigley Field situation as well, as it decided to adjourn for the summer without resolving the issue. Night baseball at Wrigley was prohibited by state law (as well as by Chicago city ordinance), so it would take an act by the Assembly to enable it. The delay caused some to worry that an anti-nocturnal stadium would keep the Cubs out of the playoffs — or make them move outside the city. Governor Jim Thompson, however, told the citizens not to worry. "I think we're getting way ahead of the horse and the cart. I don't think it's going to be the Schaumburg Cubs. It's the Chicago Cubs, and they're going to win the pennant and the World Series," he predicted boldly. Nonetheless, people were becoming nervous when they learned that the Chicago Tribune Company, which owned the team, also possessed a 100-acre tract of land in Schaumburg that was ready for development.

As the Dodgers came to St. Louis for a Fourth of July matchup with the Cardinals, the much-maligned career of their talented left-handed reliever, Steve Howe, seemed to be coming to an end. He had been suspended for the entire 1984 season for cocaine use, and was mysteriously AWOL for the Dodgers' game in Atlanta on June 30. The Dodgers released the southpaw, winner of the 1980 National League Rookie of the Year award, before the club left for its current road trip. Howe himself believed that an exit from L.A. was the best thing for him. "I have found it necessary to advise the Dodgers that I could not effectively handle many of the pressures I have here in the Los Angeles area," he stated in a press release. "Los Angeles is full of my friends and supporters. Regretfully, I daily encounter situations that cause me deep pain. I believe my continuing improvement demands a relocation and a reduction of stress." His teammates, such as fellow pitcher Dave Stewart, agreed it was best that he got out of the fishbowl in Los Angeles. "It got so bad that if he sneezed, they wanted him to take a urine test."

The problems for Howe, unfortunately, were only just beginning. He would be picked up by the Minnesota Twins later in the 1985 season, and would have future stints with the Rangers, Padres, and Yankees through 1994. He would suffer several relapses into his drug habit, but became even more infamous for the numerous "second chances" that he subsequently received to resume his major league career.

St. Louis was one of the favorite destinations for Lasorda in the National League. He could be found at one of several Italian restaurants around the area, especially Charlie Gitto's downtown and various spots on The Hill. The food and fireworks were all that Tommy got to enjoy on this July 4. Andujar became the first 14-game winner in the majors as he out-pitched Rick Honeycutt, Tom Niedenfuer, and Ken Howell of the Dodgers for over three hours in achieving a 3–2 win. And after Los Angeles came back to take the next two games against Cox and Kepshire, Tudor continued his amazing string by beating the Dodgers in the finale, his eighth win in a row, to gain a 2–2 split in the series.

Although Tudor's win wasn't another shutout, it nearly was; the left-hander logged another complete game, allowed only one run, and got three hits of support from both Pendleton and Smith as the Cards were victorious, 7–1. Coleman had saved the day defensively, as he broke back on Terry Whitfield's drive that went over his head late in the game and bounced against the left field wall. In one motion, Coleman grabbed the ball with his bare hand and threw a no-hop strike to Herr at second to get Whitfield. Also on the defensive side, Ozzie had a rare blemish as he made his first error since June 9, and only his fourth all year. Coleman had to sit out the final two games of the series after he hurt his wrist, and his status was day-to-day. Interestingly, the win put the Cardinals up by one game in the voluminous all-time series against the Dodgers, 933–932.

The morning of July 4 saw the latest-ending game in National League history, as the Mets clubbed a team-record 28 hits for a New York victory in a contest that was decided at 3:55 A.M. in Atlanta. Hernandez then hit for the cycle in the regularly-scheduled game later that day.

Looking at the Cardinals' roster, Maxvill was expecting a near return from Porter, who was to be sent to Triple-A Louisville for some rehabilitation games to test his healed finger. Even though Nieto had won the starting catching job, Herzog was looking forward to making Porter's left-handed bat available once again. Through the Fourth of July, Nieto was hitting .370 (10-for-27) in an eight-game stretch dating back to June 26.

While Herr continued to lead the National League in RBIs (63) and be second to teammate McGee in hitting (.339 to McGee's .347), he was finding it difficult to unseat Sandberg in the All-Star voting for the starting second base position. The game was a week away as the Cardinals concluded their series with the Dodgers, and Herr was behind Sandberg by 32,000 votes—despite the fact that Herr had closed the gap in recent weeks. Ozzie Smith had a commanding lead at shortstop with over a million votes, while Dale Murphy and Padres' first baseman Steve Garvey were in a tight race for being the top overall vote-getter.

The Andujar Storm raged on, as the visiting Giants and former teammate LaPoint were the next victims. Even though darkness never seems

6. The Changing of the Guard

to be a coolant for the St. Louis summer anyway, it was a particularly hot night on July 8 at Busch Stadium, and the hefty LaPoint couldn't match the stamina of Andujar. "That's another reason Joaquin is an amazing pitcher," LaPoint marveled. "He can go out in this heat time after time and throw nine innings." LaPoint knew all too well the meaning of no run support, as amazingly, he himself was outhitting the Giants team (.222 to .220) in games he had started. Andujar scattered twelve hits, but the Giants left the same number of men on base.

Coleman, having returned from his wrist injury, tripled and got his 56th steal as part of a 6–1 St. Louis win. It was another three-hit night for Smith, as the batting average for the defensive-minded shortstop had suddenly ballooned to .272. Pendleton also got another three knocks, as his average—which had been down around the .200 mark a couple of weeks prior—was presently an improving .241. Even Nieto, he of the strong arm and good work behind the plate, had demonstrated a big bat in recent days. He contributed a two-run single in the sixth inning of Andujar's win, and the nice surprise of his bat for the Cardinals made Miklasz compare it to "Billy Joel discovering that Christie Brinkley can cook."

The Cards, now 15 games over .500 at 47–32, continued to lead the Eastern Division by two-and-a-half games over the Mets and Expos. The Mets were gaining steam once again, as their recent nine-game winning streak was the club's longest since winning ten in a row in 1976, and their string of seven road wins in succession had set a team record.

A strong case could have been made for Herr as the first-half MVP of the National League, and that was what made an incident so frightening the next night for St. Louis fans. In the first inning, after he had doubled home Coleman to give the Cardinals a 1–0 lead on Giants starter Bill Laskey, Herr bolted as Clark hit a laser-shot single towards Jeff Leonard in left field. Despite the hard-hit ball, Herr was waved home by third base coach Hal Lanier. Leonard's throw went up the third base line a bit, and was retrieved by catcher Bob Brenly. Brenly reached back for a tag on Herr, and his shin guard caught Herr directly above his left kneecap. Those in the ballpark who witnessed the nasty collision feared that Herr had blown out his knee entirely. Fortunately, he was able to remain in the game as the injury was diagnosed as only a deep upper-thigh bruise, and he helped Cox improve his record to 10–4 with a 3–1 victory.

Coleman, who stole his 57th base before being driven home by Herr, was ejected by home plate umpire Joe West for arguing balls and strikes in the sixth inning. Afterwards, the Giants were able to sneak across their lone run in the ninth, and Cox just missed his fourth shutout, which would have tied Valenzuela for the league lead. The hard-luck Laskey, meanwhile

Tommy Herr smoothly turns the doubleplay with Chris Speier barreling in during the Cards' game with the Cubs at Busch Stadium on June 20, 1985. *(From the collections of the St. Louis Mercantile Library at the University of Missouri–St. Louis)*

6. The Changing of the Guard

(only one part of the Giants' hard-luck pitching staff), saw his mark fall to 1–11—partly due to a .219 overall team batting average for San Francisco. Things must have been bad financially in San Francisco, too, as the club decided to go with little-league baseballs for batting practice, which saved them $1.25 each.

Much to the surprise of the baseball world, the newspapers on July 11 announced that Herr had now taken over the lead in the All-Star balloting for second base over Sandberg, and that Herr would indeed be the starter for the National League in Minneapolis five days later. Teammate Smith was also penciled in for the third straight year at shortstop, and it was the fifth career appearance for the Wizard, who had been an All-Star with the Padres in 1980 and 1981. Murphy edged out Smith and Garvey for the league-wide lead with nearly one-and-a-half million votes. It was the first trip to the big game for Herr, and Sandberg was gracious about the turn of events in the voting. "Tommy Herr is definitely having an All-Star season, and that's what the game is for," Sandberg said. "In this case, the fans did their job."

Some in the media made the case for as many as five other Cardinals to make the squad, namely McGee, Clark, Cox, Andujar and Coleman. Dick Williams of the Padres, having the privilege of managing the National League in light of San Diego's pennant in 1984, did not yet tip his hand on who would comprise the pitching staff, or who the starting pitcher would be. "That depends on a lot of factors," he stated, "and I'm looking at all of them. Maybe tomorrow, maybe Saturday... Andujar, with the year he's had, certainly deserves the top consideration. If you go by the numbers, then he has some of the best." If the season had started in May, then Tudor would have been the hands-down choice to start for the National League.

Coleman, not on the St. Louis roster at the start of the season, did not have his name on the ballot and had to be posed as a write-in candidate. He received the most such votes in the league with over 67,000.

Coleman had certainly helped his cause the previous night, as he collected two more stolen bases (his 58th and 59th) and scored two runs in Kepshire's 7–3 beating of Vida Blue and the Giants. Smith, who was now batting .377 in his last 13 games, made one of his two hits his fourth home run of the year (with all 11 in his career still coming right-handed), and Clark added his sixteenth. It was exactly the halfway point of the season, and the Cards' record stood at 49–32, keeping their two-and-a-half game distance from Montreal and New York.

Tudor got the ball the next day against San Diego, and he furthered a new scoreless innings streak to 17 with yet another shutout, a five-hitter against the Padres. The Cards ran wild on San Diego starter Mark Thurmond and catcher Terry Kennedy, as the club stole eight bases, highlighted by the performances of Coleman and McGee (three each). "I respect speed," a shell-shocked Williams mumbled after the game. "Whitey's got it, and more power to him."

Meanwhile, down in Houston, flamethrower Nolan Ryan was getting ready for another appearance in the All-Star Game. He did so in style by fanning Danny Heep in the sixth inning against the Mets for the 4,000th strikeout of his career. The game was then halted as he got a two-minute standing ovation from the sellout crowd in the Astrodome. Heep's whiff was the first out in the inning; Ryan struck out Rafael Santana and Sid Fernandez for 4,002 before the Astros batted again. He remained 85 strikeouts ahead of Carlton on the career list, and the gap was widening as Carlton continued to struggle with a sore left shoulder.

The following day, Williams announced that McGee, Clark, and Andujar would join Herr and Smith representing that Cardinals on the National League roster. Going into the Cardinals-Padres game that night, however, it was still undecided as to who the starting pitcher would be for the National League, as Ryan and Gooden would not have enough rest to do so. So Williams left it up to the head-to-head duel that night at Busch Stadium occurring between Andujar and the Padres' right-hander Lamarr Hoyt. Hoyt, a newcomer to Williams' staff in San Diego, was appearing to regain the Cy Young form he had displayed with the Chicago White Sox in 1983. He was teaming with Hawkins to give the Padres a great duo during the first half of the season, and he took top honors in the confrontation with Andujar. Hoyt ran his record to 12–4 in seven innings of two-hit, no-walk baseball (his tenth win in a row), and Rich "Goose" Gossage finished things off with his 18th save, as San Diego took one from the Redbirds, 2–0.

Hoyt was in the middle of an incredible demonstration of control, in which he would walk only 15 batters in his first 154 innings of the 1985 season. The Padres had given up two players with major league experience plus a prime shortstop prospect in Ozzie Guillen for Hoyt, but still felt that they got the better end of the deal. And even though White Sox fans weren't happy with the trade, Chicago manager Tony LaRussa defended the move. "I'd do it again in a minute," he said. "Not only that, but I'd do it for Ozzie Guillen straight up. This kid is a special type of player. I'd like to see all the people that questioned that trade to put their names on a piece of paper and I will check with them in a few years."

Andujar (15–4) didn't pitch that badly, going eight innings and evenly distributing eight hits. In a strange turn of events, Andujar then announced

6. The Changing of the Guard 101

that he was not going to the All-Star Game after all — claiming that Williams had already made his decision before the Padres-Cardinals game that Hoyt would be the choice. "How many guys go to the All-Star Game 15–3?" Andujar complained. "Not very many." The local media had become used to this sort of thing out of him, but the act was a surprise to many on the national scene. It was imagined that his boycott would ultimately hurt his chances for the Cy Young Award to be given at the end of the season. Andujar, however, didn't seem to be bothered by that, either.

How did Williams feel about Andujar's pouting? "I really don't give a care," he said. He also made clear that Andujar's inference that Williams had something against him because he was Dominican was ridiculous. "I've got a guy 11–2 [Hawkins] not going. I've got a catcher who's not going [Kennedy] because the league office said I have to take somebody else to have a player from every team. I got a telegram from somebody in Massachusetts today who was mad at me because I didn't take John Tudor."

The Cards righted themselves to take two more wins from the Padres before the All-Star break, courtesy of Cox and Kepshire. Kepshire's effort was particularly strong, as he allowed only one run in eight innings while yielding only five hits and two walks. In that game, the offense was highlighted by a home run off the bat of Pendleton, which snapped an 0-for-22 downturn for him.

A quick look at some of the team statistics at the break showed the following:

Batter	Avg.	AB	HR	RBI	SB	Pitcher	W–L	ERA
Landrum	.362	58	2	9	0	Tudor	10–7	2.27
McGee	.340	306	3	39	36	Cox	11–4	2.36
Herr	.334	317	3	68	17	Andujar	15–4	2.37
Clark	.288	306	17	63	1	Horton	0–2	2.67
Smith	.283	290	4	24	11	Lahti	0–0	2.67
Coleman	.278	309	1	16	63	Dayley	2–0	2.80
Van Slyke	.267	217	6	29	16	Campbell	2–1	2.14
Nieto	.243	173	0	29	0	Forsch	4–4	4.47
Pendleton	.228	281	3	36	9	Kepshire	7–6	4.63
Lawless	.214	42	0	8	2	Allen	1–4	5.59
Porter	.125	64	2	6	0			

And the National League standings at the All-Star Break on July 15 looked as follows:

Eastern Division	W	L	Pct.	GB
St. Louis	52	33	.612	—
New York	50	36	.581	2½
Montreal	49	39	.557	4½
Chicago	45	41	.523	7½
Philadelphia	37	49	.430	15½
Pittsburgh	29	56	.341	23

Western Division	W	L	Pct.	GB
Los Angeles	48	37	.565	—
San Diego	49	39	.557	½
Cincinnati	44	41	.518	4
Houston	43	45	.489	6½
Atlanta	39	47	.453	9½
San Francisco	33	55	.375	16½

It had been a super run for the Cards, beginning with a start to the season that had them destined for the bottom of the division by most. The outlook had changed with the contributions of both exciting newcomers and rejuvenated veterans. "If Branch Rickey were with us," praised Bob Broeg, "the Mahatma's bushy brows would arch in excitement and he'd chomp with joy on his juicy cigar over the speed and defense of the current Cardinals, major-league baseball's most productive ball club at the All-Star break.... Rickey worshipped at the twin shrines of fast feet and strong arms."

The unrelenting drive up to the All-Star break was important for two reasons: one, the fact that the club would go on a grueling 14-game road trip after the break, and two, the possibility of an impending players' strike at any time warranted that *staying* in first place for the near future was critical. "The only thing that can stop the Cardinals is to have them run into a lot of good pitching," Kennedy said, after his Western Division champion Padres finished their series in St. Louis. "The Mets have great pitching. They're capable of shutting you down for a whole series. But they don't have the Cardinals' speed or defense."

The dominance was noted in sheer numbers, too, as the Cards led the league in hitting at .267 and in stolen bases with 172, with no other club closer than 70 steals behind them. In addition, the pitching staff paced the National League with a crisp 3.01 ERA.

It indeed looked as if nothing could stop St. Louis—at least on the field.

7

Labor Clashes and the Mid-Summer Classic

As baseball prepared for the All-Star Game — one of the hallmarks of the summer in America — a shroud of doom hung over the event, with destruction on the horizon. On the first day of the break (Monday, July 15), the player representatives met in Chicago to set a strike date. Although he was away from the meeting for his preparations for the festivities in Minneapolis, Tommy Herr's absentee ballot of support for the players' union resounded. Ricky Horton, the alternate team representative, was at the meeting in his place.

"You might as well get ready for it, because they're going to break your heart," Kevin Horrigan wrote of the impending strike by the major leaguers. "Batten down the hatches, close the shutters," he continued, as if preparing the citizens for an air raid. "Tape a bunch of games on the VCR. Plan a vacation for late August, and don't include major league baseball in your plans. Louisville is lovely that time of year."

Pittsburgh Pirates' coach Bob Skinner added, "Come January, you might be able to get a Mercedes real cheap around here."

Despite the near-unanimous feeling among the players of the need to strike, the actual date for action was still in debate. Equally divided among the roughly 700 players in the major leagues were those who wanted to strike immediately and those who wanted to keep playing through continued negotiations. One dissenting voice was Vance Law, third baseman for the Montreal Expos. "The problem is that both sides are being greedy," he explained. "Somebody has to give up something. I think the players are the ones that should be flexible."

Others, such as Sutcliffe, thought that a walkout could be avoided.

"I'm not in favor of anything that keeps us from playing," he said. "I wasn't surprised at the strike last time [in 1981]. I would be surprised if there is one this time." Progress crept along, as noted of the most recent bargaining session (July 10) by Lee MacPhail. "It was a good, businesslike meeting," he described, "but not one that marks a lot of progress. It was the type of meeting that was essential if we are going to get together." MacPhail's circular response mirrored the unproductive nature of the talks.

The major issue at stake now for the players, in addition to the continued freedom to negotiate their contracts, was a larger take from the new television contracts that were approaching a value of a hundred million dollars. The players wanted at least a third of that money; but the owners contended that they needed it, ironically, to pay the ever-increasing salaries of the players. Broeg summed up the feelings of many: "With big league players averaging about $300,000 per year and qualifying for a pension as early as age 45 — no matter how little time spent in the majors — I don't feel sorry for them. My sorrow was back there when players were underpaid, had no pension, and were subject to dismissal with ten days' salary notice."

Commissioner Ueberroth maintained that the likelihood of a strike at some point remained "a good chance," and that baseball would be better served if it happened sooner than later, if it had to happen at all. "It's not a strike date," he said of the deadline that the players were trying to set. "It's a failing date. It means that both sides have failed to come together." While understanding that the fans had turned sour with the talk of a strike, Ueberroth himself was irritated with the other fires he was being asked to put out — mainly, the on-going drug issue and the financial troubles of certain organizations, primarily Pittsburgh. He had experience with the former problem, as chairman of the 1984 Los Angeles Olympic Games. The latter he did not, and he wondered how he would bail out franchises that were failing. He was now trying to separate fact from rumor in a story that had the Pirates moving to Washington, D.C.

But baseball fans tried not to think about such things, and conversely they turned their thoughts to the grand gathering of talent at the Metrodome in Minnesota. The All-Star Game had a new look, with members of the old guard like Rod Carew (an 18-time All-Star), Reggie Jackson (14), and Mike Schmidt (9) left out of the fun for the first time in a long while. For Carew, his 18 selections had come consecutively leading up to the 1985 game in Minneapolis, and he was less than 20 hits away from the magical milestone of 3,000 for his career. Despite not being selected, the slugger Jackson appeared to be on his way to his 16th season of hitting 20 or more home runs.

7. Labor Clashes and the Mid-Summer Classic

Keeping some stretch of history going in the game, it would be the 16th visit to the gala spectacle for Pete Rose. With the appearance, Rose also became the oldest All-Star ever at 44, surpassing Carl Yastrzemski of the Red Sox.

The starters, as voted in by the fans (with the exception of the pitchers), came out this way:

	National League	American League
C	Gary Carter (NY)	Lance Parrish (DET)
1B	Steve Garvey (SD)	Eddie Murray (BAL)
2B	Tommy Herr (STL)	Lou Whitaker (DET)
SS	Ozzie Smith (STL)	Cal Ripken, Jr. (BAL)
3B	Graig Nettles (SD)	George Brett (KC)
OF	Dale Murphy (ATL)	Dave Winfield (NY)
OF	Tony Gwynn (SD)	Rickey Henderson (NY)
OF	Daryl Strawberry (NY)	Jim Rice (BOS)
P	LaMarr Hoyt (SD)	Jack Morris (DET)

And the reserves included:

National League	American League
Tony Pena, C (PIT)	Carlton Fisk, C (CHI)
Ozzie Virgil, C (PHI)	Ernie Whitt, C (TOR)
Pete Rose, 1B (CIN)	Don Mattingly, 1B (NY)
Jack Clark, 1B (STL)	Cecil Cooper, 1B (MIL)
Ryne Sandberg, 2B (CHI)	Damaso Garcia, 2B (TOR)
Garry Templeton, SS (SD)	Alan Trammell, SS (DET)
Tim Wallach, 3B (MON)	Paul Molitor, 3B (MIL)
Jose Cruz, OF (HOU)	Wade Boggs, 3B (BOS)
Glenn Wilson, OF (PHI)	Gary Ward, OF (TEX)
Willie McGee, OF (STL)	Harold Baines, OF (CHI)
Dave Parker, OF (CIN)	Phil Bradley, OF (SEA)
Tim Raines, OF (MON)	Tom Brunansky, OF (MIN)
Ron Darling, P (NY)	Bert Blyleven, P (CLE)
Scott Garrelts, P (SF)	Willie Hernandez, P (DET)
Dwight Gooden, P (NY)	Jay Howell, P (OAK)
Rich Gossage, P (SD)	Jimmy Key, P (TOR)
Jeff Reardon, P (MON)	Donnie Moore, P (CAL)
Nolan Ryan, P (HOU)	Dan Petry, P (DET)
Fernando Valenzuela, P (LA)	Dave Stieb, P (TOR)

A balloting of the major league managers had Clark instead of Garvey,

Wallach instead of Nettles, and Guerrero instead of Strawberry as their preferred starters. Wallach was very dignified in response to the fans' voting in players like Nettles, who was hitting only .244 at the break. "They have been superstars all their careers," he pointed out. "They are the ones that the fans want to see and the fans are entitled to see them. That's the way it ought to be."

Clark, meanwhile, didn't give much thought to Garvey getting the starting nod from the fans. "I'd rather be picked by my peers, people I play against and the managers," he said. "I feel better about that. That's what counts the most. The fans should have their vote, but sometimes the players most deserving don't make the team." Cruz was one that manager Dick Williams did find deserving, as the 38-year-old veteran had hit .300 five times and driven in over 900 runs, but had never made the cut.

Murphy, the top vote-getter among the fans, was the only unanimous choice with the managers in the National League, and only Henderson got all the managers' votes in the AL.

Injuries that were announced before game time kept both starting catchers, Carter and Parrish, out of the game. Carter had been suffering from a sore knee (which was later found to be torn cartilage), and Parrish a stiff back that had been hampering him from the start of the season. Terry Kennedy was moved into Carter's spot in the starting lineup, while Parrish's ailment opened the door for hard-hitting catcher Rich Gedman of Boston.

In addition, the spot vacated by Andujar's defiance was filled by Darling, and Glenn Wilson got the nod when Guerrero decided that his back spasms required a few days off in lieu of going to the game. "It's the biggest thrill of my life — next to my child being born," said Wilson, who along with having an impressive 61 RBIs also possessed one of the strongest throwing arms in the major leagues. And despite the fact that the Phillies had used 62 different lineups so far in the season, Wilson was the only Philadelphia player to be in every one of them.

There was a lot of talk surrounding Andujar, on why the only 15-game winner in baseball decided not to show. Dick Williams was still taking it well, however. "We would love for Joaquin Andujar to be here, but we didn't miss him the other day in St. Louis. We beat him for our only win in the series. We were happy he showed up for that game." Hoyt added frankly, "Actually, I'm pretty happy that Joaquin didn't want to come. It [starting the All-Star Game] is something I've wanted to do." The writers in Andujar's home country of the Dominican Republic blasted him for not being at the game, thus denying an honor to the homeland.

Williams' counterpart on the American League bench was Sparky

7. Labor Clashes and the Mid-Summer Classic

Anderson, who in guiding the Tigers to the world championship in '84 had become the first manager to win a World Series in both leagues. He had won the All-Star Game in the National League, too, and now sought his final jewel as the AL head man. "I would like very much to be the first manager to win in both leagues," Sparky admitted. "I don't ever want my name to be attached to anything to do with losing."

A packed house of over 55,000 jammed the Metrodome to see the War Between the Leagues begin. It had been a rough ride for the Americans, as the Nationals had taken 20 of the last 22 meetings. Two years prior, a 13–3 win by the AL at Comiskey Park in Chicago was powered by a grand slam off the bat of Fred Lynn, the first slam in game history. Paging back to 1971, a National League team managed by Anderson lost at Detroit, and those were the lone triumphs by the American League in recent history.

Earlier in the day, McGee and Clark had both amused and awed themselves by taking batting practice off the legendary Sandy Koufax. "It was an honor," Clark said. "I would have hated to bat against him in his prime."

And when the American League took the field, it looked like an imposter and not Lou Whitaker who was warming up at second base. Whitaker was wearing a generic Tigers uniform from a local sporting goods store, since he had left his real one in his car back at the Detroit airport. With no number on the back of the jersey, he had to use a black magic marker to inscribe his number "1" on it. He had forgotten his glove, too, and had to borrow one from Cal Ripken, Jr. The brand, however, was not the one that Whitaker typically used — or more importantly, *endorsed*— so he had to put some tape over the wrist area of the glove that revealed the company logo.

As the contest started, it was evident that the American League meant business, as they acted immediately to try and reverse the losing trend. After Morris retired Gwynn, Herr, and Garvey in the top of the first, Henderson singled and stole second off Hoyt, and wound up on third as Kennedy's throw bounced past Smith at the bag. A sacrifice fly by Brett ensued, and the American League had a rare lead.

It would be their only tally, as Hoyt (three innings), Ryan (3), Valenzuela (1), Reardon (1), and Gossage (1) silenced the AL's artillery. Herr sparked the go-ahead rally for the NL in the third, as he doubled with two out and was then driven home by a Garvey single. The NL added a pair of runs in the fifth and another pair in the ninth for a 6–1 win, making it 21 wins in the last 23 tries. Hoyt was named the MVP, and interestingly, there were no home runs in the game. The Metrodome had by then earned its nickname as the "Homerdome," but the biggest bats in the game couldn't surmount its outfield walls.

As the crowd headed home, it was back to stark reality: a strike deadline of August 6 had been set by the players if a deal was not done.

The Cardinals rested on the final day off to prepare for the long road trip that would begin in Los Angeles. During the break, Maxvill finally found a taker for Neil Allen in the New York Yankees. A player to be named later was dealt for the struggling right-hander, as the Cards agreed to pay about half of his remaining contract. "With the money he was making," commented Herzog, "he couldn't be the ninth or tenth man on the pitching staff." Apparently, the talks between the two clubs had stalled at one point, when Yankees owner George Steinbrenner and Susman entered the negotiations. The Yankees had considerable money invested in Moreno, Berra, and Ken Griffey that they wanted to unload, but the Cards still declined to have any of those players involved in the deal.

To fill the spot on the St. Louis roster, Maxvill announced that probably either Rick Ownbey or Matt Keough would be promoted from Louisville to make a start. Allen felt that the trade would relieve some of the pressure he felt in St. Louis. But Horrigan, for one, never thought the pressure on him was all that great in the first place. "He might not have made us forget Bruce Sutter," Horrigan wrote, "but he might have exorcised the ghost of Keith Hernandez for a while."

In addition, Gary Rajsich wrangled his way out of San Francisco and back to the Cardinals organization. His option was purchased by Louisville, and he immediately began playing for the Triple-A Redbirds.

It would not be Ownbey or Keough that would join the Cardinals' pitching staff, as expected. Rather, it was little-known Joe Boever, a St. Louis native and graduate of Lindbergh High School, who would be added to the relief corps. Boever had been a starter at Crowder College but had never made a start in 175 professional appearances. He had a combined record of 6–3 between Louisville and Class AA Little Rock, and Herzog believed that he would bolster the bullpen. "He's a short-armer," Whitey noticed. "The kind of guy who, if you only see him once or twice, might be very effective."

A blister in Andujar's right middle finger limited his work to only five innings in the opener in L.A., in which he gave up one hit. He was replaced by Horton, who allowed a single to Greg Brock to permit the tying run to score. The Dodgers added a run in the seventh off Campbell, and the score remained 2–1. It was the first time in 20 starts that Andujar did not get a decision, but he was still ahead of his games-won pace in 1984, when he had 20 victories and did not record his fifteenth until August 1.

Horton had to come back and labor $4\frac{1}{3}$ innings the next night, as Cox was uncharacteristically knocked out early in the third frame during a four-run Dodger assault. Boever made his major league debut with a scoreless eighth, but it was too late as Los Angeles won again, 5–2. The Cards' bats had seemed to have gone into hiding; especially Pendleton, who was enduring a 1-for-31 streak after his slump-busting home run against the Padres a couple weeks before.

A bright sign was the long-awaited return of Porter, who caught Boever's opening act and contributed a base hit in his only at-bat. Otherwise, it looked like the entire team was headed into a cold spell at the plate. In addition, Tudor (10–8) had his nine-game winning streak snapped in the third game as the Dodgers were victorious by a 3–0 score behind Valenzuela.

Then came Steve Braun to the rescue — almost exclusively a nondescript pinch-hitter to this point (with an occasional venture into the outfield) — to salvage the Redbird bats and the final game of the Dodgers series. He had been only 6-for-37 on the year, his main quality being a left-handed bat for Herzog in certain late-game situations. "Sunday [July 21], against the Los Angeles Dodgers, Pendleton and Braun were unlikely heroes for the Cardinals," wrote Hummel. "However, with the strike date of August 6 looming large, this is an unlikely season."

After a stellar .324 season as a rookie in 1984, Pendleton's average had dropped to .219, but Herzog still would not give up on him. With both men pinch-hitting with the game tied at two in the tenth inning against Niedenfuer, Pendleton's double was followed by Braun's first home run in two years, which gave the Cards a 4–2 lead. Horton and Forsch finished up for the winner Lahti, with Forsch gaining his second save.

Pendleton and Braun came through in the same roles the next day in San Francisco. Andujar and LaPoint locked horns in an equal fight for seven innings, and then gave way to Lahti and Garrelts. Pendleton was sent in as a pinch-hitter with two out in the eighth, and singled home McGee to tie the game at three. Next was Braun, and he plated Landrum with a base hit for the lead. Lahti got his tenth save for Andujar (16–4), as the Cards had put together back-to-back wins after their initial slide coming off the All-Star break, and stood at 54–36, a game-and-a-half ahead of the Mets and three-and-a-half in front of the Expos.

On July 23, Porter returned to the starting lineup. He had caught a few games in rehab at Louisville, but complained that his broken finger still hurt, so he had been relegated to designated-hitter duty. Nonetheless, he felt good enough to be behind the plate in the opener against the Giants, as Herzog was looking to give Nieto a night off. It was a perfect time to get him in the lineup, as he had a career average of .489 against Giants starter Mike Krukow. Porter did nothing to hurt that mark, as he went 2-

for-3 with his third homer of the season (and his second against Krukow on the year — in addition to a double and a triple against him) and Cox (12–5) went the distance in a 6–3 win. Porter knew, however, that the catching job now belonged to Nieto, and that he would mostly be a spot starter and pinch-hitter against certain right-handers for Herzog. "We've been playing well," Porter said after the game. "If there was ever a team that you wanted to sit on the bench for, this would be the one. When I was out, it was fun to watch them play." The other star on the day was McGee, who added three hits to his league-leading .342 average.

Tudor was not about to let himself go into another bad binge, as he rebounded from his first loss in over a month to nip the Giants and sweep the series, 4–0. The outing was his fifth shutout in his last 11 starts (and fifth on the year, which tied Valenzuela for the major league lead), a stretch that included only nine runs permitted in 83 innings of work. It was also the 11th time that the Giants had been shut out on the year, most in the league. Tudor's nine strikeouts against the Giants also equaled his Cardinal (and National League) career-high for a game. The big blow for the Cardinals once again came from McGee, as his fifth-inning, opposite-field, three-run home run off Mark Davis provided Tudor all he needed. The sweep in San Francisco had put the Cardinals back in front by three-and-a-half games over the Mets, four over Montreal, and a big seven over the fading Cubs, who finally made the announcement official that there would be no night postseason games at Wrigley Field (the idea of installing temporary lights atop the roof had been considered).

The Cards next brought their speed show to San Diego, where the Padres had relinquished their Western Division lead to the Dodgers and now trailed Los Angeles by two games. They had seen their biggest lead over the Dodgers grow to five games on the Fourth of July, but the team had fallen since. The Padres had been relying on the long ball, for in contrast to the Cardinals, they had stolen only 30 bases through 97 games.

Kepshire, battling inconsistency all season, got the start for St. Louis in the opener. He was hit early and often by the Padres, and by the fifth inning had given San Diego a 6–0 advantage. The deficit would have been larger, though, if McGee hadn't taken away Nettles' second home run of the game with a leaping grab over the wall in the fourth.

Learning ever more about themselves each day, the young Redbirds mounted a fierce counterattack, ignited by a pinch-hit single in the seventh by Braun (the 108th pinch hit of his career, tying Gates Brown of the Tigers for seventh on the all-time list) and another safety by Coleman, which sent starter Eric Show out of the game. The baton was then picked up by Clark as he belted a long three-run homer, his 19th on the year.

7. Labor Clashes and the Mid-Summer Classic   111

Then in the ninth, trailing 6–4, the Cardinals let loose on Gossage, the intimidating veteran reliever. Braun doubled to start the inning (after staying in the game in right field for the struggling Van Slyke, who was in the midst of a slump), and Coleman singled him home to put the Cards within one. After getting his fourth hit of the game, Vince then promptly stole second — his second on the day and 68th of the year — and moved to third on a McGee groundout. Coleman was now only four steals away from the rookie record set the year before by Juan Samuel of Philadelphia. After Herr reached on an error (a fly ball that Carmelo Martinez dropped and allowed Coleman to tie the game), the Padres took no chances with the big bat, and promptly walked Clark. This enabled Pendleton to drive home Herr with a single to put the Cardinals ahead, 7–6. Padre errors made by Kennedy and center fielder Al Bumbry — the team's second and third miscues of the inning — plated two more runs, and Lahti held on for his 11th save and a rousing 9–6 Cards win. Lahti had retired 27 straight batters over the past several weeks until he walked Tim Flannery to start the inning, but then righted himself to seal the triumph.

This victory, perhaps as much as any other, proved to the league and the Cardinals that they were a team to be reckoned with in the pennant race. "This team has character," Smith announced to the press after the game. "I have never questioned this team's character." The veteran shortstop, who was starting to struggle in the field a bit and even more at the plate, was being helped through his 3-for-25 slump by his eager young teammates.

The next evening, Andujar was scheduled to face his old friend in San Diego skipper Dick Williams. Andujar said before the game that revenge was not a motive for him, but he did find the energy from somewhere to pitch 11 innings of one-run ball — after which he gave way to Dayley — as Ozzie Smith broke out of his doldrums at the plate with a single to score Clark in the twelfth, which gave Joaquin his 17th victory by a 2–1 score. "I don't have to show Dick Williams anything," the Cards' pitcher mentioned afterwards. "I don't know why people make such a big deal of it. It's in the past."

Cox got the ball on Saturday, and lost once again — this time to Hawkins, the Padres' pitcher whose own manager didn't have room for him on the All-Star roster but who still ran his record to 13–3 with the win. The Cardinals, understandably with their speed, had been the toughest club in baseball to double up, hitting into only 50 double plays in their first 94 games. But they batted themselves into five twin-killings on this day, as Hawkins combined with Gossage on a 2–0 blanking of St. Louis.

But Old Reliable was there for the Cardinals in the Sunday matchup, as Tudor bested Hoyt, 4–2. The win ended Hoyt's personal winning streak at 11, and it meant that Cards had taken five out of their last six on the California trip. Most impressively, perhaps, was that Tudor had only walked five men in his last ten starts, including none in this game. While not possessing an overpowering array of "stuff," Tudor knew that a pitcher like himself had to have pinpoint control to be successful. "The less guys you can put on for free, the better off you are," he stated. "I try not to walk anybody unless I have to." McGee, Porter, and Pendleton led the way, each with multiple-hit games, as Porter crushed his fourth home run and an RBI double. He was now batting .321 since rejoining the club near the All-Star break.

Also on that Sunday (July 28), with more and more talk of a players' strike being near, baseball tried to take its mind off its labor problems with another happy diversion. Two of the greatest outfielders the Cardinals had ever known, Enos Slaughter and Lou Brock, were inducted into the National Baseball Hall of Fame, along with former Pittsburgh shortstop Arky Vaughan and durable relief pitcher Hoyt Wilhelm. In his acceptance speech, Brock traced his love of Cardinal baseball all the way back to his boyhood days in Colliston, Louisiana, when he would listen to games on KMOX radio from St. Louis, and hear the exploits of his predecessor Slaughter as he tromped around the base paths and the outfield of Sportsman's Park.

On the last part of the road trip, the Cardinals returned to the wasteland that was Wrigley Field; it did not resemble the same place they had visited a few weeks earlier when they began their drive on the weakening Cubs. Chicago was still a battered team, decimated by injuries at key positions, which now had put them in a distant fourth place in the National League East. Although Sandberg was putting together a fine encore to his MVP season in 1984, there was not much left to be said of the North Side. Dernier and Matthews had returned to the outfield, but pitchers with names like Meredith and Engel, whom Cub fans had never heard of, were strolling to the mound with their meager offerings. The potent Cub batting order had been put back together, but its pitching staff was still in shambles. In addition to Sutcliffe, Trout was back on the injured list, joined by newly-hurt Eckersley and Scott Sanderson, too.

There were no tears of sympathy shed from the Cardinals, however. "You don't feel sorry for anybody," stated Herr. "Injuries are a part of the game. You can empathize with them and whatever dilemma they're in, but you've just got to worry about yourself."

"The pressure was on them since spring training," added Jack Clark. "It was like everybody predicted they [the Cubs] were supposed to be in the World Series before spring training. It doesn't work that way."

7. Labor Clashes and the Mid-Summer Classic 113

The star of the first game was McGee, and he erased all memories of "Sandberg Day" in June of '84. His benefactor, sixty feet and six inches away, was rookie Steve Engel, just brought up from Triple-A Iowa to take the place of Sutcliffe. It was now a shoulder problem for the defending Cy Young winner, and it looked like he would be on the shelf for the rest of the season. McGee greeted Engel with a first-inning home run that bumped his league-leading average to .345. Clark would follow later with his 20th, Coleman with his 70th stolen base, and McGee with four more hits on the day as the Cardinals ran away with an 11–3 win. Engel lasted until the fourth, at which point he was put to rest by Warren Brusstar, after the Cards had already built a 7–0 lead. By the time the game had ended, as the Chicago sportswriters pecked away at the Cubs' carcass in the press box, the men from St. Louis had amassed a season-high 17 hits.

Meanwhile, there was something to cheer about for the team from the other side of town. Tom Seaver and the White Sox beat Boston, 7–5, at Fenway Park for Seaver's 299th career win. Phil Niekro, the ageless knuckleballer now twirling for the Yankees, was also close to the 300 milestone, as his lifetime total stood at 294. And right behind Niekro was Don Sutton with 289, who at the time was with the Oakland A's. It was possible for Seaver to make one more start before the players' presumed strike date of August 6.

The standings on August 1, less than one week away from Donald Fehr's Doomsday, looked like this:

Eastern Division	W	L	Pct.	GB
St. Louis	60	38	.612	—
New York	59	41	.590	2
Montreal	56	46	.549	6
Chicago	52	47	.525	8½
Philadelphia	45	54	.455	15½
Pittsburgh	32	66	.327	28
Western Division	W	L	Pct.	GB
Los Angeles	58	40	.592	—
San Diego	54	47	.535	5½
Cincinnati	52	46	.531	6
Houston	46	55	.455	13½
Atlanta	44	55	.444	14½
San Francisco	39	62	.386	20½

Not being able to beat the Cardinals player-for-player in the first game of the series, the Cubs turned to their groundskeeper for help. The grass turf, always high at Wrigley Field anyway, appeared higher than normal as the fleet Redbirds came to town. Some speculated that the grass was left to grow in order to slow down the Cardinals' running game; but there were also other ideas, like Horrigan's. "The high grass Wednesday helped make a hero out of a young man named Ray Fontenot, a left-handed sinker ball pitcher who coaxed 13 ground balls off Cardinal bats in the seven innings he worked," he wrote. "Balls that would have scooted through on artificial surface — or even an orthodox grass surface — became candy-hoppers for the refugees from the geriatric ward who play shortstop and third base for the Cubs.

"The shortstops—Larry Bowa and Chris Speier—are 39 and 35, respectively. The third basemen, Ron Cey and Richie Hebner, are 37."

Fontenot outdistanced Andujar (17–5), but Coleman got steals number 71 and 72, tying Samuel's mark for a first-year player. "With the frame of mind I'm in the last two or three days, there's no telling how many bases I can steal," he warned.

The Cubs found more life the next day, too, as a 14th-inning squeeze bunt off the bat of Bowa scored Moreland with the game-winner, five hours and three minutes after the marathon affair had begun. It was yet another tough start for Cox, who had lost his fine rhythm from earlier in the year. He lasted only three innings, as Chicago pounded him for six runs on six hits and four walks. "Cox didn't have anything," Herzog assessed simply afterwards. The Cards' offense kept him off the hook for the loss, however, as Coleman's legs toyed with the Cubs in getting a pair of triples.

In the loss, McGee matched Coleman with two more stolen bases (McGee now had 41). The incredible part was that all four steals occurred *on the same play*. In the first inning, Coleman singled to left, and McGee walked. On the next pitch to Herr, they bolted on a double steal attempt. Coleman then got into a rundown between third and home. He got catcher Jody Davis to run him back towards third and then make a throw to Cey, upon which Coleman sprinted back for home. No one was there to cover as Coleman scored, McGee went to third, and the "quadruple steal" was unofficially believed to be some sort of record. "That goes in the Guinness Book," Coleman jokingly had hoped, as he now had more stolen bases than five entire teams in the National League.

Dayley (3–1) was charged with his first loss of the year, as he allowed Moreland to double, gave up walks to Dernier and Davis, and then threw wildly to home after fielding Bowa's squeeze bunt. The Cardinals thought that Dayley had gotten Dernier swinging on a 2–2 count, but on an appeal, first base umpire Billy Williams said that Dernier had not swung. "You know he swung — tell the truth about it," Herzog said to the reporters and the absent Williams after the game. "There wasn't even any doubt about it … we play all day, and then you let these guys take it away from you. It's amazing." Herzog was never confused with Gashousers Frankie Frisch or Leo Durocher in his rage towards umpires, but he could raise his ire when needed.

Perhaps everyone's temper was short, as it was the end of the arduous 14-game road trip and all were looking forward to the friendly confines of Busch Stadium. During the epic voyage in the previous two weeks, the Cardinals were able to hold serve with a respectable 8–6 mark away from home. They maintained a game-and-a-half lead over the Mets, even though the New Yorkers had blitzed through July with a 21–7 record for the month. As the dog days of August approached and the pennant races heated, everyone sensed the omnipresent feeling of a work stoppage.

8

The Clock Strikes Midnight

The Cardinals were able to stretch their lead to two-and-a-half after their first night back on the Mississippi. Tudor (13–8) slipped by Charles Hudson and the Phillies, 3–2, for his twelfth win in his last thirteen decisions; while in Chicago, Matthews' home run provided a difference in the Cubs' 2–1 win over the Mets. The margin in the Cards' victory came in the seventh inning while leading 2–1. Tudor lifted a routine pop fly behind second base as Samuel and shortstop Luis Aguayo gave chase.

Miscommunication then occurred as the two fielders collided, the ball fell free, and Smith was able to score the deciding run. The resilient Phillies came back to take the next two games in the series, 6–4 and 6–0, which included an impressive four-hit shutout by Kevin Gross over Andujar (17–6); Gross had taken over as the ace of Philadelphia staff with the injury to Carlton. Carlton had been on the disabled list since June 21 and had a 2.43 ERA despite a 1–7 record when he went down. There was one more game with the Phillies on a Monday before the Strike Clock struck midnight on August 6.

As people waited for news on the strike talks, the Pirates made a preemptive strike of their own. Candelaria finally got his wish, as he was dealt out of Pittsburgh along with Hendrick and pitcher Al Holland. The three veterans were sent to the California Angels in exchange for three prospects, a move that was obviously a cost-cutting measure on the part of the troubled Pirate franchise. To general manager Joe Brown, it was addition by subtraction. "The Pirates and I will be accused of or credited with getting rid of big contracts," he predicted. "We simply wanted players who want to play in Pittsburgh." It was clear that Candelaria did not; that Hendrick was having trouble getting his game back, and Holland was trying to evade ghosts from the drug scandal. For their benefit, the three were sent to a

8. The Clock Strikes Midnight

pennant contender, as the Angels were leading the American League West by a game-and-a-half over Kansas City.

And in perhaps an attempt to fortify the people with good news amidst the labor negotiations, two old veterans delivered. In New York, Seaver became the 17th pitcher in history to win 300 games, as he went the distance in leading the White Sox over the Yankees, 4–1, in the 231st complete game of his career before a capacity crowd of over 54,000. He was also close behind Ryan and Carlton on the all-time strikeout list with over 3,500. The durable right-hander owned major league records for consecutive strikeouts in a game (10), as well as the most total (10) and consecutive (9) seasons with 200 or more strikeouts. In California, Carew got a third-inning single for the Angels against the team that raised him, the Minnesota Twins, as the sleek left-handed batter got his 3,000th hit off Frank Viola. Both Seaver and Carew had broken into the big leagues in 1967.

The calendar seemed like it was going to be cruel for St. Louis, as the Mets were beating the Cubs 7–2 in New York behind Strawberry's three home runs, and the Cards lost for the fifth time in their last six games, as Rawley went the distance in a 9–1 shellacking by Philadelphia. It meant that, going into the players' strike deadline in the morning, the Cardinals now trailed the Mets by one-half game.

"If they turned out the lights at Busch Stadium for the final time this season Monday night," John Sonderegger worried, "baseball fans in St. Louis will have to carry around a nasty memory for a l-o-n-g time.... The lights officially went out at 10:27... but the Cardinals looked like they were playing in the dark all night long."

Cox's struggles continued as he matched the three-inning, six-run performance of his previous start, and Boever, Forsch, and Campbell mopped up the mess. The Cardinals now went home to a restless night, wondering if all they had worked for on the field during the summer had been lost.

Was there any hope of an immediate settlement? "My gut feeling is there's a 50–50 chance," Horton offered. The Cardinals remembered the last strike of 1981 all too well, as the infamous "split season" saw the team finish second in the National League East for both halves of the schedule — the first half by a game-and-a-half to the Phillies, and the second portion by a mere half-game to the Expos.

The latest round of talks between the negotiating teams led by MacPhail and Fehr had reached an impasse. However, there were the first signs of compromise coming from the players' side, as they showed a small willingness to budge on their demand of one-third of the new television revenue for their pension funds. "With each passing hour, it becomes more difficult," Fehr said. "But the players are not about to go backward and give up the rights that any other citizen has to earn as much as he can in the free market."

It was not only baseball people who were worried about the situation. The City of Chicago, for example, forecasted that it would lose $25 million directly and upwards of $60 million in residual effects if the home schedules of the Cubs and White Sox were canceled for the remainder of the year. "Residual effects" included the adverse ramifications that local businesses would incur, such as restaurants, bars, and souvenir vendors. The Cardinals were to host the Cubs beginning on the August 6, and if the typically well-attended series were not played, the Cards estimated that over $700,000 in ticket sales alone would be sacrificed.

In addition to all of the cold figures, there would also be the natural backlash expected among the fans. "The fans will definitely look at the players for blame," Tom Brunansky of the Twins said. "We're in a no-win situation. If we end up striking for what we feel we deserve, the fans will hate us, but at the same time we end up cutting our own throats if we don't strike. We have to protect ourselves." Ueberroth had said for weeks that he wouldn't allow a strike, but that threat didn't seem to coerce the two sides into getting closer together (he had no official power to keep the players from striking, but when he arrived on the job in 1984, he did successfully keep the umpires' union from striking after the season was over).

Although the TV revenue was still a hot item, other prime issues remained. The gulf between the players and owners on salary arbitration (the owners wanted the minimum service time increased to three years—from the existing two—before players would be eligible to file) was not resolved, nor was the owners' proposal of a salary cap and a revision of free agency.

Then, after one last meeting on the afternoon of Tuesday, August 6, the word officially came. "We're on strike," said players' lawyer Gene Orza. The main sticking point was arbitration, as the owners held to their claim that its misuse had caused the skyrocketing of salaries. "No two-year player — except for the Dwight Goodens of this world — deserves $500,000 a year," chimed in Horrigan for the owners' side on this point. The bargaining teams met the evening of the 6th as all of the major league games for that day and night were canceled. A sign outside the east parking garage of Busch Stadium said it all in big, chalked letters: "NO GAME TONITE." The Cubs were ready to leave for St. Louis at a moment's notice, as their bus was running at 4:00 P.M. to take them to O'Hare Airport outside Chicago. After a while the players were told to go home.

8. The Clock Strikes Midnight

Meanwhile, dejected fans sat in the lobby of the Marriott Pavillion Hotel across the street from Busch Stadium, now wondering what they were going to do in lieu of their lost series. "It's very disappointing," said one of the patrons at the hotel, 17-year-old Lesley Murray. "But we're going to stay and do our best to enjoy ourselves." Tempers were short back across the street at the Cardinals' ticket offices at the stadium, as fans stood in the rain in a complicated attempt to get their Tuesday tickets refunded. When it was announced that all games for Wednesday the 7th would be canceled, too, another rush of refund-seekers hit the windows.

But in a startling turn of events, the winds shifted and common ground was found between the parties. The players pulled back further from their original one-third demand for television revenue, and the owners agreed to mostly preserve the existing arbitration system. A five-year deal was struck, and the games were back on. Herr and Braun were playing golf at the Glen Echo Country Club when they got word of the progress. "I played two more holes, and then I got a call from my wife, who said that I'd better get home," Herr reported. "She was getting tired of answering the phone because of what was going on." Added Don Sutton, who was serving as the Oakland A's' player representative, "I have to have surgery to remove the phone from my left ear."

Herr and Horton quickly made calls to the other Cardinal players to let them know that a deal had been reached.

Players around the majors, some of whom had considered taking vacations if no resolution were made, now rushed to get back to their clubs. Andujar had considered going home to the Dominican Republic, but did not; Pedro Guerrero of the Dodgers and Tony Pena and Cecilio Guante of the Pirates, however, did have to be traced to the island by their clubs. Guerrero's flight did not leave the D.R. in time for the Dodgers' first game with Cincinnati. Pascual Perez, a pitcher for the Braves, had disappeared from the club a few days *before* the strike even occurred. And even though the Yankees had a doubleheader with Cleveland, they found out that their left fielder, Rickey Henderson, was still at his home in Oakland. "A lot of guys were unhappy when the strike was settled," revealed Giants pitcher Greg Minton. "They were looking for a few weeks off."

It was also time to resume thinking about records, titles, streaks, and other pleasant thoughts, as Boggs, the rising star of the Boston Red Sox, had been leading the American League in hitting at the time of the walkout and owned a 25-game hitting streak from earlier in the summer. "I didn't even want to think of winning a batting title because of a strike," a relieved Boggs said. "It would have been a cheap way to win the title."

As play resumed around the National League, Pete Rose was now only

15 hits away from Cobb's record. As the games got going again, Rose looked at the situation from his other standpoint as the Reds' manager. "Hopefully, the closer I get [to the record], the more enthusiasm will be in the ballpark," he said. "Then there will be more electricity, and it will help my players."

So in the end, what was feared for so long turned out to be nothing more than a second All-Star break in duration. As in Cleveland, many major league clubs set up doubleheaders on August 8 to help make up for the two lost days, but the Cubs and Cardinals did not bother since Chicago would be visiting St. Louis again in September (the make-ups were set for previously-scheduled open dates on the 5th and 9th of that month, which left the 30th as the only day off for the Cards in September).

It was figured that the extra rest from the short strike would benefit the ailing Cubs; but they still played like a beaten team, and John Tudor was still pitching like a Cy Young candidate. Durham's fifth-inning tapped single that just evaded Clark was the only Chicago hit on the evening, as Tudor also allowed only one walk, and spun his league-leading sixth shutout of the season in nailing the Cubs again, 8–0.

The Cards didn't even give their opponents a chance, as a five-run barrage in the first inning helped make it a short night for Cubs starter Sanderson, who had been the last Chicago pitcher to throw a complete game (back on June 30th). Coleman started things with a rocket down the right field line, which Moreland had trouble handling. Taking a peek at the ball bouncing around in the corner, Coleman rounded second and streaked for third on what was ruled a double and an error. McGee and Herr followed with hits, and after Clark was retired, Van Slyke lofted a long, high home run into the right field corner, his seventh on the year. Pendleton then cracked his own dinger, the first time the Cardinals had gone back-to-back with homers since September 22, 1984. Later, Clark's sacrifice fly would increase the Cardinal lead, and increase his own National League lead in RBIs to 80. And a couple of days later, when Sanderson went on the disabled list with a bad knee, it meant that all five main Chicago starters—Sutcliffe, Trout, Eckersley, Ruthven, and him—had all spent time out of action during the year.

A lot of people were thinking of Gooden or Guerrero as the MVP favorites in the National League (Herzog himself currently thought that Gooden was the hands-down choice), but they may have changed their minds with McGee's performance in Philadelphia on August 10. After taking the opener from the Phillies, 5–4, the night before, the two clubs met in a "twi-night" doubleheader the following day (the old term given to a doubleheader in which the first game was played during the day, and the

8. The Clock Strikes Midnight

second one at night). McGee had three hits in the first contest to help Cox win his thirteenth, 5–4. Not satisfied, Willie came back with a spectacular four-hit explosion in the nightcap, including a three-run homer, as the Cardinals romped 13–4.

Kepshire made the start but could not record an out past the first inning. Horton came in and made the longest relief appearance in the National League for the year — eight innings — to get the win. Also in that game, Herr stole the Cardinals' 200th base of the season. The major league record was 347, set by the 1911 New York Giants — and not too many folks wanted to bet against the Cards matching it. And though Coleman had the gaudy individual numbers in that department, it was McGee who was really flashing the all-around game, and his teammates thought he would be a strong MVP candidate.

"He can play," Ozzie Smith said simply. "This is his year, and he's doing everything. He's a first-rate ballplayer and a first-rate guy." McGee's batting mark had swelled to .354, and seemed to only keep going up at a time of year when most averages start going down. He led the league by a wide margin in front of Guerrero (.331) and Herr (.322). McGee was threatening the major league record for the highest single-season average by a switch-hitter, set by Mickey Mantle at .365 in 1957. The National League mark was held jointly by Rose (1969) and Frisch (1923), each of whom batted .348. In addition, Rose had been the only switch-hitter to win the National League batting title. After the Philadelphia series, McGee also had accumulated an impressive total of 14 triples, a league high as well.

Winning the first three games in Philadelphia kept the Cardinals in a first place tie with the streaking Mets, but they fell a game behind the next day as Rawley beat them again in the finale, 4–1. The Phillies attack was led by Schmidt, who hit the 444th homer of his career and his ninth off Bob Forsch — the most he had had off any pitcher to that point in his career. Gary Carter and his two home runs beat the Cubs at Shea, 6–2, and the Mets had won seven in a row. It was the first time since June 29 that the Cards were behind by a full game.

The Mets made it eight in a row the next day against the Phillies, as the Cardinals kept pace in St. Louis against the Pirates with Tudor (15–8) winning yet again, 8–1, and McGee piling three more hits onto his mounting season total. And the "roadrunner show" went on and on, as Willie added his 42nd steal, Coleman three of his own for a total of 81, and Van Slyke his 19th against beleaguered catcher Tony Pena, who happened to have one the best throwing arms among catchers in baseball history.

Andujar (19–6) won the next night, a 6–5 squeaker over Don Robinson and the Pirates. Smith went 3-for-3 and Dayley picked up his eighth save after an inning of perfect work. Dishearteningly, though, the Mets won again, 4–2, over the Phillies—their ninth straight victory. Rain in St. Louis on August 14 pushed that day's contest into a doubleheader between the Cards and Pirates 24 hours later, while the Phillies finally cooled off New York, 2–1.

These were the standings on August 15:

Eastern Division	W	L	Pct.	GB
New York	68	43	.613	—
St. Louis	67	43	.609	½
Montreal	64	49	.566	5
Chicago	55	56	.495	13
Philadelphia	52	60	.464	16½
Pittsburgh	33	76	.303	34
Western Division	W	L	Pct.	GB
Los Angeles	66	44	.600	—
San Diego	60	53	.531	7½
Cincinnati	58	53	.523	8½
Houston	52	60	.464	15
Atlanta	49	61	.445	17
San Francisco	43	69	.384	24

The Cubs, looking for any spark at all, called Dunston back up and gave Bowa, the veteran hitting .246, his unconditional release. Bowa said that he did not plan on playing again, but when the Mets called him the following week, he signed on. Bowa's record of fewest errors by a shortstop in a season (9) was being somewhat challenged by Smith (8), but was likely to be upheld with a large chunk of the schedule remaining. In addition, Bowa's career fielding percentage of .980 was a record for shortstops (as was his single-season figure of .991 in 1979), and his 2,212 games played at the position were also an all-time standard.

"Larry is a proven veteran who has been through the pennant race before," Mets general manager Frank Cashen reasoned about the acquisition. "With [Ron] Gardenhire hurt, we're most fortunate to find a player with Larry's know-how, ready to step in and fill the back-up role [behind starter Rafael Santana]." Despite the struggles of the shortstops in Chicago, the other side of the second base bag was fine, as Sandberg had recently become the first Cub in history to steal 30 bases and hit 20 homers in the same season.

Some of the Cubs, for sure, were losing their confidence, such as Bob

8. The Clock Strikes Midnight

Dernier. "I'm not writing off '85," he said, "but when you're out double figures in mid–August and you've got three teams to hurdle, you're not looking very good. We have to finish with a Detroit start." He was referring to the Tigers' rocket launch to the 1984 season, in which they found themselves with their incredible 35–5 record in late May en route to the title. A couple of days later, the Phillies would pound out six home runs against the Cubs, including three off emergency starter Sorensen in a 10–4 pasting at Wrigley Field, described by a dejected Frey as "a pretty unpleasant day that kept getting progressively worse." The last time the Phillies had hit six homers in a game was also at Wrigley, seven years earlier.

One true test of a championship-caliber ball club in August is the ability to continuously beat teams that should be beaten, and the Cardinals took care of the business at hand. They took two more from the Pirates behind Kepshire (9–6) in the first game and Cox (no decision, still at 13–7) in the second, 3–1 and 4–3. Kepshire had a perfect game with one out in the seventh inning when Pittsburgh second baseman Johnny Ray blooped a single in front of McGee in center to spoil the bid. Kepshire rebounded to make it through the seventh and eighth, and was aided by Lahti and Dayley in the ninth. Lahti's stretch of not allowing 27 straight batters to reach base had lasted from June 18 to August 1, which also included 15 games and 16 innings without allowing a run.

Herr, looking to catch his teammate in the batting race, duplicated McGee's seven-hit effort in Philadelphia, including four hits in the nightcap. McGee had five more himself on the evening, but had to leave the second game in the sixth inning after he hurt his ankle in pursuit of a fly ball. Fortunately, no fractures were found in post game x-rays, but he was doubtful to start for the next day or two. After the pair of victories, the Cards were now dead even at 69–43 with the Mets, who had beaten the Phillies again, 10–7.

The Expos next came calling to Busch Stadium, and the St. Louis bullpen took advantage of the rest with a complete game by Forsch during a 6–1 win. It was the first nine-inning piece of work for Forsch since April 15, and the siesta for the relievers was sorely needed in the wake of crunched-together games from the strike and recent rainouts. The Cardinals also took advantage of a rare Pittsburgh win over New York to climb back in front by a full game in the National League East. They fell right back into a tie the next day (August 17), however, as Tudor got a no-decision in seven innings of work and Campbell (3–3) got charged with a 5–4 loss. A huge factor in the Cardinals' favor on the horizon, however, was the fact that two-thirds of their remaining games would be at Busch, while the Mets would play the same amount on the road.

The Dodgers were starting to run away with the Western Division. They had opened up a nine-game lead on the Padres and Reds, and 15 or more on everyone else, due in part to the .769 ball (20–6) they played during the month of July.

The hottest part of the summer had certainly arrived, as the temperatures at major league ballparks during the third week of August reached the upper-90s. While officiating a game at Shea Stadium in New York, the large umpire McSherry had to take a break, as he was getting light-headed. It was the time of year when players were starting to get a little worn out, too, and they had to find it within themselves to gear up for one last gasp: the trip through August, through September, and into October for the pennant fight.

One of the workhorses in the St. Louis heat was Joaquin Andujar, and he continued to take the ball regularly. His overall total for wins (19) still outpaced Tudor, though the lefty was closing fast, and it was on August 18 that Andujar would make his bid for 20 victories against the Expos at Busch. He was staked to a two-run lead in the first, thanks to a Coleman double, a Smith single, and a Landrum triple. Montreal tied it in the second on a home run by Sal Butera, after which the teams traded blows into the tenth inning with the score tied at four. Andujar was still firing the ball, straining for the 20-victory milestone that he had achieved in 1984. After he allowed Raines and Law to reach base, Andujar was lifted in favor of Dayley to face the left-handed-batting Terry Francona. Francona promptly banged home the two runners, which made the difference in a 6–5 final score. The Cards had still been without McGee and his sore ankle, but he would return the following night at Houston.

Though working through almost ten hot innings, Andujar had apparently saved enough energy to besmear the reporters in the Cardinal clubhouse — something which left the local writing staff perplexed, especially Sonderegger.

"Because Andujar comes off as a rebel without a cause, I haven't tried to crack the insecure wall he throws up around himself after games," he wrote, finally having had enough of Andujar's attitude. "When a guy says he doesn't want to talk, I respect that. But don't complain then about not getting enough publicity. I've really found Andujar a little amusing in the past. He'd wave off reporters, cuss them out in Spanish, and then grin…. Andujar isn't a very popular fellow in other cities. He's considered a hot dog and a hothead," Sonderegger wrote.

Understandably, the press had grown tired of his antics, and Andujar seemed to be willing to grab at any straws that would make himself look good, which Sonderegger also noticed: "'Americans first, Domincans

8. The Clock Strikes Midnight

last,' he said, obviously ignoring the fact that he makes more than a million dollars a year in this country throwing a baseball every four days." Rick Hummel was also frustrated with Andujar's demeanor. "It's been an exasperating four years," he sighed in reflection on his job as the Cardinals' beat writer for the *Post-Dispatch*.

It was possible that Andujar's decision to skip the All-Star Game was causing repercussions far wider than what he had bargained for. His concentration on the mound seemed to be off, his temper even shorter, and the blame for his mistakes — usually pointed in someone else's direction besides himself — was even more often placed at the feet of others. The team could not afford to encumber itself with such a poor mindset from one of its leading pitchers in the stretch run, but no one appeared to know how to handle him.

The Astros knew how to handle Kepshire, though, as the Cards began a series in Houston by getting thumped 17–2. The Astros pounded out 19 hits — including a grand slam by Mark Bailey — while Gooden struck out 16 Giants in New York as part of a 3–0 win for the Mets, the thirteenth win in a row for the second-year wonder, which put the Cards behind by a game-and-a-half. With the effort, Gooden joined Herb Score as one of the only two pitchers in history to register 200 or more strikeouts in their first two seasons.

Thanks to the St. Louis bullpen, however, the Cardinals won the next two nights with no decisions for Cox or Tudor. Porter's pinch-hit homer (his seventh on the year) helped win the first one, while seldom-used Brian Harper had the game-winning RBI single the next evening. The relievers stole the show, as in the two victories Dayley, Lahti, and Horton went five innings while allowing only one run. More testimony was found in the fact that the Cards were now 56–2 in games they led after the sixth inning.

No one was mentioning Bruce Sutter's name anymore, as by the middle of August the Cardinals' staff ranked fourth in the National League in saves; and no one in St. Louis felt sorry for the bearded one, as he had failed in half of his last 16 save chances for the Braves. "It seems like I make one bad pitch and it hurts me," Sutter told a reporter in Atlanta about his newfound woes. "Last year I could get away with that pitch. That's what happens when you're going bad." Did being away from Roarke, his former pitching coach, have anything to do with Sutter's demise? "That has a lot to do with it," affirmed Herzog. "Especially when you believe in someone the way he believed in Mike. Every time he got in trouble before, he called Mike. Mike knows every mechanical thing about him." With the Cardinals newfound success in 1985, some wondered if Sutter was having second thoughts about the lucrative deal he signed with the fifth-place Braves, but he said it wasn't bothering him that much. "I've made my choice," he said. "I can't think about it. Every night, if I wish I had stayed, that would drive me crazy." Sutter also complained about a sore pitching arm that had been bothering him. "I can't deny it," he said of the pain. "I've never had this before. It's really been hard. It's okay when I throw a fast ball, but when I have to get my arm up for the split-fingered fast ball, I just haven't been able to do it."

The Redbirds got a chance to see their old friend, as Atlanta was the next stop on the trip. Andujar finally got the elusive 20th win, 6–2, even though he allowed 14 base runners (ten hits and four walks) in just over seven innings. It was also the first time that a Cardinal pitcher had posted back-to-back seasons of 20 wins since Bob Gibson did it three times from 1968 to 1970. Ironically, the notable win cost Andujar some money — but it was of his own doing. He had promised before the game to give $1,000 to the player who scored the winning run in his 20th triumph, and an extra thousand to a relief pitcher who would save it. As Andujar later enjoyed a bottle of champagne that cooled by his locker during the game, he cut a personal check to McGee (whose three hits raised his league-leading average to .365) and another to Lahti.

The clubhouse got even happier when it was learned that the Padres had swept a doubleheader from the Mets, winning by scores of 6–1 and 3–0 behind two home runs by Garvey. Starting the day (August 23) a half-game out, the Cards ended it by being a game ahead once again.

It was a costly victory, though, in that Clark strained a rib cage in the first inning, the result of a violent swing of the bat. At first, it looked as if Clark would only be out a couple of days; upon further examination of the injury, the strain was actually a pulled muscle, and it was forecast that he would be sitting for up to two weeks. Clark himself, though, was more optimistic. "Hopefully by the time we get to Cincinnati [in two days], I'll be ready to play. I don't think I'll be out that long to make a difference. With the miracles of modern medicine, I ought to be back in no time."

Rather than make a roster move, Maxvill decided to go with 24 players for the time being, until it was more accurately determined just how long Clark would be out. Veteran Mike Jorgensen, who had seen limited duty in the outfield as well as at first base, would attempt to make up for Clark's absence. "Jorgy's done a good job when he's gotten to play," said Herr, who also pointed to the Gold Glove that Jorgensen won at first base in 1973 while with the Expos.

With Clark missing in the lineup, it was presumed that the Cardinals would turn to their speed game even more. That facet of the offense notched a new high in the first game in Atlanta, as Herr's stolen base in the ninth inning (his 24th on the year) set a new club record for a season with 221. Furthermore, it was their third straight season with 200 or more. And still charging towards the individual records was Coleman, who snared his 84th.

General Sherman would have been proud, as the Cardinals fought past the casualties and rolled through Atlanta with a sweep. "Sunday's winner was Kurt Kepshire," Hummel wrote, "whose performances have suggested Jekyll-Hyde characteristics. In two of his previous three starts, Kepshire had not made it out of the third inning. In the other, he had a perfect game until the seventh. It was a Day of the Jekyll for him on Sunday...." Kepshire threw 7⅔ innings of one-run ball, and Lahti saved the day by striking out Murphy with two runners on in the eighth to preserve a 5–2 win.

The end of the road was nearing for Eddie Haas, as it would be announced later in the week by Ted Turner that Bobby Wine would be taking over as the Braves' manager. "We needed it around here," pitcher Len Barker said about Wine's taking over. "It was just like a graveyard. Everybody got a new life. You can't blame Eddie. Eddie knows baseball. He just didn't communicate with the players. He hired the coaches but didn't communicate with them, either. That's the bottom line."

And on the same day that the Cards completed their sweep, the 20-year-old Gooden became the youngest pitcher in history to win 20 games as he beat San Diego, 9–3. He was also only the third Met in history to turn the trick, with Seaver and Koosman being the others, since the club was founded in 1962.

Cincinnati was next, and it was Cox's turn to take the mound. Through the first half of the season, it looked like he could make as strong a run at the Cy Young as Andujar or Tudor. Come August 26 at Riverfront Stadium, however, Cox had been victorious only once in the previous month. "Everyone's been pitching well when they go out there," he noticed of those around him, "and you don't want to be the one to give it up." He didn't give it up — instead, he ran his scoreless steak against the Reds to 20 innings, as he posted his fourth shutout and 14th victory of the year, 3–0. The win put the Cards 30 games over the .500 mark (76–46) for first time since their pennant-winning year of 1968.

Cox did not have overpowering stuff, as Cincinnati pitcher Jay Tibbs was his only strikeout victim. Nonetheless, he had the Reds hitters off balance with an effective breaking ball and change-up that he kept down in the strike zone. One of the six hits that he allowed came off the bat of Rose, who was now only 11 shy of Cobb's record; and as the Reds were scheduled to come to St. Louis in a week, it was predicted that he might break the mark during that series. Even though Rose was a switch-hitter, he was starting to platoon himself against right-handed pitchers only, and place fellow veteran masher from the Big Red Machine of the '70s, Tony Perez, against the lefties.

A new face arrived in the bullpen the second night in Cincinnati. Todd Worrell, the Cardinals' number-one draft pick in 1982, had picked up 11 saves at Louisville during the season, and was striking out more than one batter per inning after the Triple-A club moved him from the starting rotation to the bullpen. He had been undrafted out of high school despite a perfect 10–0 record for his team in Arcadia, California. He went on to college, and reportedly had scared teams off from the draft by saying that he wanted to stay in school and finish his degree. St. Louis was one of the few teams that knew he had aspirations to play pro ball, and they did not hesitate in making him their first choice. In his place, Boever was sent back to Louisville after compiling a 4.09 ERA in nine appearances.

Looking to bolster the bullpen even further, Herzog had former Cardinal Doug Bair throw in the bullpen after the first game. Bair, who was living in the Cincinnati area, had just been released by the Tigers. Herzog said that even if the Cardinals were interested, Bair would not be able to be picked up until the rosters expanded on September 1. Bair had been a member of the Cards' bullpen on the '82 World Series championship team.

The hot streak continued, although Tudor was roughed up a bit the following game. He surrendered eight hits and four runs over 6⅔ innings, but the usual accomplices of Horton, Campbell, and Lahti bailed him out in a 6–4 triumph. Their lead in the Eastern Division had stretched to three games with the Mets' loss to the Dodgers in New York. It was yet another big night for McGee, as the high-flying center fielder had two hits (including a triple that plated the go-ahead runs in the eighth inning) and scored twice. "Remember in spring training, I told you," Smith reminded. "I told you it was about time he put it all together." There was no question that McGee had turned into a solid leader on the club. "It's an MVP year," Coleman added about his outfield mate, after he himself had stolen his 87th base, and kept his pace ahead of Brock's National League record of 118 steals from 1974. McGee was now up to .362 at the plate.

Boever found himself right back on the Cards' roster the next day, as it was decided that Clark needed to go on the disabled list after all, putting him out until at least September 8. He itched to return, but he knew that his valor might get the best of him — and Herzog knew it, too. "I knew that Jack was going to try to force it. He would go out there a day or two early and take a rip and put himself out for the year." So, instead of making a deal for another first baseman, Maxvill chose to sit on the issue for 72 hours until the roster expansion date.

Meanwhile, the club played its last game of the road trip at Cincinnati. They had won seven in a row on the voyage, after the humiliating 17–2 loss to begin the trip at Houston. After traveling the next day back home, they would play 32 games in the next 31 days. Andujar took the mound to try for the club's eighth straight, but it wasn't meant to be. He had one of his worst outings of the year, permitting six runs through five innings that helped the Reds erase a 6–0 Cardinals lead. The game stayed tied at six into the bottom of the 12th when Horton walked Rose with the bases loaded to give Cincinnati the win.

The Cards then figured they couldn't put off a bona fide replacement for Clark any longer, so on August 29 they sent minor league outfielder Mark Jackson to the Reds for veteran Cesar Cedeno. In order to have Cedeno eligible for postseason play, a roster spot had to be vacated — and Boever got the bad news that he was headed to Louisville once again. Cedeno was acquired two days before he would have been ineligible for the playoff roster.

Cedeno, who broke into the majors with Houston in 1970, was considered one of the more athletically gifted young outfielders to come into the game in a while. He spent 12 productive years with the Astros, and then went on to Cincinnati. He had been batting .241 with three home runs and 30 RBIs in 83 games for the Reds on the year. "I'm thrilled an organization like the Cardinals has interest in me," the 34-year-old said. "It's a great feeling to be wanted. Whatever they want, I'm willing to do it." He noted that the Cardinals were the team he almost had signed with back in 1968. "They were the first team to approach, and they already had a contract mailed out," he recalled. "But the Houston Astros came by the next day and made a better offer. My father wanted that one."

His professionalism was also figured to be a calming influence on Andujar, as the two Domincans had played together in Houston for six years before both being traded in 1981. Another former Houston teammate, Astros relief pitcher Dave Smith, thought that the Cardinals had made a good move in picking up Cedeno. "If he feels like he's needed, playing for a contender, he'll help them," Smith predicted. The Toronto Blue Jays, chasing the pennant in the American League, almost beat out the Cardinals for Cedeno's services, as they were looking for a right-handed bat to spell outfielder Lloyd Moseby against left-handed pitchers. But the Blue Jays pulled out when they decided that Cedeno could no longer play center field (Moseby's position), and St. Louis moved into the picture.

Cedeno made his Cardinals debut with a bang, knocking out a seventh-inning home run off Houston starter Mike Scott in his first at-bat, which evoked a standing ovation from the crowd as he crossed the plate. And McGee had a four-hit night, boosting his mark to .367 that was best in the league by over 40 points. (Herr remained second at .322.) But it was hardly enough, as Kepshire had one of his "Mr. Hyde" days, being yanked by Herzog with nobody out in the second inning after already granting the Astros to a 4–1 lead. "He got behind on everybody," Herzog said about his pitcher's problem this time out. "This is a fast ball–hitting club and if you throw them a fast ball, these guys can wring your neck." Kepshire was booed loudly by the Busch Stadium crowd from the very beginning, as Houston leadoff hitter Bill Doran singled to start the onslaught.

The season had reached its final sprint, as the papers on September 1 showed the standings like this:

Eastern Division	W	L	Pct.	GB
St. Louis	77	49	.611	—
New York	76	52	.594	2
Montreal	70	57	.551	7½
Chicago	62	65	.488	15½
Philadelphia	60	66	.476	17
Pittsburgh	40	86	.317	37
Western Division	W	L	Pct.	GB
Los Angeles	74	51	.592	—
San Diego	68	59	.535	7
Cincinnati	67	60	.528	8
Houston	60	67	.472	15
Atlanta	55	72	.433	20
San Francisco	51	76	.402	24

The Cards were in the midst of a battle in which no one thought they would be at the beginning of the season — they were fighting for the National League pennant.

9

It's Up to You, New York

The races in the American League were becoming as exciting as the one being played out in the NL East. Detroit had slipped from its throne of invincibility, as they stood 11 games in back of Toronto in the Eastern Division, but the Yankees were close on the Blue Jays' tail at three-and-a-half games back. In the West, California held onto a slim one-and-a-half game margin over the Royals, and a six-game advantage over the A's.

Houston left-hander Bob Knepper out-pitched Cox 3–1 in the middle game of the series with the Astros, but Tudor came back to get the finale, 5–0, for his 16th win and seventh shutout. Tudor seemed especially to enjoy throwing at Busch Stadium, as Herzog noticed. "There's no [big] left field wall like he had in Boston," Whitey pointed out. "A left-handed pitcher should be successful here if he throws strikes." Throw strikes Tudor did, as he didn't walk a single Houston batter on the day.

Also as important as architecture, Herzog knew, was a good defense behind the pitcher; and he brought out another example from the recent past. "I'll say it now and I'll say it again," he went on. "There's a reason — well, three reasons— why Mike Cuellar and Dave McNally [both lefties] won in Baltimore. Paul Blair, Mark Belanger, and Brooks Robinson." Herzog was obviously referring to the inspired play of McGee, Smith, and Pendleton on defense, among the other stars with the glove on the team, like Herr, Van Slyke, Coleman, and Nieto. Pendleton continued to struggle at the plate, as his .228 average was nearly a hundred points lower than his '84 mark. Someone not struggling was McGee, who with three more hits (including his seventh homer) raised his average to a whopping .368.

Attention was diverted from the pennant only slightly as Rose and his Reds came to town on September 2. As expected, he had closed in on the record before making his way to St. Louis, and came into the three-game series only six hits away. "All 112 press box seats are gone," announced Cardinals publicist Jim Toomey. "And that does not include any of the TV people. I'd say there's 40 writers over and above what we always have, and God only knows how many radio and TV people." To the loads of photographers also on hand, Toomey had a warning. "I told some of them that they may have some trouble finding a place to stand and take their pictures," he said. "But you can't stop them from coming, really." Some of the more obscure papers that found their way to St. Louis included the *Wichita Eagle*, the *Virginian-Pilot*, and the *Providence Journal*.

What was Herzog's explanation for all of the media's being in the visiting manager's clubhouse for a change? "Because the other guy's got 3,800 more hits than I do." Whitey did not give himself enough credit, though — he was actually only about 3,600 hits behind Rose.

And why were so few (159) of Rose's career hits home runs? Rose, as with every question on hitting, had an answer. "In order to hit homers, you have to pull the ball," he reasoned. "And the second thing is, you've got to hit the ball in the air. Those are two things I try not to do." Also, Hummel interestingly pointed out that nearly a fourth of Rose's hits— 1,025—had come in stadiums that no longer existed in 1985.

What the big press crowd and average paid crowd (29,000) saw the first night was primarily a dominating performance by Reds rookie left-hander Tom Browning over seven innings. Browning, trying to keep up with Coleman for the Rookie-of-the-Year honors, allowed only one run. "He reminds me of Catfish Hunter," Rose said in praise of his young hurler. "He's always around the plate. He goes at you. He challenges you and gets you out." Browning would go on to become the first rookie in 31 years to win 20 games. Andujar (20–8) took the loss in giving up three runs in six innings of work, as the final turned out to be 4–1. Rose went hitless in three at-bats (the only Reds starter not to get a hit, in fact), although he scored a run in the sixth on Parker's home run off Andujar, a long blast that cleared the first deck in right field. And two more hits from McGee inched his average up to .369, as the Cards scattered eight safeties as a club.

Much to the disappointment of fans the following night, Rose sat himself down in favor of Perez, but St. Louis turned the tables on him, as Harper doubled home a pair of runs in the seventh to give Lahti (3–2) the win in relief of Forsch, Horton, and Worrell. Rose returned for the last game, and Worrell (after seven strong innings by Kepshire) shut down his club for his first major league victory, a 4–3 final, while two more stolen bases by Coleman gave him 90 for the season. Rose did manage an eighth-inning single that put Cincinnati ahead temporarily, 3–2, as he moved to within five of Cobb.

But Jorgensen, getting a chance to shine in Clark's absence, singled home Pendleton for the game-winner in the ninth after Van Slyke scored from second on Concepcion's error, which had allowed Pendleton to reach. Jorgensen had appeared in only 40 of the Cardinals' first 118 games when Clark went down, but the club knew that the veteran could be counted on. The Cards had taken two out of three from Cincinnati to improve to 80–50 on the year—but still only a game ahead of the Mets.

Meanwhile, the National League had named McGee as the Player of the Month for August, in light of his dazzling 44-for-101 hitting (.436) and 22 runs scored. He continued to lead the circuit in average (.365), hits (175), and triples (16). Before Rose left town, he had a one-liner for the press about the Cardinals' new star. "I told Willie," Rose said, "'Quit making a joke out of the league.'" Elsewhere on the team, Herr continued to be a quiet hero by batting .318 and was second in the league in doubles with 31.

The Cubs then limped into St. Louis for another meeting with the Cardinals at Busch, as the clubs made up one game they had lost with the strike in August. Things had gotten progressively worse for Chicago, as they had just lost three straight at home to Houston and now were five games below .500 at 63–68. Cox (15–8) took matters into his own hands as he twirled a two-hit complete game for a 6–1 Redbird romp.

The Cards came after Engel with 13 hits, with McGee and Cedeno logging three each and Landrum two, the latter getting his first stolen base and fourth home run of the year. (Herzog's plan continued to be to play Cedeno for Jorgensen against left-handers like Engel, and the same with Landrum for Van Slyke.) McGee was back at .369, four points ahead of Mantle's 1957 pace for the modern single-season record for a switch-hitter.

Cox disposed of the Cubs in a little over two hours, as at one point he had retired 16 batters in a row. His streak ended when Dunston shot a ball over Coleman's head in left in the sixth inning, as Coleman had trouble retrieving it. Trying to generate some excitement for his club, Dunston ran all the way around the bases in an attempt for an inside-the-park home run. He actually beat Smith's relay throw home, but Nieto blocked the plate deftly, applied the tag, and thus ended the inning.

Engel had been thrust into another starting role as the Cubs' "Big Five" had now missed a total of 45 starts for the season. Mourned one of the infirm, Rick Sutcliffe, "It's frustrating to see people laughing at you and stepping on you and not be able to do anything about it." And it was the ninth win in 11 tries versus Chicago for St. Louis in '85, a true reversal of fortunes from the year before.

All was not rosy with the home folks, however. Andujar's name had been brought up in the drug investigation, as Lonnie Smith got immunity from federal charges in exchange for testimony against Strong, one of his main suppliers, the Associated Press reported. "We're going to find out if a jury will believe the testimony of junkies," said Strong's attorney, Adam Renfroe, before the proceedings began — although he was not specifically speaking of Smith or any other player in particular. As Smith began spilling the beans on September 5, he claimed that the cocaine that Strong provided was used frequently by himself, Andujar, and Keith Hernandez in the Cardinals' clubhouse. When asked by the local media about what Smith had said, Andujar quickly replied "no comment." More testimony from other players around the league was still to come, and most in the press warned the public of a lot of dirty laundry about to be aired. Not too long after Smith's participation, Parker testified, claiming that Strong was so popular among the players that he was invited to the Pirates' 1981 New Year's Eve party at the house of Bill Madlock, the team captain.

"A baseball season is a marathon, not a sprint," Tom Wheatley of the *Post-Dispatch* reminded readers on September 7. "Rick Mahler and John Tudor, running in opposite directions, are proof of that." While the Braves' Mahler had begun the season with his red-hot 7–0 start, Tudor was suffering through his 1–7 misfire. As Atlanta came to Busch, however, Mahler sported a highly cooled 17–13 mark while Tudor's exploits were becoming nationally famous. He added his eighth shutout of the season against the Braves, spreading seven hits over his nine innings in an 8–0 Cardinal win, and the fourth loss in as many decisions for Mahler against St. Louis on the year. With the performance, Tudor's ERA dropped to 1.95 (second in the league only to Gooden's 1.81); he had won 16 of his last 17 decisions, and became the winningest left-hander in a Cardinals season since Carlton's 20–9 campaign in 1971.

Tudor earned applause for his masterful pitching from the Busch Stadium faithful, but also for the little things, too — for although it was a terribly humid September evening in St. Louis, he sprinted out a routine fly ball that he hit in the fifth inning, which aroused an isolated standing ovation from the fans behind the Cardinals' first base dugout. Later, coming to bat again in the eighth inning, he legged out an infield hit. "If I run out of gas from sprinting 90 feet," he said afterwards, "I don't belong out there."

Coleman switched his contributions to the defensive side for a change. Although he was thrown out by Bruce Benedict in his only steal attempt (his total still stood at 90), he made two great plays in left field — one off the bat of Rafael Ramirez in the seventh, a diving catch near the foul line, and he then held Horner to single on a ball hit to the wall in the eighth.

9. It's Up to You, New York

Despite his disdain of home runs, Pete Rose hit one in windy Wrigley Field, along with another hit, and his distance from Cobb had shortened to three.

The Cards hoped to fatten their division lead with the lowly Braves in town, as their advantage stood at only a game-and-a-half over New York. The Braves were almost 20 games below .500, and still a distant fifth in the National League West. While tougher games lay ahead on the schedule for St. Louis, the Cardinals knew that they had to keep making progress against the lesser teams. In addition, the Atlanta series—plus the one final make-up game with the Cubs on September 9—marked the last home games before the club embarked on an 11-game road trip on the East Coast.

The Cards thought they could turn to Andujar to do what needed to be done. Unfortunately, he remained stuck on 20 wins, perhaps distracted by the drug controversy, as he gave the Atlanta club too many chances in taking a 3–1 loss. The victory for the Braves' starter Steve Bedrosian was saved by Sutter, his 22nd, who met a loud chorus of "boos" when he entered the game in the ninth.

In other reminders for the fans of the Cardinals' 1982 championship club, Ken Oberkfell, the third baseman on that team from nearby Highland, Illinois, got a two-out, run-scoring single in the fourth that proved to be the difference. "There's no question it's a good feeling to go out and beat your former teammates," Obie admitted. "They're in a pennant race, and this will slow them down a little." They were slowed down some more the next day, thanks to the bat of Horner. The powerful Braves infielder was used in a pinch-hitting role by Bobby Wine in the last game of the series, and he responded with a broken-bat, bases-loaded triple to send Atlanta to a 7–3 victory.

Three hundred miles up the road, a standing ovation by the crowd of 28,000 at Wrigley greeted Rose after his fifth-inning single off Reggie Patterson tied Cobb at 4,191. Cobb had spent 23 years in the big leagues, and Rose had caught him in his 23rd (the result of which was approximately 2,300 more at-bats than Cobb, with the changes in scheduling and other factors). He later grounded out in the seventh and struck out in the ninth in pursuit of a new mark.

The Cardinals had one more home game before heading east, and they did not send themselves to New York in the manner they had wanted. Their local rival came in again on the 9th to play the final strike make-up, and Hummel described the scene: "Kurt Kepshire, alternately horrid and torrid in his last seven starts, was much the former Monday night as he didn't make it out of the second inning in a 3–1 loss to the Chicago Cubs." Kepshire surrendered four hits and all three runs before exiting, as Cub hurlers Fontenot and Jay Baller kept the St. Louis bats in check. The Mets were idle, waiting for the Cardinals' invasion, so the clubs were exactly tied at 82–53 as the battle would begin at Shea Stadium.

"It's an important series," Herzog affirmed, "but it's not what you'd call crucial. If we sweep them or they sweep us, it won't be the death of either one of us." Jack Clark, now back on the active roster, thought it was critical that the Cards go at least 6–5 on the 11-game trip. He took extended batting practice before leaving St. Louis, and although Jorgensen and Cedeno were still getting all the time at first, he hoped to crack the lineup at some point against the Mets. To help the pitching staff, Boever was recalled from Louisville once again, as well as left-hander Pat Perry, who had 14 saves and a 2.37 ERA with the Triple-A club. Perry called home not too far up the road in Taylorville, Illinois, near Springfield.

Thinking of their offensive strategy, the Cardinals figured they could take advantage of their speed, as the New York pitchers were not doing a good job of holding runners on base. Carter was having one of his better years throwing the ball, but was given few chances to actually throw runners out because of the big jumps they had been getting.

Round One in the Fight for the East took place on Tuesday night, September 10, with Cox going up against Darling, who was 14–5 on the year for the Mets. The fireworks started immediately, as after Herr homered in the top of the first for St. Louis, Cox ran into trouble. New York left fielder George Foster took his time getting into the batter's box, which annoyed Cox to the point of drilling Foster in the left thigh with his next pitch. The benches cleared, as small skirmishes broke out between pairs of players. Cox said later that he wasn't trying to throw at Foster, but in any event, the melee rattled Cox more than it did the Mets. He promptly then served up a fat one to Howard Johnson, who launched the pitch over the right field wall for a grand slam as part of a five-run first inning for the Mets.

Cox ultimately settled down, however, and gave the Cards three more innings before yielding to Horton. In the fifth, Coleman blooped a single into shallow center to score Smith, who had doubled, and the Cardinals added two more in the seventh. That was as close as they would get, as McDowell fired scoreless innings for the last two-and-two-thirds in relief of Darling, giving New York a 5–4 win. The Mets had ascended to first place by a full game, as Herzog gave the ball to Tudor for the second tilt in hopes that the left-hander could continue his magic.

It was *the* matchup of National League baseball in 1985. A summer full of drug scandals and talks of player strikes had mostly vanished, as all eyes focused on Shea for a monumental standoff. Gooden would be taking

9. It's Up to You, New York

the mound for the Mets, as the two top candidates for the National League Cy Young Award went toe-to-toe with first place on the line in front of over 52,000 spectators. If it had been 50 years earlier, one could have easily substituted Dizzy Dean and Carl Hubbell into the main roles and it could not have been more dramatic.

"Pitching duels are overrated. Usually," wrote Horrigan. "But sometimes you get a pitching duel that transcends the cliché that describes it, a duel that is a duel, indeed. That's what you got here Wednesday night [the 14th]."

Similar to a gunfight, one false move — allowing a single run to score — might have spelled death for the one who faltered. And like two great gunfighters, neither Tudor nor Gooden blinked, but rather stared each other down for hours in the sinking New York sun. After each going nine scoreless innings, one of the men tired out, but didn't blink. Gooden was lifted by Davey Johnson in the tenth in favor of Orosco, who offered an 0–2 slider to Cedeno. Cedeno got his bat around and planted the pitch over the left field wall, and the tie was broken.

Not to be outdone, Tudor took the mound in the 10th inning, and coolly retired the Mets in order for his ninth shutout, boosting his record to 18–8. He now had a streak of 28 consecutive scoreless innings going, longest in the league for the year, as no Met player ever reached second base. "I'm sure there will be a lot of important games before the season is over," the humble Tudor said. He would be right.

But even with this fantastic display, the focus of the baseball world on this day was in Cincinnati. Rose stepped to the plate in the bottom of the first inning against San Diego right-hander Eric Show and lined a 2–1 pitch to left-center for a single and hit number 4,192 that separated himself from Cobb. The game was stopped for seven minutes, as the crowd cheered maniacally and snapped flashbulb after flashbulb. "No other record in no other sport has the impact of this," said his counterpart Garvey, as the Padres' first baseman watched the scene unfold. And young Tony Gwynn, who in the past year had won his first National League batting title, also witnessed it from his right field position. "I can't comprehend 4,000 hits," he said. "I don't think anyone else can, either. It was a typical Pete Rose hit to left field." Rose tripled off Show later in the game as well, and fittingly he scored both Reds' runs in a 2–0 shutout for Browning.

"This record will never be broken," claimed National League umpire Lee Weyer who worked the plate for the game, and who also had monitored third base when Hank Aaron broke Babe Ruth's career home run mark in 1974. "It was a slider about belt high. As soon as he hit it, I knew there was no way they were going to catch it. I talked to Pete about three, four, five years ago, and I told him I would be behind the plate when he broke Cobb's record."

"I can't really explain my feelings," the new king said among the storm of media folk after the game. "I wish every player in baseball could experience what I did at first base tonight." Mike Downey of the *Los Angeles Times* took amusement in Rose's response to President Ronald Reagan, who had phoned from Washington to offer his congratulations. "You missed a good game," Rose told the leader of the nation.

The hallowed newspaper of baseball, *The Sporting News*, had said on September 27, 1923: "In the end, Cobb's record probably will be one never to be equaled — though never is a long time." At that point, Cobb had just passed Honus Wagner for the all-time hits mark. Cobb got his final hit on the same day that Rose set the record — September 11 — but 57 years earlier in 1928. "No active player poses anything resembling a threat to Rose," assured writer Joe Reichler in a tone similar to *The Sporting News*. "The 40-year-old Carew's chances of reaching 4,000 hits, let alone overtaking Rose, appear nil."

Andujar could not keep the momentum going that was ignited by Tudor, as the struggling hurler lost his fourth straight bid for his 21st victory. He lasted only an inning and a third, getting blasted for seven hits and six runs as New York later held on for a 7–6 win. "You've got to wonder if he's going to help us down the stretch," a puzzled Ozzie Smith pondered afterwards about Andujar, now carrying an ERA of 5.81 over his last ten games. "You've got to wonder if you've got to put somebody else in the rotation."

The Cardinals did fight back from the early explosion, capped by McGee's dramatic game-tying home run in the ninth inning. But in the bottom half, Mets outfielder Mookie Wilson beat out an infield hit, was sacrificed to second by Wally Backman, and then Hernandez delivered the final blow with a single to left for the winning tally off Dayley. On the play on which Wilson reached, Smith had to make a quick throw off a tough hop that bounced in front of Cedeno at first, allowing Wilson to be safe. "I made the pitch," Dayley said of the curve ball that induced the grounder. "When you make the pitch you want and they hit it, there's nothing you can do about it. I jammed him, and he just didn't hit it hard enough for Ozzie to get it."

A bright spot in the bullpen was the debut of Perry, who threw scoreless frames in the third, fourth, fifth, and sixth after Horton put out Andujar's fire in the second.

So the Mets were back to a one-game lead once again, with Cardinals off to Wrigley Field in Chicago to try and keep pace.

9. It's Up to You, New York

The running game had somewhat stagnated during the three games in New York, as the Cards managed only three steals (one each by Coleman, McGee, and Smith). As the first game unraveled in Chicago, so did the Cubs once again — and the speedsters took advantage. Two wild pitches and ten walks by Chicago pitchers (including five by starter Steve Trout in only 1⅔ innings), plus a passed ball by Jody Davis and an error by Dernier in center, helped the Redbirds circle the bases in a 9–3 St. Louis rout. The Cardinals helped themselves, too, as stolen bases by Coleman (94) and Smith (23), as well as two each by Van Slyke (27) and McGee (45), made the Cubs woozy watching the merry-go-round. The Cards' eight total steals on the day matched a club high for the year, set previously on July 11 against San Diego. Cubs manager Jim Frey was his usual displeased self after the game, and Trout was the main target of his anger.

"You start the ball game walking a guy [Coleman]," he began with his voice trembling. "And you know he's going to run. We just kept walking them. Why the [expletive] are you going to walk a team that's going to steal 300 [expletive] bases?"

What did Frey say on his visit to Trout at the mound in the first inning, after he had walked Coleman, allowed a hit to McGee, and walked Herr?

"I said, 'Throw the ball over the stinking plate and get some stinking outs.'"

Trout had been 4–0 lifetime against the Cardinals coming into this game. He still had been dealing with his rash of injuries — the latest of which, he claimed, occurred when he fell off his stationary bicycle at home while glancing to check on his young daughter.

Forsch (7–6) went six solid innings for St. Louis, and Worrell picked up his first major league save in working the ninth. The Mets and Expos split a doubleheader in Montreal, so that meant the Cards were back on top by the slimmest of margins on September 15:

Eastern Division	W	L	Pct.	GB
St. Louis	85	55	.607	—
New York	85	56	.603	½
Montreal	76	65	.539	9½
Philadelphia	69	70	.496	15½
Chicago	66	74	.471	19
Pittsburgh	46	92	.333	38 |//
Western Division	W	L	Pct.	GB
Los Angeles	84	57	.596	—
Cincinnati	74	66	.529	9½

Western Division	W	L	Pct.	GB
Houston	71	70	.504	13
San Diego	71	70	.504	13
Atlanta	59	82	.418	25
San Francisco	56	85	.397	28

Coleman's stolen base in that game was his 95th on the year, the eighth-most ever in one season. Next up on the list at number seven was Cobb, who stole 96 for the Tigers in 1915, which was matched by Omar Moreno while with the Pirates in 1980.

The Cards had the Cubs' number so convincingly, in fact, that they were able to beat them on a day in which Ozzie Smith made two errors—"which would fall into the Halley's Comet category," informed Hummel, in terms of its frequency. It was just as obvious to Herzog about a change being needed at shortstop. "If he keeps making errors, I've got to bench him," a phrase he couldn't even finish before neither he nor the reporters could keep from laughing.

Despite their "poor fielding" shortstop, the Cardinals pieced together enough runs and defense to defeat the Cubs, 5–4. Smith himself contributed to the offense with a nifty 2-for-2 day with a couple of stolen bases thrown in. And Herzog once again wasted no time in taking the ball away from Kurt Kepshire. The St. Louis starter threw only 14 pitches—13 of them for balls—when the Cardinals' manager made a slow walk to the Wrigley Field mound. Kepshire was not even credited with a third of an inning pitched, as he walked the first three Cub batters in the bottom half of the first (Dunston, Matthews, and Sandberg), and then started off Moreland with another ball. To at least eat up some innings, Herzog then put the veteran Matt Keough in charge, another pitcher only recently brought up from Louisville to shore up the bullpen for the playoff run. Keough had spent seven years in the American League, almost exclusively with Oakland and mostly as a starter.

What kind of stuff did Kepshire have, Herzog was asked, that caused his removal? "I don't know," Whitey replied. "Nobody hit it."

The speculation was Herzog wasn't going to give Kepshire too many more chances, as the bullpen couldn't handle being taxed for seven, eight, or nine innings of work on a regular basis. That speculation soon festered into fact, as Kepshire was banished to bullpen after making 29 starts on the year. Ricky Horton was temporarily selected to take the fifth spot in the rotation behind Tudor, Andujar, Cox, and Forsch. After one more game in Chicago on Sunday the 15th, Horton would start the second game of a doubleheader at Pittsburgh on Monday.

9. It's Up to You, New York 141

People kept asking about Clark: when he would come back, how much batting practice he was taking, how sharp he would be for the playoffs, and so on. The questions halted for a little while, though, as his understudy, Cedeno, knocked Chicago pitchers around for five hits and four RBIs in the Cards' 5–1 win in the last Cards-Cubs game at Wrigley for the year. He capped the day with a two-run homer in the seventh off hard-luck Steve Engel, who lost to St. Louis for the third time in the past six weeks. Cox (16–9) shook off his recent woes to go seven strong frames with relief help from Worrell.

The Cardinals had beaten the Pirates 10 out of 13 times on the season, and they stretched that ledger to 12 wins in 15 tries by sweeping the unusual Monday doubleheader. The Pirates were still looking for a new ownership group to take over the waning franchise, and one of the groups was headed by manager Chuck Tanner. Pittsburgh had recently gone six weeks (7/22 to 9/3) without winning a road game. "To my way of thinking," Madlock assessed, "it takes two or three things to win — speed, defense, and power. Right now, we're 0-for-3."

Tudor (19–8) wasn't his typically sharp self in allowing 12 base runners over six innings of work. But he got plenty of offense in an 8–4 win in the first game, highlighted by Van Slyke's RBI triple, as Jose DeLeon was the loser for Pittsburgh. DeLeon, with an unbelievable 2–18 mark, was finishing one of the worst individual records for a pitcher ever seen. "Stuff-wise," Herzog stated, "he's the best 2–18 pitcher in history. He walks guys and he can't hold runners on (a bad mix in facing the Cardinals), but he's got a great chance to be a helluva pitcher. His stuff is as good as anybody's." Tudor, a teammate of DeLeon's in Pittsburgh, echoed Herzog's comments about his potential. "He's got a great arm, but he just doesn't throw strikes. When he does throw strikes, then they don't score any runs for him. So he's kind of in a Catch-22 situation." Evidence of DeLeon's potential was seen back on April 16, when he struck out 14 Mets for a Pittsburgh club record — although he lost the game to New York as Darling and Orosco fired a one-hitter back at the feeble Pirates.

Horton followed up with a sparkling performance in the nightcap, throwing six innings of one-run ball with help from Campbell and Perry, the latter picking up his first big league win and pushing his personal scoreless-inning string to seven.

The club had now won five in a row, and still held a one-game lead over the Mets with 19 games left to play. It was hoped that Andujar could capitalize on the team's momentum, and not only gain his elusive 21st victory but right himself for the postseason. Understandably, the Pirates provided the right opponent for a confidence boost, and Andujar took advantage with a complete-game 10–4 win. He had not won since August 23—the same day that Clark went on the shelf with his injured rib cage—and it was the first time he had gone nine innings since ten days prior to that date. He credited Herzog's close monitoring during pre-game throwing stints in the bullpen for the turnaround. "I had been a little lazy," Andujar admitted. "Whitey worked me. That's why I thought I had a better fast ball [against the Pirates]."

Coleman's two steals, putting him at 98 for the year, meant that only Brock and Maury Wills (who had 104 stolen bases in 1962) had more in a single National League season, as Coleman passed the 97 that Montreal's Ron LeFlore swiped in 1980. The Cards also had a rare three-homer game, as Smith (his 5th), Cedeno (6) and McGee (10) all went deep. And as the team moved on to Philadelphia, more power was coming as Jack Clark announced that he was finally ready to play and might be in the lineup against the Phillies—depending on what Herzog wanted to do.

The issue of drug abuse in baseball was still hanging around, as the problem always happened to surface with someone or another. On September 17 it was Steve Howe again, who had been given another chance with the Minnesota Twins after being freed from the self-described fishbowl in Los Angeles. He had missed the entire Twins series with the Indians the previous weekend, and nobody with the club knew where he was. When he finally showed up in Minneapolis on Monday, he claimed that he had gone to Detroit to be with his wife's grandfather, whom he said had suffered a stroke. Members of Howe's family, though, said that he never showed up. Howe admitted to Twins' officials that he was still using cocaine, and he was released.

Bob Forsch, the dignified knight and dean of the St. Louis team, had been overshadowed by some of his flashier teammates during the season. He himself knew in spring training that his role would be diminished, but that role became all the more important in light of the recent struggles of Kepshire. Exhibiting himself as the true professional that he was, Forsch answered the bell when called and shut out the Phillies on their home field, 7–0. It was the first shutout for Forsch since his second no-hitter two years before, and his teammates were quite impressed. "He was as good as I've ever seen," claimed Tommy Herr. "His ball was moving and he was putting it right where he wanted to."

Coleman's run pace was slightly ahead of his stolen bases, as he scored for the 100th time on the year after stealing his 99th bag. Porter knocked his tenth homer (and eighth since the All-Star break), and McGee's three hits in the game increased his average to .363, still more than 40 points better than Guerrero for second place in the league. Guerrero had become a lame-duck candidate, as he had been out of the Dodgers' lineup since September 8 with a broken hand.

Clark returned to the starting lineup on the 19th, as the full impact of the Cedeno trade now became clear. Against left-handed pitchers (as the Cardinals were facing that night in the Phillies' Dave Rucker—a former Cardinal who was involved with the Campbell-DeJesus trade back on April 6), Herzog was now able to put another powerful right-handed bat in the lineup, as Cedeno moved to his more customary position in right field. Although Van Slyke's bat had been steadily improving for the past couple of months, Cedeno had been hitting over .400 since joining the Redbirds, and Herzog did not want to take him off the field.

The second game against the Phillies also produced a pair of significant "100s." After walking in the fifth inning, Vince Coleman became the first rookie in baseball history to steal 100 bases. He was believed to also be the first player to steal 100 bases in three consecutive seasons in three different leagues (in addition to his 145 at Macon in 1983, he had stolen 101 at Louisville in '84). Two innings earlier, Herr had doubled home McGee to reach the century mark in RBIs, the first time in 35 years a player had a 100 runs batted in for a season with fewer than ten home runs (George Kell of the Detroit Tigers had been the last). He also joined fellow Cardinals Frisch and Rogers Hornsby as three of only seven National League second basemen to have 100 RBIs in a season. The milestones notwithstanding, Keough did not make good use of a trial start as he lost to Rucker and the Phils, 6–3.

The Mets, meanwhile, refused to go away; their tough lefty Fernandez struck out 11 Cubs in winning for New York, 5–1. The St. Louis lead was once again whittled to a single game.

Down in Atlanta, Rose set another record while the world was still buzzing about the all-time hits mark. His third hit of the game was his 100th of the season, the 23rd consecutive time he had accomplished the feat, in the Reds' 15–5 drubbing of the Braves—breaking away from Boston's Carl Yastrzemski and his 22 straight seasons of 100 or more.

It was then back home, where the third-place Expos were at the ballpark. The Cards and Cox fell behind in the first match, trailing 3–2 in the bottom of the seventh. Smith then singled, stole second, and was driven home on McGee's hit to tie the game. And in the eighth, Pendleton and Cedeno smacked back-to-back triples for the lead. As he had done in Cox's last start, Worrell came to the rescue out of the pen. The rookie was showing like he was intent on taking over the closer's role, as he shut down the big Expo bats of Andre Dawson, Brooks, and Wallach, and gained his second big-league win with two perfect innings (save an error by Smith and a passed ball by Nieto) in the Cards' 5–3 triumph. Unbelievably, the Mets let an extra-inning game slip to the bumbling Pirates, so the Redbirds saw their lead grow to two games again.

Even though Cedeno was filling in tremendously, the Redbirds knew that Clark's bat was needed back in the lineup. They were 18–9 without Clark, but common sense told everyone that he would make a strong club stronger. Clark was finally feeling back in the groove of playing an entire nine innings, and he came through late in the game the following night. His two-run homer in the bottom of the seventh capped a five-run Cardinal comeback, as Lahti (4–2) got the win and Worrell the save (his third) in a thrilling 7–6 victory at Busch in front of over 32,000 fans.

However, the Mets righted themselves against Pittsburgh, and Gooden upped his record to 22–4 in a 12–1 pounding of the Bucs, so the Cards' lead stayed at two. While the Expos jumped out to a 6–1 lead, Raines looked his usual formidable self, stealing three bases for a total of 63 on the season; it was hard to imagine, though, that he trailed Coleman for the league title by almost *forty*. Tudor had gotten knocked around, allowing five runs in the same number of innings before giving way to Kepshire. The big hit was a grand slam off the bat of Dawson, which put Montreal up 5–0 in the third inning.

Mets manager Davey Johnson was already thinking about the three games he had to play in St. Louis beginning on October 1. Even though the series was over a week away, he was shuffling his starting rotation to ensure that Gooden would throw the first game in Busch Stadium. And over in the American League West, the Royals and the Angels were in a tooth-and-nail struggle for the division crown, tied with identical 83–64 records. "Forget the Subway Series and the All-Canadian Series," wrote Craig Horst of the Associated Press, in reference to the possibility of the Yankees, Mets, Expos, or Blue Jays making it to the final round. "Missouri is ready for the Interstate 70 Series."

Things were indeed getting pretty rough in New York, as salty Yankees manager Billy Martin broke his arm in a fight with his pitcher Ed Whitson in a Baltimore hotel. The two started their early Sunday morning scrap in the hotel bar, then into the parking lot, and then onto the third floor of the building. Other team members noticed that Martin had gotten into a shoving match with a patron in the same bar the previous Friday evening. Apparently, Whitson had unloaded some frustration on Martin after being removed from his turn in the starting rotation for the Friday night game against the Orioles.

The Mets took another step backwards on September 22, as they bowed again to Pittsburgh and rookie pitcher Bob Kipper at Shea Stadium,

5–3. And in St. Louis, Tommy Herr drove a 2–2 fastball from Montreal pitcher Jack O' Connor towards Raines in left. The outfielder drifted back and watched the ball fly fittingly over the Mets' sign on the wall for a stunning 6–5 victory before a crowd of over 38,000 that was crazed with joy. Dayley (4–2) got the win in relief of Andujar, as the lefty pitched a scoreless eighth and ninth to keep the Redbirds in the game. The Cards entered the inning down 5–4, but McGee singled in front of Herr's heroics to bring the winning run to the plate (it was McGee's 200th hit of the year, the first Cardinal to reach that plateau since Templeton and Hernandez both did it in 1979). Also in the game, Braun notched his 54th pinch hit as a Cardinal, which broke the club record previously held by Schoendienst.

"There's a new hero every day," noticed Andy Van Slyke about his team. "Every guy who has been here has made a major contribution this year at one time or another. How many times is Tommy Herr going to win a ball game in the bottom of the ninth with a home run?" Herr himself conceded that the scene was surreal. "I think every kid who's ever played baseball has fantasized about doing something like that," he said afterwards about his feat. "As a big leaguer, you fantasize about doing something like that, too. When I was going up to the plate in the ninth inning, I was thinking how great it would be to hit a home run and win the game. But the type of hitter I am, I can't go up to the plate in that frame of mind too often." His contributions to the team had been many, as talk centered around Herr and McGee being the front-runners for the National League MVP award.

"We're capable of beating you in a lot of ways," McGee added about his company. "We've got the speed, the gloves, and the long ball. We're not a one-dimensional team. We've got a little bit of everything. We've got a lot of all-around players on this team." With his Mets teammates watching Herr sock the game-winning homer on television, pitcher Roger McDowell was sick. "It was as though we had been stabbed in the back," he described.

In the first game in a series with Pittsburgh at Busch, Pendleton delivered the goods with a two-out triple to drive in the tying and winning runs for a 5–4 St. Louis victory. It was the fourth comeback win in a row for the Cards, and made for 11 successes in their last 12 tries overall. Even though they had their smallest home crowd since May 1 with 17,611, the Cardinals broke their single-season attendance record set in 1983 with over 2.3 million supporters. Even errors by three of the most iron-clad defensive men the next night—Smith, Herr, and McGee—could not offset the team, as Horton (3–2) pitched through the miscues towards another 5–4 win over the Pirates.

The Mets were keeping pace in Philadelphia by trouncing the Phillies, 7–1, but still trailed St. Louis by three full games. It lengthened to four the next night, as the Cards' train kept rolling towards the playoffs with a 6–3 win over the Phillies at Busch, while New York suffered a crushing 5–4 defeat at the hands of the Cubs at Wrigley Field. The Mets had won 13 of 16 games against Chicago on the year going into the game (including all nine at Shea Stadium), but Speier's single off Orosco scored Lopes with the game-winner in the ninth. Coleman ran wild back in St. Louis, stealing three bases for a new total of 105, as he made child's play out of the Philadelphia battery of Hudson and Virgil. He now had passed Wills on the National League single-season list, and only Brock stood in his way.

There were ten games left for both the Mets and the Cardinals, and ten also happened to be the Cardinals' magic number (the combination of St. Louis wins and New York losses needed to clinch). The standings appeared as follows on the morning of September 26:

Eastern Division	W	L	Pct.	GB
St. Louis	96	56	.632	—
New York	92	60	.605	4
Montreal	79	73	.520	17
Philadelphia	71	79	.473	24
Chicago	71	80	.470	24½
Pittsburgh	52	98	.347	43

Western Division	W	L	Pct.	GB
Los Angeles	89	63	.586	—
Cincinnati	82	68	.547	6
Houston	78	74	.513	11
San Diego	76	75	.503	12½
Atlanta	62	89	.411	26½
San Francisco	59	92	.391	29½

Tudor got his twentieth win against the Phillies that evening, along with his tenth shutout, as he dominated Philadelphia on four hits and no walks, 5–0. It was the first time in the National League two pitchers from the same club had won 20 games in the same season, when Fergie Jenkins and Bill Hands for Chicago and Claude Osteen and Bill Singer for Los Angeles accomplished it. In addition, it was more shutouts in one season than any left-hander in history, except for the 11 posted by Koufax in 1963, and the first time anyone had reached ten in a single year since Jim Palmer of Baltimore in 1975. Tudor had gone an astonishing 19–1 since May 29,

9. It's Up to You, New York

as he and Gooden were on a collision course for the Cy Young. "I wasn't even thinking about winning 15 games," Tudor recalled about being in the middle of his funk in late May. "I was just thinking about battling back and getting in gear." The offensive stars were Pendleton and Van Slyke — the former hitting .375 in the past two weeks, and the latter grabbing three stolen bases for 33 on the year. The Cards then made one more road trip for the regular season, and lost two out of three in Montreal, as the Mets prepared to invade St. Louis, trailing the Cardinals by three games with six left to play.

10

"How Do You Like Us Now?"

Although the math said otherwise, the Mets knew that they had to sweep the Cardinals to have any realistic shot at overtaking the division. After the series at Busch, New York would finish the season by hosting Montreal for three games, while the Cubs would play three at St. Louis. Davey Johnson backed off of his original idea and decided to start Darling instead of Gooden in the first game against the Cardinals on Tuesday, October 1. Herzog had already announced that Tudor would take the mound in the opener for Cardinals, and perhaps Johnson felt that Tudor, still on his hot streak, couldn't be beaten—even by the seemingly-indomitable Gooden. For St. Louis in the second game, Herzog wasn't sure beforehand if he was going to go with Andujar or Cox. "Sometimes you can outsmart yourself," he cautioned.

The Cardinals were dealing with several minor injuries—not just Clark's ribs. The most significant were a gash on Coleman's knee that wouldn't seem to heal, a hurting right elbow for Cox, and a sore right shoulder that had been hampering Smith every time he threw across the diamond from his shortstop position. But Ozzie didn't have time to be hurt. "That's what championship seasons are about—playing hurt," he said. "It's not about sitting down and resting. Hey, we're all banged up. We're all tired. Any time you get to this point in the season, you're going to be tired. If you're not tired, you're not human." Though Smith had struggled throughout parts of the regular season with his bat, a recent hot streak had him hitting .275 going into the Mets series, the highest in his career.

As there was when Rose was pursuing the hit record, a flock of reporters had descended on Busch Stadium to witness the decisive games. As usual, they sought out the good-willed Gary Carter, who offered his feelings. "This is what it's all about," the smiling, gifted, curly-haired catcher said. "You play 162 games and it comes down to this. It is the way it should be." Carter was also playing through a bunch of bumps and bruises, nearing the end of a painful year that started with being hit by a pitch on the elbow (in the first game of the season against the Cardinals—the game he won with a home run in the tenth inning). Despite all his pain, Carter played well enough to be named the National League's Player of the Month for September, belting 13 home runs and driving in 34. And Gooden was the pitcher of the month, going a span of 49 innings without allowing an earned run.

As the first pitch approached, the home crowd grew to about 46,000, and yelled wildly as Tudor emerged from the dugout to take the hill. He was as good as advertised, but so was Darling; the two hurlers shut down each side, inning by inning, as it looked like a repeat of Tudor's joust with Gooden a couple weeks earlier. Darling proved a worthy adversary, as the game went into extra innings and he was relieved by Orosco, who blanked the Cards in the tenth after Tudor did the same in the top half. In the top of the eleventh, Dayley was brought in to face the tough left-handed bats of Hernandez and Strawberry. He got the former, but not the latter. Strawberry knocked a hanging curve ball out of the park for a 1–0 New York lead, a booming blow that broke ten lights on the Busch Stadium scoreboard clock, and Orosco pitched a scoreless bottom half for the Mets' win. To add insult, the Cardinals had a consecutive stolen base streak that was stopped at 33 by Carter, as he gunned down Pendleton in the sixth. After the game in the locker room, Strawberry said of the destructive homer that "it was the biggest hit of my career." The 23-year-old had been in the major leagues for three seasons, and New Yorkers looked forward to the franchise's holding onto their two young gems, Strawberry and Gooden, for years to come.

St. Louis had to deal with the other gem on the second night, as Gooden was capping off one of the greatest seasons by a pitcher in recent memory. He was leading the league in wins (23), earned run average (1.51), and strikeouts (258), and like Tudor, seemed to be getting stronger with each passing week. Andujar, going after win number 22 for himself, was penciled in by Herzog as his choice.

The Mets opened the scoring in the first, as Backman singled and stole second. The throw by Porter appeared to be in time, but it hit umpire Fred Brocklander. The play was followed by an infield hit for Hernandez and another single by Carter, which scored Backman. Gooden got the Mets another run in the second, as he beat out a double-play grounder that allowed Foster to score. A triple by Porter got the Redbirds their first tally in the bottom of the second, but the Mets added more offense in the fifth and seventh to take a 5–1 lead, which included Foster's 21st homer of the year.

Andujar was lifted in favor of Perry, as the lefty and Bill Campbell held the Mets in check in the eighth and ninth. The bats could not come through, however, as an RBI single by Coleman in the ninth was all that could be mustered in a 5–2 loss. After Coleman's hit, McGee added an infield single, and Herr crushed a line drive that seemed to be headed for the gap. But Backman reached out and plucked it with his glove, and the game was over. The lead for St. Louis was back to one game.

Now, a serious situation had become critical. The Cardinals had not been swept in a three-game series at Busch all year, and they wanted to keep it that way. Meanwhile, neither of the races in the American League had been decided, as the Angels were only a game behind the Royals in the West, and the Yankees were three games off Toronto's pace in the East. The Dodgers had wrapped up the National League West, leading the Reds by an insurmountable seven games, in a great rebound from a 79–83 record a season ago. It was the third time in the last five years that Los Angeles had won the division title, as well as having done it five times in the previous nine seasons. One major loss in the playoffs for the Dodgers, though, would be veteran shortstop Bill Russell, who was suffering from blurred vision.

Cox, sore elbow and all, took the mound for the Cards against right-hander Rick Aguilera as the Mets looked to bring out the brooms. Once again, the visitors jumped out on top in the first, as Hernandez doubled to score Wilson. The Cardinals thought, however, that Wilson should have been out on a previous play. Backman had hit a tapper to Smith at short, as Ozzie glided across the bag and threw to first in an apparent double play. But second base umpire Dutch Rennert claimed that Smith never touched the bag and called Wilson safe. Herzog shot like a dart out of the dugout and protested the call, with Clark, Herr, and Smith alongside.

The Cardinals tied things up in the second when Pendleton, who had singled, went all the way to third on a throwing error by Aguilera, and was ultimately driven home on a ground out by Smith. A pair of runs in the bottom of the fourth gave St. Louis their first lead in the series, 3–1. The teams then traded punches through the sixth and seventh, as the starting pitchers were relieved by McDowell and Dayley. The Mets crept to within one run at 4–3 in the eighth, but Worrell, Horton, and Lahti shut the door the rest of the way. When Lahti got Carter to fly out to Van Slyke in the ninth on his only pitch, and the final one of the game, his team led the division by two games with three left to play. It had been the eleventh one-run game that the Cards and Mets had played for the season, with New York winning six and St. Louis five.

Just as the excitement was building, another labor problem took center stage. The umpires' union, which had nearly authorized a strike before the decisive fifth game of the 1984 National League Championship Series between the Cubs and Padres, threatened again to walk out. The problem was the pay involved for working the postseason games. Through 1984, the league championship series were best-of-five series; starting in 1985, they would be best-of-seven. "Our contract calls for working best-of-five series," union chief Richie Phillips said. "They [the league] have not negotiated a deal for a best-of-seven series with us." But neither National League president Chub Feeney or American League president Bobby Brown envisioned it's being a serious stalemate, and figured it would be resolved by the time the regular season ended on Sunday, October 6.

Some Cards fans feared the worst scenario for the season's last series, in reference to the visitors from the North. The Cubs actually arrived in St. Louis on a bit of a hot streak, winning five out of their last six games. But John Sonderegger offered a calming voice. "The Cardinals have carved out 12 victories in the first 15 games against Chicago in 1985," he pointed out. "There is no reason to think that would change, despite some hysterical rantings from Cubs fans about knocking the Cardinals out of the race on the final weekend. That would be sort of like every dog having his day, but the Flubs are *real* bow-wows this year."

Forsch was Herzog's choice against Eckersley in the first tilt, and the veteran continued his consistent pitching. He went eight innings, as Coleman ripped off his 110th steal and Van Slyke his 13th homer, and beat the Cubs 4–2 in front of over 40,000 at the ballpark. It was Forsch's third straight win and the team's 100th on the year. "I'm grateful Whitey gave me a chance," he said. "We had four starters doing a good job; we really didn't need me."

His effort allowed Herzog to rest most of the bullpen, as only Worrell was used for an inning in picking up his fifth save. Worrell threw only fastballs in his appearance, which including a strikeout of Matthews after falling behind on him 3–0. "He was definitely waiting for a walk," Worrell commented after the game, speaking like a seasoned veteran. "He's always been a little tardy on my fast ball." Meanwhile, the accolades kept pouring in for Forsch from his teammates. "Forschie's got more lives than a cat," said Ozzie Smith. "People keep counting him out, but he comes back again. The same thing happened in 1982. He's quality. You hold onto those guys because at some point in time, they're going to help you."

The win did not clinch the division for St. Louis, however, as the Mets rallied to beat the Expos, 9–4, in New York. The magic number was down to one, and any Cards win or Mets loss in the last two days would secure the title for St. Louis. "We can come out here and end it tomorrow, and that's a nice feeling," Herr wished. "But we haven't won anything yet." Van Slyke agreed. "Being in control of your destiny is a pretty good feeling."

The possible clincher the next day was put on national television as *NBC Game of the Week*, with Tudor going up against Trout.

"It was just another game, and I had to look at it that way."

Those were Tudor's words after the game, as he was speaking about his mindset beforehand. As it turned out, it was indeed just another ho-hum outing for the hottest lefty in the game. He had picked up the slack for Andujar's slide, as the two had earlier become the first pair of Cardinal pitchers to win 20 games in the same season since Mort Cooper and Johnny Beazley in 1942.

He threw only 85 pitches in going the whole nine innings once again, as he tamed the Cubs on four hits and no walks, 7–1, for his 11th straight victory and his 20th in his last 21 decisions. The last out was caught by Van Slyke, a running, one-handed grab in the gap off the bat of Sandberg — which was fitting, as if the defending National League MVP of the defending Eastern Division champions was passing the torch to the new rulers. Hummel noted that the Cardinals' starting five of Tudor, Andujar, Cox, Kepshire, and Forsch had amassed 76 victories, the most by any fivesome in baseball.

Horton had his own philosophy for the success of the "Bullpen by Committee." "Everybody was kind of a specialist," he said. "And everybody knew there was more than one person in the bullpen who could do the job. We knew we were going to get our chances and we also knew that if we messed up, there would be somebody else there to pick us up."

"It's been amazing," Campbell observed, in describing the orchestral talents of Herzog. "I've watched him and it just seems like no matter how many moves are made, it always seems to come out where he's got the guy he wants in the right place — and somebody ready to back him up just in case." Campbell's four saves on the year gave him a total of 123 for his career, good for 13th on the all-time list.

The Cards had a tough time breaking through on Trout, as the game remained tied at one into the sixth inning. That was when Herr scored on a sacrifice fly to put St. Louis ahead, and later, Baller walked Tudor with the bases loaded to break things open. The Mets had lost 8–3 to the Expos in New York anyway, but there wasn't a man to be found on the Cardinals that would have wanted the division won in that manner; the club wanted to win its way in. When news of the St. Louis victory reached Shea Stadium

10. "How Do You Like Us Now?"

in New York, the fans gave their Mets a long standing ovation. The cheering went on for several minutes, and didn't end until Carter tipped his hat in front of the dugout after grounding out.

In the joyous clubhouse, Smith and Tudor embraced in a hug as Coleman doused them both with a full bottle of champagne. Pendleton then returned the favor to Coleman. "They were all wrong!" Ozzie yelled from atop a stool, speaking of the writers that had picked the Cardinals last at the beginning of the season. His speech met with cheers from his teammates. "What's that tell you? They ought to stop picking, that's what. Games are not played on paper." Herzog and the Cards were joined in the locker room by a proud Gussie Busch. "I couldn't be happier," the 86-year-old beer colonel said. "I'm so happy I can't see straight." It was soon after announced that Tudor would face cult-hero Fernando Valenzuela in the first game of the National League Championship Series on Wednesday, October 9, in Los Angeles. Ironically, their only previous match up of the year was when Valenzuela beat Tudor 3–0 in Los Angeles on July 20, which was Tudor's only loss since the end of May.

Although Andujar was starting the last regular season game against the Cubs, it was already decided that he would pitch only two innings, and then Kepshire would take over. Among the starting position players were Lawless, DeJesus, Braun, and Ford, as Coleman appeared as a pinch-runner only, while McGee and Herr did not enter at all. In the contest dubbed "the hangover game" by Herzog, the Cubs got to Andujar early for three runs, and coasted in to an 8–2 win for some consolation. Andujar was tagged with the loss, as he sputtered to a final record of 21–12. The crowd of 43,665 pushed the record total for the year to 2,662,875, for an average of over 33,000 per home contest. When these figures were announced during the seventh inning, the Redbirds emerged from the dugout and gave their loyal fans a salute. The spectators gave one final cheer after the game, despite the loss, as organist Ernie Hays tooted out "California, Here I Come" on the stadium keyboard. The Cardinals finished the regular season with 314 stolen bases, which was the fourth-most in the history of the game, behind only the 1911 New York Giants (347), the 1976 Oakland A's (341) and the 1912 Giants (319).

As for the Cubs, Dallas Green warned that no jobs were safe for 1986. "Every effort will be made to bring in new blood to increase the competitive spirit," he said. In particular, he cited the disappointing performances of Matthews and Sanderson. "They will be given every opportunity to remain with the team," Green continued, "but we will not become involved in lengthy negotiations to keep them in Chicago." He also had some thoughts on the struggles of Ron Cey. "You have to wonder, is it the beginning of the end, is it the end, or just one of those things that a player goes through?" Cey, now 37, had a considerable drop-off from his contributions to the Cubs' playoff drive in 1984. "All I know is he hasn't helped us as much as we'd like," Green said.

On a bright note, the Cubs had also set a new attendance record in 1985, drawing over 2.1 million fans at Wrigley Field. But that didn't guarantee that the hallowed ballpark would be the home of the Cubs in the future. "We're working to stay in Wrigley and play in Wrigley Field," Green said. "That's our priority and our first thought. But we're getting banged around by the courts and have to look at the alternatives, other stadiums, other ideas."

In Toronto, the Blue Jays had already taken hold of the American League East title, the first time a Canadian team would head to the playoffs (except for the appearance of the Expos in the 1981 split season "playoff," as they finished first in the second half of the season and met the first-half champion Phillies in what was called the "Divisional Series"). Back in spring training, Moseby had walked up to Kirk Gibson of the defending-champion Tigers and brashly stated, "This year, it's our turn."

Even though the drama in the standings had ended, there was still some history to be made. Phil Niekro of the Yankees got the 300th win of his career in an 8–0 shutout of the Jays, albeit with Toronto starting a number of minor-leaguers in their final game. The Blue Jays, like the Cardinals, wanted to give an extra day's rest to their main everyday players. At the age of 46, Niekro became the oldest pitcher to reach the mark. What did it prove? Niekro had the answer. "It does show that you don't have to throw a 95-mile-per-hour fast ball or a Dwight Gooden curve ball to get by in the major leagues." Toronto manager Bobby Cox, though, thought that Niekro was quite dominating. "I don't think the 1927 Yankees would have hit him today, not the way he was throwing," Cox told the press. "He had great stuff." Amazingly, Niekro and his catcher, Butch Wynegar, purposely deviated from his famous knuckler. "The last three pitches of the game [in which he struck out Jeff Burroughs] were the only knuckle balls," Wynegar revealed in the locker room. In the Western Division of the American League, Kansas City won out with a 91–71 final record, one game better than the Angels.

There were a number of individual honors to be passed around among the Cardinals as the regular season ended. McGee ran away with the batting title (.353), while also leading the league in hits (216) and triples (18). Coleman did as well with the stolen base crown (110), while Coleman and McGee had set a new major league record for stolen bases by two teammates in the same season. In addition, their combined total of 166 was more than every team in the National League, save Chicago and Montreal. Andujar and Tudor tied for second in the league with 21 wins each, and Tudor paced the circuit in shutouts (10). Andujar also dubiously led the league with 11 hit batsmen. From the bullpen, Lahti and Dayley gave the Cardinals their first teammates with double figures in saves since 1975. The bullpen had gotten some help too, as the Cardinal starters had doubled their total of 19 complete games from 1984.

McGee's batting mark couldn't top all of baseball, however, as Boggs put up an impressive .368 figure. "Two hits a day keeps the doctor away," Boggs said of his philosophy on hitting. "And in this case, the doctor was George Brett." (Brett finished second to Boggs in the AL at .335.) Boggs' 187 singles were the most ever in one season, while his total of 240 hits was the highest in baseball since Babe Herman of the Brooklyn Dodgers collected 241 in 1930. In addition, the 135 games in which Boggs hit safely tied the record of Chuck Klein of the Phillies, set in 1930 as well. Also in the American League, Carlton Fisk at 38 became the oldest player to win a home run championship. He also broke the American League home run record for catchers, recently set by Detroit's Lance Parrish. Lastly (and notoriously), Don Baylor of the Yankees tied an all-time standard as he was hit by pitched balls 24 times on the year.

It was now on to the postseason for the Cardinals, where the Dodgers stood between St. Louis and its 14th pennant.

Going into the playoffs, the Dodgers were the favorites in Vegas to win the World Series, at 8–5 odds. They were followed by the Blue Jays at 2–1, the Cardinals next at 11–5, and then the Royals at 7–2. The odds panned out in the first game of the ALCS, played the day before the NLCS got underway, as Dave Stieb and his Blue Jays beat up on the Royals 6–1 at Exhibition Stadium in Toronto. Stieb, who was the regular season ERA champ in the American League with his 2.48 mark, was 0–3 against Kansas City during the year. He pitched eight scoreless innings and left the finishing work to Taos, Missouri, native Tom Henke. Perhaps Stieb got some extra luck from Juanita Smith, a 19-year-old Blue Jays fan who ran onto the field and planted a big kiss on his cheek after the took the mound.

As Los Angeles and St. Louis got ready to commence the National League rumble, the Dodgers weren't sure if their main slugger, Guerrero, would be ready. He had been playing with his busted hand for the past month, and it gave no indications of getting better. To help make up the difference, Los Angeles had acquired a new hit man since the Cardinals had last faced them. Bill Madlock, who escaped the pits of Pittsburgh, had hit .360 in 114 at-bats since joining the Dodgers in September, and provided a new challenge for Herzog and his pitchers when going over the opponent's lineup. "He hasn't played well for a couple of years," Herzog said of Madlock, the four-time winner of the National League batting crown. "This [coming to Los Angeles] was probably the best thing that could have happened to him." Madlock won two batting titles with the Cubs in 1975 and 1976, spent three years with the Giants, and then won two more with the Pirates in 1981 and 1983.

It was indeed a different Dodgers club than the championship teams of the '70s that fans knew. "The Dodgers won because [team vice president Al] Campanis succeeded in dismantling one championship team — the Garvey-Cey-Lopes-Baker Dodgers— and found the replacement parts within the Dodgers' system for another," explained Gordon Edes of the *Los Angeles Times*. "Just as he said he would. And Dodgers manager Tom Lasorda exercised the patience to let them develop." The Garveys and the Ceys had been juxtaposed by the Brocks and the Marshalls, as a new identity was born in Chavez Ravine.

One holdover was catcher Steve Yeager, who was gradually relinquishing the job to Mike Scioscia. What worried the Dodgers, though, was that the Cardinals stole 12 bases in 13 tries off Scioscia during the regular season. How did Lasorda plan to counter Coleman, in particular? "Fake a throw to second, and then try to catch him going to third," he joked.

Always a threat to steal, Coleman dives back safely on a pick-off attempt under the tag of Padres first baseman Steve Garvey. *(From the collections of the St. Louis Mercantile Library at the University of Missouri–St. Louis)*

Even though the series hadn't yet started, Andujar was already pointing the finger away from himself. "The playoffs don't start yet, and they start blaming me," he complained about a story in a St. Louis newspaper that quoted Herzog as saying Andujar was key to the team's success. "I'm only pitching Game 2, not 1, 3, and 4. It's not going to be Joaquin Andujar's fault." It seemed as if he was trying to beat the papers to punch, and expecting something bad to happen for himself, if not for the entire club.

10. "How Do You Like Us Now?" 157

Valenzuela was indeed the people's choice, and his popularity had not worn off since his screwball first arrived at Dodger Stadium from the hills of Mexico in 1981. That year, he twisted bats around to the tune of a Rookie of the Year award, as Los Angeles topped the Yankees in the World Series to avenge a couple of beatings in the late '70s. He was larger than life, and larger than most pitchers—his considerable girth seemed to gently rotate around the pitcher's rubber as he sailed the ball towards home. "He is the Chicano version of the Pillsbury Doughboy," described Horrigan, "but oh boy, can he pitch." He had finished the regular season with a 17–10 record and a 2.45 ERA. Tudor was looking to take back the one game that tarnished his remarkable streak during the summer, as the two best lefties in the National League got the Senior Circuit's postseason underway in front of 55,000 fans. Valenzuela had actually been going in the opposite direction of Tudor, as he was winless in his last five starts and had been victorious only once since the 26th of August.

Both pitchers seemed to be in complete command through three innings, and did not offer the opposition many chances to score. The Dodgers drew first blood in the bottom of the fourth, courtesy of an error by Pendleton. Madlock hit a cue shot that produced a funny spin on the ball, and it handcuffed the Cardinal third baseman. On the next pitch, Madlock stole second while Porter held onto the ball, and subsequently scored on a single by Guerrero for a 1–0 advantage. Madlock started the game's next runs in the sixth, when he doubled and was followed by an intentional walk to Guerrero. After a single by Scioscia scored Madlock, a bunt down the third base line by Candy Maldonado was handled by Pendleton, but in throwing home he hit Tudor instead, and Guerrero waltzed across the plate with L.A.'s third run. It had appeared earlier that Pendleton had righted himself defensively, as he committed only three errors in the Cardinals' last 40 games of the regular season. Then second baseman Steve Sax, who followed up Valenzuela's Rookie of the Year award with his own in 1982 (in addition to former Dodgers Sutcliffe and Howe in '79 and '80 to make it four in a row), doubled in Scioscia for a 4–0 lead. Tudor was lifted for Dayley, and the inning ended with no further damage.

The Cards finally got some offense going in the seventh, as Pendleton atoned for his miscues by reaching base and being driven home on a Landrum hit. After that point, however, Niedenfuer shut the door completely for the next 2⅓ innings as he preserved the 4–1 Los Angeles lead as the final score. "We just don't do much with Fernando," a frustrated Herzog said in review of the game. "When Fernando is on the black (the edges of the plate), he gives us fits, and he gave us fits tonight."

And it looked like the Blue Jays were going to run away from the

Royals in the ALCS, as Al Oliver's single in the tenth scored Moseby and Toronto edged Kansas City 6–5 to take a 2–0 lead in their series.

Unfortunately, the Cardinals' sloppy play continued on into Game Two, as Hershiser was going up against Andujar. Hershiser had actually been more dominant than Valenzuela during the regular season, as the second-year pitcher sported a 19–3 record (for an .864 winning percentage, tops in baseball, as he also had 14 no-decision starts) with a miniscule ERA of 2.03. Coleman and McGee were each thrown out trying to steal in the first inning, and later, defensive lapses such as Andujar's wild pickoff throw to Clark, Pendleton's and Porter's misplay of a bunt, and an array of missed cutoff men from the outfielders led to big Dodger innings. By contrast, Hershiser limited his mistakes, although one was a wild pitch that allowed McGee to score the first run of the game in the third.

But Los Angeles capitalized on the St. Louis miscues, and by the fifth inning had rolled up a 6–1 lead on Andujar. They feasted on an eight-hit bounty from him, and Andujar then left the game to a chorus of jeers—to which he gave an "I-don't-really-care" smile towards the stands. "How could anyone go so bad so fast?" Horrigan wondered about the two-month free fall of the right-hander. "Everyone has a theory. Joaquin says that he's not getting the close calls from the umpire, that he's just unlucky. Others figure that what's wrong with Andujar is between his ears." Andujar had dug a hole out of which his club could not get out, and the Dodgers ran away from the Redbirds in the second game, 8–2. The Cardinals now had to win four out five contests, beginning with a three-game stretch back home in St. Louis.

Another poor performance by Andujar now meant that Forsch would get the ball if there was a Game Five on Monday, October 14. Thomas Boswell of the *Washington Post* thought that Andujar would eventually do himself in with his temper. "What happened to him — losing a ball game and making a clown of himself in the process—is enough punishment to fit his petty misdemeanors."

It was Danny Cox starting Game Three for the Cards, and it had been a rough week for him personally. The ex-husband of his sister had been harassing her, and Cox took matters into his own hands—he went over to the man's workplace and slugged him a couple of times. "When you mess with my family," Cox said, "you get hurt." He said he felt just fine about what he did. "A lot of people came up to me and said, 'I would have done the same thing.' I wouldn't change anything about it."

It was just the fighting spirit the Cardinals needed, for a 3–0 deficit would not be acceptable. The incident showed that Cox would not back down from a challenge, and he faced a considerable one in tough Dodger

10. "How Do You Like Us Now?" 159

right-hander Bob Welch. Did L.A. have it wrapped up? No, said Lasorda. "There are no guarantees, but it's a lot better than 0–2."

There was a definite lack of the Cardinals' feared running game in the first two contests, and being back at home, Herzog looked to get it back in the picture. It showed up in the very first inning, as Coleman led off with a single and then drew 14 throws over to first from Welch. He finally was able to break for second, and he had his first playoff steal. McGee then walked, and as Welch was getting more unnerved, he turned and threw wildly in trying to pick Coleman off second. The ball nearly ricocheted off umpire Paul Runge, but rather flew cleanly into right-center as Coleman scored and McGee scooted into third. As Pendleton grounded out, McGee crossed the dish for a 2–0 St. Louis lead.

Coleman again sent the Dodgers into a panic in the second inning, when, after getting his second hit, he drew two pitch-outs from Scioscia. On the latter one, a rushing Scioscia fired the ball down the right field line as Coleman galloped for third. "I had more time than I thought," the Dodgers' catcher said later about the play. "I saw him way off first, and started to run down there." Coleman was actually caught between first and second on the play, as he headed back towards first and Scioscia started running towards him. McGee then knocked him in with a single, and was caught stealing on the ensuing pitch to Herr. But Tommy followed up with a home run that moved the lead to 4–0, as Cox settled in and went to work. He gave up a run in the fourth on a pair of doubles by Guerrero and Marshall, and another Dodger run crossed the plate in the seventh on a combination of hits. Cox had to leave in the seventh with a sore elbow, as Horton, Worrell, and Dayley finished up effectively for a 4–2 win. The teams combined for 13 walks on the day, which was a championship series game record; six of those belonged to Welch, and five were the work of Cox.

Dayley got the save, although some in the media thought that it figuratively should have gone to Pendleton. The third baseman came up with two brilliant catches in the eighth and ninth to preserve the victory. On the first play, he turned 180 degrees and sprinted down the left field line to catch a pop-up off the bat of Brock in the Cardinals bullpen, a grab that reminded Herzog of Willie Mays' renowned catch in the 1954 World Series. In the ninth, he kept the potential tying run off base by leaving his feet to snatch a hot grounder by Maldonado, rising, and throwing him out at first. "Not many third basemen could have made that catch," asserted Dodgers third base coach Joey Amalfitano, who witnessed the stop made on Maldonado from only a few feet away. Helping out was particularly sweet for Pendleton after his rough defensive days back in Los Angeles.

Herzog claimed that the Dodgers were "quick-pitching" in the first three games of series, as he had protested in Los Angeles earlier in the season. He meant that the pitchers were not coming to a complete stop in the stretch, in an effort to slow down the St. Louis running game. He figured his complaint would fall on deaf ears, though. "They're [the umpires] just going to stick it to me," he predicted regarding the presumed ignorance of the umpires about the violations.

Game Four, pitting Tudor against Reuss, would be the first Sunday night game ever played in St. Louis. Night baseball in the playoffs had begun with the 1971 World Series between Pittsburgh and Baltimore, and many considered it strange, even though regular season night games had been played since 1938. In preparation for the lighted contest, the Cardinals held their usual routine for pre-game practice for a night home game. At a few minutes after five o' clock, a light drizzle started falling from the sky, so the players and groundskeepers scrambled to gather equipment in the surprise rain. Most of the players were mindful of the automatic tarp machine that was built into the field, and for good reason, as Horrigan described: "Like a Zombie, it rises from its grave, a three-foot-wide, 180-foot-long section of the stadium floor that comes up, unrolling a motorized aluminum tube on which the rubberized canvas infield tarp is stored."

The machine started its customary rumble, and a couple minutes later, Horrigan and others in the press box heard someone yell, "HEY!" When everyone turned to look, the tarp machine had caught Vince Coleman's left leg, as he had turned for only an instant to toss his glove to someone. The handful of onlookers in the seats watched dumbfounded, as if at an auto accident scene. And Horrigan claimed that "very few reporters, even the most hardened, had ever seen a man attacked by a tarp." After he was freed from under the roller by several teammates, it was presumed that Coleman had broken either his leg or his ankle, or both, as he was carried off on a stretcher by Pendleton and Smith. "The worst part of it was they had to roll the tarp back over my leg," Coleman later said in a pain-filled laugh.

Herzog placed a call to Coleman's worried mother in Jacksonville, Florida, to assure her that everything was okay.

"Are you sure that I don't need to come up there?" Mrs. Coleman asked.

"No," Whitey replied. "We've got Willie and Ozzie to mother him."

Tito Landrum got his chance as a result of the freak incident, as he was inserted into the number-six position in the lineup in Coleman's absence. "You'll have to look that one up," Landrum said jokingly, when asked by the reporters when his last starting assignment had occurred. "If I had to play, it might have been a blessing in disguise for me to find out at the last

10. "How Do You Like Us Now?"

minute." It surely was a blessing, as Landrum rapped out four of the Cardinals' 15 hits in a 12–2 dismantling of Reuss and the Dodgers.

Tudor had a no-hitter going with two out in the sixth, as he coasted through seven total innings with assistance from Horton and Campbell, one inning each. Reuss, on the other hand, did not make it out of the second, as the Cards exploded for nine runs in that frame, with Clark getting two of the Cards' eight hits in the inning. Landrum also drove in three of the St. Louis runs, as did Pendleton.

People were starting to notice Landrum's defense, too, as through the end of the '85 season, he had committed only three errors in six big-league seasons. Landrum's pinch-hitting average of .391 was second in the National League in 1985, and

Terry Pendleton. *(From the collections of the St. Louis Mercantile Library at the University of Missouri–St. Louis)*

reporters across the country were beginning to take notice of him. "Landrum's clubhouse demeanor is hardly an indication of his aggressive style of play," wrote Jim Henneman of the *Baltimore Sun*. "He is polite to the point of beginning, or ending, every sentence with yes sir or no sir." The series was now tied at two, with the assurances that a Game Six in Los Angeles would now be necessary after one more battle in Busch Stadium.

It was later learned that Coleman had suffered contusions from his foot to his mid-thigh, but no broken bones, according to team surgeon Dr. Stan London. He was out indefinitely, as Landrum would take his place once again in Game Five. And as promised, Forsch took Andujar's spot in Game Five as well, while the Dodgers countered with Cardinal-killer Valenzuela in the pivotal game.

St. Louis kept the momentum going, jumping on Valenzuela early for two runs in the first inning by way of a Herr double. The pitcher gathered himself, however, and turned away other Cardinal attacks as Madlock tied the game with a two-run homer off Forsch in the fourth inning. Then, after Brock hit a long drive foul, Herzog jogged to the mound and summoned Dayley from the bullpen in favor of a lefty-versus-lefty matchup. "If we didn't win this game, I didn't think we had a chance to win the series," Herzog explained in bringing in Dayley, normally not seen before the seventh inning. He retired Brock, and thus ended any further Los Angeles threat in the fourth.

Valenzuela continued to keep the Redbirds at bay, despite walking a playoff-record eight batters by the time he had completed the eighth inning as the score remained tied, 2–2. The Cardinals' bullpen, meanwhile, was doing its usual superb job as Worrell followed Dayley's 2⅔ scoreless innings with two of his own, and then Lahti got the Dodgers in order in the ninth. Lasorda then brought in Niedenfuer, expecting him to shut down the St. Louis bats as he had done in Game One. The Cards needed just one run to take the lead in the series, no matter how that run came. "I had it set up how I wanted," Herzog recalled in his use of the bullpen that day. "But if we'd gone past 11 innings, we were in trouble."

Niedenfuer got Ozzie Smith behind in the count at 1–2. Then, in one of his trademark calls, Jack Buck relayed the action as Niedenfuer flung a fast ball towards the inner part of the plate.

"Smith corks one into right down the line ... it may go!... GO CRAZY FOLKS, GO CRAZY!!! It's a home run, and the Cardinals have won the game ... by a score of three to two ... on a home run by the Wizard!!!"

Ozzie was high-fived by third base coach Hal Lanier as he prepared to leap onto the plate and into a throng of celebratory Cardinal arms. His first-ever left-handed home run in professional baseball lifted the Cards to a 3–2 win, a series lead by the same amount, and one victory away from the pennant.

Lasorda was gracious about the event. "Naturally, I'm dumbstruck," he said calmly in the clubhouse. "In all my years in baseball, you learn one thing—never expect the expected to happen. If Ozzie had 25 or 30 home runs, you could understand it. But this is what makes baseball so great. It's hard to believe, but you never know in this game."

"Call it a 3,000-to-1 shot," Rick Hummel wrote, struggling as was everyone to put the surreal scene into words. "That's how many times Ozzie Smith had batted left-handed in the major leagues—actually 3,009—without hitting a home run."

To be sure, nearly equal to the importance of Ozzie's dramatic homer was the performance of the Cardinals' relievers. "If you listed 1,000 scenarios for a Cardinals victory," Horrigan challenged St. Louis fans, "a left-handed

10. "How Do You Like Us Now?"

homer by Smith wouldn't be among them. But a strong bullpen performance would be part of nearly all of them." They shut down Los Angeles for nearly six innings, as the image of Bruce Sutter became an all-the-more-distant memory.

Coleman did not dress for Game Five, but hoped to be back in uniform as the series shifted to Dodger Stadium once again.

In the American League, the Royals had fought back from a torrid start by the Blue Jays to knot the series at three games apiece. Mark Gubicza beat Doyle Alexander 5–3 at Exhibition Stadium, setting up a winner-take-all Game Seven in Toronto. In other news, former President Richard Nixon was chosen by Ueberroth as the arbitrator in the umpires' dispute with the leagues over postseason pay. Nixon ultimately decided that the umpires would receive a 40 percent increase in pay for their extended postseason work.

Ozzie pumps his fist in the air after his dramatic game-winning home run in Game Five of the 1985 National League Championship Series. *(From the collections of the St. Louis Mercantile Library at the University of Missouri–St. Louis)*

Partly because of Cox's sore elbow, and partly because of getting a second chance from Herzog, Andujar got the start for Game Six in Los Angeles against Hershiser. Herzog stated that Cox would not be available at all in Game Six, although he might be ready for bullpen duty in a possible Game Seven to be started by Tudor. Andujar had lost 9 of his last 13 decisions and had only one complete game in his last 20 starts entering the game, but he retained the confidence of most of his teammates. "I think he's due," predicted Cesar Cedeno. "As long as he keeps his cool, he will pitch a great game."

"I don't have to show anybody who I am," Andujar said in his unique style of last-minute, pre-game thoughts. "If they don't know who I am, they're never going to know."

While the Dodgers were being introduced before the game, and in doing so taking their places along the third base foul line, Herzog had the Cardinals stay in the dugout in a move of protest. He was told by a Dodgers official that it was a tradition at the ballpark, and that he was supposed to have his club out there. "I say taking infield is a tradition, too," Herzog fumed. "But we couldn't do it because there was always some band out there. Who cares about the Dodger tradition?"

Andujar continued the protest as he took the mound in the bottom of the first, chomping away at the dirt in front of the rubber with his cleats. He and Hershiser used opposites sides of the rubber in their deliveries, and Andujar dug away with his foot until the umpire and Dodger leadoff hitter Mariano Duncan became annoyed.

Los Angeles jumped on him early, scoring a run in each of the first two innings. A Madlock single scored Duncan in the first, and then Duncan did likewise for Brock in the second. It was Andujar who started the Cards' offense in the third, as he doubled to the left field wall. After a McGee groundout moved him over to third, Herr came through with a big two-out hit to cut the score in half. Things got more bleak, however, as Madlock drove in Duncan again — this time, on a home run — as the Dodgers upped their advantage to 4–1. Feelings were not too depressed, however, on the St. Louis bench. "We were fired up when it was 4–1," Herr said. "They were over in their dugout celebrating. They thought the game was over. But a lot was said in our dugout about having four more shots at them and having been in worse situations than this."

Andujar made it through one more inning, as it became obvious that Herzog would pinch-hit for him in the seventh. Porter started things with a sharp single to center, and Landrum followed suit to put runners at first and second with nobody out. Braun, inserted for Andujar, hit a chopper that advanced the runners to second and third. McGee then hit a liner to center — the Cards' third hit in the inning in that direction — that plated both runners to bring the score to 4–3. At that point, Lasorda played the odds and lifted Hershiser in favor of Niedenfuer. It was a calculated gamble because at plate was recent hero Ozzie Smith, and Lasorda figured that the Wizard's lightning wouldn't strike Niedenfuer twice. He was wrong. Ozzie sliced a triple into the outfield which scored McGee and raised his series average to .435, tops on either club. Smith's triple almost went out of the park, and landed in almost exactly the same spot as his blast in Busch Stadium.

The momentum lasted only an inning, however, as Marshall socked a long home run off Worrell in the bottom of the eighth, and Los Angeles re-took the lead, 5–4.

10. "How Do You Like Us Now?" 165

Despite allowing the game-tying triple to Smith, Niedenfuer was left in by Lasorda, and he rewarded him initially by retiring Cedeno, who led off the ninth pinch-hitting for Worrell. In September, Cedeno had built a 12-game hitting streak, the Cardinals' longest of the year. The locals became jittery again, though, when McGee rapped his third hit of the game to the left and promptly stole second, leaving the Cardinals only 180 feet away from tying the game once more. McGee was on a mission in Game Six, for he had come into the contest hitting only .190 in the series and being successful on only one of three steal attempts. Noticeably unnerved by Smith's presence at the plate, Niedenfuer walked Ozzie, and then got Herr to ground out, which moved both the tying and go-ahead runs into scoring position, with McGee at third, Smith at second, and Clark coming to the plate.

Clark indicated before the game that his sore rib still wasn't quite right. Behind Clark was Van Slyke, who was 0-for-5 on the day and 1-for-10 in the series. A consideration of Lasorda may have been to walk Clark, since the go-ahead run was already on second, and first base was open. But Niedenfuer seemed to have settled down, and besides, he had struck out Clark in that fateful inning back at Busch when Ozzie hit his home run. So in a classic power match-up, the fastballer Niedenfuer went toe-to-toe with the fastball-hitting Clark. His couple of innings of recent success behind him, Niedenfuer figured himself to be the more powerful. At about 5:30 P.M. St. Louis time, he tried to blow his fastball past Clark on the inner-half at the knees, thinking that Clark would be looking for a slider on the first pitch. Clark responded with one of his patented quick swings, among the best in the game at the point of contact. The result was a long drive, up and away, that landed 20 rows deep in the left field stands as 55,208 at Dodger Stadium went nearly silent. In the Los Angeles dugout, Lasorda ripped off his cap and rubbed his brow in anger as the Cardinals took a 7–5 lead. It was only Clark's second home run since August 23, but the biggest one of his life. He told Kevin Horrigan that, somewhere between first and third on his jaunt towards home plate, he recalled his boyhood dreams of someday playing for Los Angeles in Dodger Stadium.

"Maybe I wasn't expecting them to walk me intentionally," Clark said in reflection. "But I thought they might at least work around me. Maybe some pitches away, but not a fastball in on me." Cardinal players already on the field had the best vantage point, such as McGee and Smith on base who saw the rocket pass over their heads. "That thing looked like a laser beam," added Van Slyke as he watched from the on-deck circle. "Like something out of the lab at General Dynamics." They joined the rest of the team in a joyful mob at home plate, a replay of the scene in Game Five at

Busch, compliments of Ozzie. There were a few in the Cardinals' bullpen in left field who couldn't join the party. "It [the home run] had a trajectory which left no doubt," said one of them, Tom Nieto, as he described the flight of the ball.

Dayley took to the mound to wrap things up in the bottom of the ninth, with the men from L.A. completely demoralized. He smoothly struck out Ken Landreaux; he then did the same to pinch-hitter Enos Cabell. Finally, he busted Guerrero in on the hands, and he popped a short fly to McGee in center. Willie handled it easily, and the Cardinals were champions of the National League.

"It sent the folks in the National League offices scrambling to launder the 1985 pennant flag and dispatch it to St. Louis," Mike Smith of the *Post-Dispatch* cheered, "home of the franchise which was projected in the spring to be one of the league's worst."

The champagne and hugs were once again plentiful in the clubhouse. Word soon came down that Smith was named Most Valuable Player of the series. Campbell found Cedeno and suggested that they send telegrams to Philadelphia and Cincinnati, respectively, to thank them for setting them free. Willie McGee then rose to speak, as he summarized the year-long effort. "This is a team victory," he announced to one and all. "There are no superstars on this team. We just go out and do our jobs, and it seems like there's a different hero every day."

How long would this celebration last, Willie?

"Now I'm going home to prepare," he answered. "We've still got the World Series to play." Home was a condominium in west St. Louis County, where he had invited the rookie Coleman to join him during the summer.

Unable to face reality, Guerrero's comment left many to wonder: "What have they [the Cardinals] got? One guy who steals more than a hundred bases and another guy who hits .350. That's all. We're still the best team." Perhaps Guerrero had forgotten that with McGee and Coleman (the two players to whom he was referring), one had an off-series, and one played in only half the series.

"Crank up the Clydesdales again, put the Dalmation on the beer truck and roll out that famous brewery's theme song," instructed Kent Baker of the *Baltimore Sun*. "The World Series is returning to the muddy banks of the Mississippi and that red sea of frenzied St. Louis Cardinal fanatics who never lost the faith."

"They need no introduction now," added Gordon Edes about Herzog's refusal to send his players out to the base line before the game. "Just call them National League champions."

And in Toronto, the Blue Jays had bumbled their way to a third straight loss to the Royals, 6–2, sending Kansas City to the final round against St. Louis.

The "I-70 Series" that everyone in the Show-Me State had hoped for was now a reality.

11

A Collision on the Interstate

A few individuals on the national scene, such as Thomas Boswell, were disappointed for some reason that one or two of the "powerhouse" teams weren't involved in the series. "When we have to watch teams with a limp, like the 1983 Phillies, the '84 Padres or the '85 Royals as they try to reach beyond themselves to make the Series competitive," he complained, "we find ourselves longing for the days when October was baseball.... The World Series has been in a slump lately. When it comes to Classics worthy of the name, baseball is 0 for the '80s."

Even if people on the coasts didn't notice, folks in the Midwest were happy as could be with the matchup. "Let's be honest," the misguided Boswell continued. "The St. Louis Cardinals and Kansas City Royals are, by Series standards, drab collections." Someone failed to inform Boswell, apparently, that the "non–Classic" Cardinals had nine world championships and 14 pennants behind them, most of any city in the National League. And the "limping" Royals played in one of the more beautiful baseball stadiums to be found in the American League, again unbeknownst to those away from the heart of America.

Furthermore, by the time the 1985 playoffs had rolled around, the Royals had been in post season play more than any other team over the previous ten years. "Consistency is the hallmark of our organization," Schuerholz said. "I'd put our record up against any other team in baseball." The turning point in their 1985 season could be traced to July 22, at which time the club had a record of 46–44, jammed in third place in the American League West and 7½ games behind the front-running Angels. Kansas City then swept the Yankees and Indians at home, touching off a seven-game winning streak as they found themselves only two back of California by August 2. They stayed within striking distance before taking over the top spot on September 6, the first time since June 8 they found themselves atop the division (and June 8 had been the only date to that point they had been in first place). Their rise was compliments of an 8–0 home stand in early September, despite missing starting catcher Jim Sundberg for three weeks with torn cartilage in his left rib cage. Sundberg, who had been acquired in an off-season trade with the Milwaukee Brewers, had become a team leader with his experience and excellent defense behind the plate.

Earlier in the season, it looked as if Kansas City was an organization that might be falling apart. During a stretch in May when the Royals lost five straight games, Schuerholz was nonetheless given a long contract extension. This drew the attention of many, including Royals catcher John Wathan. "That's what's good about Kansas City," he smirked. "You lose five in a row in New York and you get fired. You lose five in a row here and you get a lifetime contract."

It was obvious that Lonnie Smith eventually made the Royals a better offensive club. Wilson, the club's fleet center fielder, noticed the change immediately. "If we [Wilson or Smith] are on third, we can score runs on ground balls or medium fly balls. It makes George [Brett] a better player because he can get more RBIs. It will help make us better players because if we get to third, he's going to drive us in."

Royals manager Dick Howser agreed. "You take Wilson's bat and speed and add Smith's bat and speed to it, and you have a couple of guys who can create a lot of RBI opportunities for Brett."

In 1985, the Royals also discovered some power in their bats, as first baseman Steve "Bye-Bye" Balboni set a club record with 36 home runs, while Brett (30) and second baseman Frank White (22) both had career highs. Right fielder Daryl Motley and designated hitter Hal McRae also had a hand in the long ball department with 17 and 14 home runs, respectively. Wilson led the AL in triples with 21, and when he was injured in September, the club acquired the speedy veteran Moreno from the Yankees to help out in center field.

In the winter of 1984, Brett had re-dedicated himself to a vigorous training regimen, which contributed in '85 to his best year since 1980, when he won the American League MVP award and challenged the .400 mark. He wound up batting .335 for the '85 regular season, and led the AL in slugging percentage at .585. He found his peak at mid-season, hitting a scorching .432 in July and being named the league's Player of the Month. By the end of the year, Brett had become the first American League player since Darrell Porter in 1979 to have 100 RBIs, 100 walks, and 100 runs scored in the same season.

Howser was extremely confident in his starting pitchers as well. "No other club in the league runs out a better starting five than Bret Saberhagen, Charlie Leibrandt, Danny Jackson, Mark Gubicza, and Bud Black," he claimed. They were certainly good, and reliable, if nothing else — for going into the last month of the season, only Steve Farr had made a start for the Royals besides the aforementioned five, who accounted for more wins than any starting staff in club history. Leibrandt, Jackson, Saberhagen, and Gubicza all recorded career-highs in wins in '85, while Black achieved his lifetime high-water mark at 17–12 the year before.

The main man was Saberhagen, whose rising story nearly paralleled that of Gooden. He was only 21 years old, but was the favorite for the American League Cy Young award, winning 20 games. He was even younger than Babe Ruth when the Red Sox left-hander reached the 20-win plateau in 1916. "There's something about Bret that gives you confidence when he pitches," Frank White said. "He's not cocky, but confident. We felt like we were going to win when he was on the mound."

The force in the bullpen was Dan Quisenberry, a part-time poet who was one of the more intelligent players in baseball. He led the league in saves for the fifth time in six seasons in 1985, and had finished the year fifth on the all-time saves list. His side-winding style elicited ground ball after ground ball from the bats of stifled hitters.

This was a year in which the pitchers would hit in the World Series and a designated hitter would not be used, which was obviously to the Cardinals' advantage (the DH rule was alternated in the series each year). Herzog believed that it would be a better idea to every year use the DH when the American League team was at home, and to have the pitchers hit when playing in the National League park. The 1985 showdown would also be the first World Series in which all the games would be played at night.

The series would be a sort of reunion with familiar faces and familiar cities for Herzog and Lonnie Smith. Herzog had managed the Royals successfully for several years, and Smith was trying to establish a new home with the Royals. Some of Herzog's fondest memories included the pleasure of having George Brett on his team. "George never needed a manager," Whitey said. "He plays the way the game should be played. Even when he's hurt, he comes out by himself, fills the whirlpool and treats himself." Brett had been the heart of multiple division championship teams that Herzog managed in Kansas City.

Smith, meanwhile, had finally reconciled about why he was traded. "Vince Coleman was doing the job. They wanted to give Vince a chance to play, and I can understand that. Just look at what Vince is doing over there." It had been a tough adjustment for Smith, as evidenced by his .145

11. A Collision on the Interstate

batting average on June 5, but he had worked to get his American League average up to .257 by season's end. "I didn't give myself time to realize coming here was to my advantage," he continued. "It took a while before I started accepting it and enjoying it. I don't want to go anywhere else." If the Royals beat the Cardinals in the series, Smith would become only the third player of all time to win championships with three different clubs. He also felt as free as he had ever been from his drug problems.

"Lonnie Smith can deal with his problems; he can laugh at them now," he said about himself. "I'm more in control. I even go to chapel a lot more."

It was rumored that Coleman would be ready to play in Game One, but as the week went along, it looked less and less likely. He had been on crutches since the accident, but leapt off of them when Clark hit his home run off Niedenfuer in Los Angeles, and was actually the second man to the plate to greet him when he reached home. With the first game on Saturday, October 19, Coleman took his first batting practice on the previous Wednesday, and then spent much of Thursday and Friday in a whirlpool to try and hasten the rehabilitation of the leg. By Friday afternoon, however, he was still unable to run at full speed. With Howser starting the 24-year-old left-hander Jackson in Game One, Herzog was going to go with Landrum anyway (for Van Slyke in right field, as had typically been the case against lefties), but now planned to have Cedeno in the outfield as well. Saberhagen was hurting for the Royals, as he had to leave the seventh game of the ALCS after a line drive bruised his hand. The injury wasn't considered serious, however, and Saberhagen was expected to take his normal turn in Game Three. With Coleman's status still up in the air, Herzog finally decided to wait until game time to make the decision. "If he's not 100 percent, he won't play," he said plainly.

The weather forecast also looked grim, as reports issued a 30 percent chance of rain for the Kansas City area for Saturday. Jackson, winner of 14 games on the year, would be matched up against Tudor.

The storm clouds held off, and play began as scheduled. Coleman was not ready to go, so Landrum took his spot in left field while Cedeno patrolled right. Jackson, not displaying any jitters, ripped through the Cardinal bats in order in the first, including a strikeout of McGee to lead off the game. Tudor did the same in the bottom half, finishing in a flourish by fanning Brett, the golden boy of KC.

The Royals opened the scoring in their half of the second. After Sundberg walked and Motley singled to left, the big Balboni shot another single through the infield for a 1–0 lead. Tudor recovered to keep it from being a big inning, however, as he got shortstop Buddy Biancalana to miss a pitch on a squeeze play, which got Motley caught up in a rundown. The

Cardinals evened things in the third, as Pendleton walked and Porter singled him to third. Next came Tudor, who laid a perfect sacrifice bunt to move Porter into scoring position as well. McGee then bounced the ball on the carpet to White at second, enabling Pendleton to score and tie the game.

The Cards got their first lead the next inning when Landrum and Cedeno slapped back-to-back doubles, with Cedeno actually breaking his bat on a tough fast ball from Jackson that he was still able to drive into the outfield. Then, in the Royals' half of the fourth, came one of the best defensive plays of the series. With Sundberg on third with only one out, Balboni lifted a pop foul down the left field line. Much like the play he made against Brock in the NLCS, Pendleton sprinted to it and made an over-the-shoulder catch. Taking his NLCS dramatics a step further, however, he wheeled and threw a perfect shot to Porter to easily get Sundberg at the plate, and kept the Cards ahead. "It was instinct to turn around and try to get the ball back to the infield," Pendleton said later. "I was surprised it didn't bounce, to be honest ... the first one [the play in Los Angeles] I had to run farther, but this one, I had to make a good throw, too."

While holding the lead at 2–1 through the sixth, Tudor began to tire in the seventh. He allowed a two-out triple to pinch-hitter Lynn Jones, and followed that up by hitting McRae, who was batting for Jackson. After throwing 102 pitches (with an uncharacteristically high 42 balls versus 60 strikes), Tudor relinquished the ball and Herzog brought in the rookie Worrell, as he wanted the hard-throwing right-hander against the right-handed–batting Lonnie Smith. Smith walked to load the bases, but Worrell recovered to get Wilson to fly out to Landrum in left field, as the Royals wasted a great opportunity.

After a scoreless eighth for the Cardinals, Van Slyke made a game-saving play in the bottom half. Inserted for Cedeno for defensive purposes in the previous inning, he robbed a home run from Brett at the right field wall, who had already hit three homers in the ALCS. The Cards picked up an insurance run in the top of the ninth when Herr singled to open the inning and Clark shot a laser into the gap in left that scored him. It was a ball that Smith should have caught, but was hit so hard it froze him in his tracks. In rounding second base, however, Clark strayed too far off as the relay throw nailed him.

Herzog left the game in Worrell's hands in the ninth, and he got off to a shaky start. Pat Sheridan, batting for Motley, doubled into the right field corner to open the inning. As Balboni grounded out to Clark, the Cardinals gladly traded the base for the out as Sheridan went on to third. Worrell then got pinch-hitter Jorge Orta to fly weakly to center, and then

11. A Collision on the Interstate

Cardinals pitcher John Tudor catches the Royals' Daryl Motley in a run-down in the second inning of Game One of the 1985 World Series, after Buddy Biancalana missed a squeeze bunt attempt. Jack Clark follows the play in the background. *(From the collections of the St. Louis Mercantile Library at the University of Missouri–St. Louis)*

induced Dane Iorg, a member of the Cards '82 championship club, to do the same to Van Slyke on a belt-high fast ball that ended the game 3–1 in favor of St. Louis. Iorg had been one of the heroes in the 1982 Fall Classic for St. Louis, in which he batted a blistering .529 (9-for-17) as the designated hitter.

Despite a somewhat shaky outing by Tudor, Roarke was happy with the way he righted himself and did what was necessary to win. "When he was missing the strike zone, he would come back and make the good pitches when he had to," Roarke noticed. "He would get in a jam—and it was by his own doing—but then he would step up to another level and get himself out of it. That's a tribute to the fellow." Tudor himself knew that it was an off-night for him, in spite of the victory. "I never felt in the groove tonight," he told reporters after the game. "I had a lot of problems. But you saw the bottom line. That's the difference between this year and my other years. I may be a little older, a little wiser, and that's helped, but what I've got behind me is the reason for my success."

People were waiting for Coleman to come around, but it was announced before Game Two that his leg was still too sore to play. "He's got a bad bruise on that knee," Herzog explained. "When he puts pressure on it, it bothers him." It was evident that Coleman was getting edgy, wanting either to play or to have reporters stop asking him when he'd be ready. "If I knew that, I would be playing now," he responded to the question. "This has never happened to me. It doesn't happen every day when fifteen hundred pounds roll over you." Pendleton was also smarting, trying to ignore a stiff neck and recovering from a cyst removal from the back of his leg the prior week. The outfield decision wasn't too difficult for Herzog, as he simply went with the big hitters from Game One once again in left and right, Landrum and Cedeno.

Cox, sore elbow and all, took the mound against another Royals left-hander in Leibrandt. Cox's arm shot with pain with every throw, but he was determined to make it through this start, plus one more. "I've got all winter to rest," he reasoned. Both pitchers were masterful at the start, allowing only two hits a side through the Cardinals' turn in the fourth. In the bottom half, Wilson got things going with a lead off single, and then Brett nailed a double into the right-center gap for the first run of the game. The other veteran infielder, White, then knocked home Brett with a double of his own for a 2–0 Kansas City lead. Leibrandt continued to be dominant, not allowing any more hits into the St. Louis ninth. The only Redbird safeties came on two bloop hits, one by Pendleton in the third and one by Landrum in the fourth.

Sensing urgency, McGee doubled to start the 9th inning, turning on an inside pitch and rifling a ball down the left field line. After Smith grounded out and Herr flied out, the Royals were within one out of tying the series. Clark then cut the Kansas City lead in half, as he singled to score McGee. An opposite-field double by Landrum then put the tying and go-ahead runs in scoring position, as Cedeno was intentionally walked to load the bases for Pendleton. The Royals felt they had an advantage in making Pendleton hit from the right side against Leibrandt. But Terry, looking to prove that his bat had returned as well as his glove, took advantage of a Leibrandt mistake to smack a double down the line in left to clear the bases and suddenly give the Cards a 4–2 lead.

"Some will nit-pick that the hit paled in comparison to Smith's ninth-inning homer in Game Five of the National League playoffs or Jack Clark's moon shot in the ninth inning of Game Six," figured Mike Smith, "But it was no less decisive." Quisenberry was then brought in to face Van Slyke, pinch-hitting for Dayley who had replaced Cox in the eighth, and he got him to fly out to center to end the blitzkrieg. But the damage had been done.

11. A Collision on the Interstate

Lahti, giving the Royals a different power pitcher to look at in place of Worrell, decimated the Royals' bats in the bottom half for a resounding 4–2 Cardinal win, and a 2–0 series lead.

The series shifted to Busch Stadium for Game Three, as the teams had Monday the 21st off for travel in preparation for the Tuesday matchup that pitted 20-game-winners Saberhagen and Andujar against one another. Saberhagen's hand, injured by the line drive he sustained in the ALCS, had appeared to heal completely. Next to Valenzuela, he would be the youngest pitcher ever to start a World Series game.

"I think we're relaxed and we're confident," George Brett said in description of his Royals teammates. "We feel we can win."

Andujar had a good deal of respect for the Royals. "Kansas City is a good ball club," he said. "I cannot say we're going to sweep the Kansas City Royals. You cannot have a big head or a big mouth. There's a long way to go. That's one word I like about America—youneverknow. That's why I say 'God bless America.'"

Among the several feel-good stories in the first two games for the Cardinals, Herzog was especially proud of Landrum, who was able to contribute so greatly on such short notice. "He understands his role," Herzog said. "The only time you get in trouble in baseball is when the guys on the bench think they're better than the guys playing."

Coleman's injury, meanwhile, was still somewhat of a mystery. When asked if Coleman would play at all in the series, Dr. Stan London said, "I'm beginning to have some doubt." As the teams arrived in St. Louis, Coleman underwent further x-rays and other tests to see if the original diagnosis was wrong. As it turned out, it was not wrong, but unfortunately incomplete. Further examination by London revealed a small bone chip in Coleman's knee, and it was recommended that he get complete rest for six weeks. "It's not a significant injury, except for the extreme pain," London said. "But it should heal and I don't anticipate it causing him any problems." Just like that, the season was over for the Rookie of the Year; retroactively, it had actually been over since the second game of the Dodgers series.

Now more than just a fill-in, Landrum was being mentioned as a possible series MVP candidate if he and the Cardinals kept their winning ways. Through Game Two, has was hitting .461 in the postseason (12-for-26). "I never dreamed I'd be playing as big a role as I am now," he admitted. "I thought I'd be watching and maybe pinch-hitting and playing some defensively."

Howser had been taking heat from the Kansas City media and some Royals fans for what they considered some questionable moves. Primarily, they were upset with his delayed involvement of Quisenberry in Game Two. "Somebody said I have a buddy now in Tommy Lasorda," Howser grimaced in description of the second-guesser sharks that were circling around him. "That's a compliment. I'm not Italian, I'm not left-handed and I'm in better shape, but other than that, it's a compliment."

About a half-hour before game time in St. Louis, the crowd rose to its feet in excitement when the wagon gate along the right field wall opened up. Out of it rolled Gussie Busch, riding atop the Budweiser wagon drawn by eight Clydesdales as Ernie Hays cranked out "Here Comes the King" (the Anheuser-Busch theme song) on the stadium organ. With such intangibles in the air and a 2–0 lead back at home, it seemed as if nothing would stop the Cardinals.

The bats in Game Three started in relatively slow fashion, just as they had in the first two. The Cards threatened in the first, as with McGee on second and Herr at first, they tried a double-steal. Clark missed the pitch for strike three as McGee was thrown out at third by Sundberg, ending the attack. The Royals loaded the bases in the third inning, but Andujar put out the fire he had set by fanning Sheridan swinging.

Kansas City got to him in the fourth, as Sundberg led off with a walk and Biancalana beat out a high-hop single to the mound with one out. After a sacrifice by Saberhagen, Lonnie Smith drove home two runs with a single. The Royals upped it to 4–0 in the fifth, thanks to a home run off the bat of White, which pushed Andujar out of the game with nobody out in the inning. A Clark single plated Ozzie in the sixth to put the Cardinals on the board, but KC added two additional runs in the seventh off Horton.

Saberhagen dominated the rest of the way, as the youngster went the distance in a 6–1 Royals win, allowing only one walk and six hits over the duration. He seemed to handle the Cards much too easily, as Clark had noticed with his three strikeouts to go along with his RBI single. "I don't like to face guys I've never faced before," he said, frustrated. "Usually, about the third or fourth time around you figure out how they try to pitch." Ron Cobb of the *Post-Dispatch* was impressed as well. "He looked every bit like the leading Cy Young Award candidate in the American League," he wrote. The Cards' big bats were indeed starting to struggle, as Clark, McGee, and Herr were a combined 8-for-34, not to mention 1-for-11 and 1-for-9 performances by Smith and Porter, respectively. "Bret Saberhagen has a great idea of what he wants to do on the mound," Van Slyke asserted, who himself was 0-for-4 for the game. "And he throws it for strikes. That's why he's so effective." Herr compared him to a Steve Rogers in his prime.

11. A Collision on the Interstate

It almost appeared to be a last chance for Andujar, who staked the Royals to their original four-run lead. He still had won only once in the previous two months, and his future in St. Louis looked a bit tenuous. "White's homer in the fifth finished him," Horrigan pointed out. "For the series, probably. As a Cardinal, quite possibly. He followed the Budweiser Clydesdales to the mound. They didn't befoul it, but he sure did."

Herzog felt comfortable in starting Tudor on three days' rest in Game Four, as a full house of 53,634 closed in to watch. A victory would mean that the Redbirds could end it at home in Game Five.

The Cardinals had served a special petition to Commissioner Ueberroth's office, seeking allowance for a replacement on the roster spot vacated by Coleman's injury. They were turned down, despite the fact that Ueberroth agreed with Herzog that the denial was a poor rule to have. "Suppose we get a bus to the airport, and it crashes and we get 17 guys hurt," Herzog hypothesized. "You've got to forfeit. I said it's stupid [the rule]." Was Herzog, in light of Coleman's mishap, out of caution going to prohibit Ozzie from doing his customary back-flip when he took the field before the game? "No," Whitey decided, "because Mr. and Mrs. Busch are here, and they like it."

Despite his outstanding year and his victory in Game One, Tudor was out to prove that it wasn't a fluke. He went up against another left-hander, Bud Black, who after his fine performance in '84 had dropped to fourth in the Royals' talented rotation during the regular season. Tudor took the hill with confidence for the fourth game, as the Cards looked to take a commanding lead in the series. The KC men began marching to and from their dugout with regularity, as the lefty put it in cruise control and allowed only two hits through the Royals' first six chances at the plate.

Meanwhile, his troops tried to push some runs across on his behalf. In the Cardinal second, Landrum continued his refusal to be put out, as he homered over the left field wall for the first St. Louis run. The lead was doubled in the third, when McGee hit a round-tripper with two out near the same spot. As he crossed home plate, a chant began to rise in the stands that grew in intensity throughout the rest of the game — "M-V-P! M-V-P! M-V-P!"

In the fifth, the dinger-happy Redbirds showed that Whiteyball was alive and well, as Nieto scored Pendleton with a squeeze bunt after Pendleton had tripled. Nieto got the ball down on a full-count pitch, but mistakenly pushed it right back at Black at the mound. The pitcher threw wildly home, however, and St. Louis had built a 3–0 head start. The triple and two homers were three of the mere four hits that Black would allow through five innings, but they had given the Cards three runs. "I've squeezed a lot this year, but never on 3–2," Nieto later revealed. "Still it didn't surprise me when I saw the sign." Herzog counted that as the 16th time in 19 tries that the Cardinals had successfully squeezed on the year. He wanted to take advantage of Black, as the left-hander had his back to the runner at third and could not see Pendleton break for home. "Nieto also said he didn't feel any extra pressure in a squeeze situation," the Associated Press reported. "There is already enough built in."

The Royals mounted a slight rally in the seventh, as Brett and Sundberg reached on singles and Balboni walked to load the bases. Next up was McRae, the 39-year-old who was making only his second appearance in the series as he was pinch-hitting for Biancalana. Tudor got him to ground out harmlessly into a force to Pendleton at third on the first pitch, and the threat was over. The Busch faithful roared as the home club left the field with the lead and shutout still intact.

The crescendo of the crowd reached its peak when Tudor struck out Brett swinging to end the eighth, as if indicating that he couldn't be touched by anyone carrying a bat. "The ovation Tudor got for his conquest was not unlike that reserved for the dramatic home runs of Smith and Tom Herr in the last month," Mike Smith wrote in describing the scene at Busch. Brett swung wildly at two pitches, unlike anything Herzog had ever seen before in his former batting star. "Anytime you strike out George Brett, it's a great strikeout," Tudor's manager observed. "But that one — you don't see George swing like that too much." The crowd noise, said observers, was different from any reaction to a pitching performance since Bob Gibson was on the same mound for the Cardinals. As Tudor walked into the Cardinals' dugout, the fans were still standing and cheering.

Motley ended a 1-2-3 ninth for the Royals by flying out to McGee in center, and St. Louis was a lone win away from its tenth World Championship. It was Tudor's 14th straight win at home, as he threw 78 strikes out of 106 pitches in going the distance — a much better ratio than his Game-One numbers. "He's got better control," Howser said afterwards, in comparing Tudor to previous years when he had seen him throw in the American League. "And his change-up acts like a screwball. Then he doesn't walk anybody. And they don't make any mistakes in the field. That's a tough combination."

The Cards were flying high, and the Royals were hanging their heads. Only five times in history had a team come back to win the World Series down three games to one, and it had happened only three times in the last 60 years. "They want to end it right here," said Motley in full understanding of the gravity of the situation. "I think if we could get them back in KC, we would have a chance to win the whole thing."

11. A Collision on the Interstate

"This is nothing new," said Saberhagen, unconcerned, as he munched on a sandwich in the Royals' calm locker room. "It's the same old stuff. They fell right into our trap, like Toronto."

Forsch was looking for personal redemption, as he had lost his only two previous World Series decisions, both at the hands of the Milwaukee Brewers in 1982. Despite having confidence in himself, Forsch thought that Cox would be the better choice for the game. "When you're doing this [competing in the World Series], you want your best guys out there regularly," he said. Herzog had wanted to bring Cox back on three days' rest, as he did with Tudor, but the bone spurs in Cox's elbow had become too painful for him to throw. So it was the veteran Forsch going up against Jackson, the young left-hander of the Royals, brimming with confidence after his solid outing in Game One.

Kansas City wasted no time in their urgent situation, as Lonnie Smith scored in the top of the first on a White ground out. The Cardinals tied the game on a pair of two-out doubles by Herr and Clark in the bottom half, but the Royals retaliated by unleashing a barrage of offense against Forsch in the second. Sundberg doubled to left with one out on a ball that Landrum nearly grabbed with a diving attempt. Biancalana then singled Sundberg home, as he dove head-first around the reach of Nieto. Nieto thought he had tagged him in time, which evoked his protests, as well as the presence of Herzog from the dugout. On the play, Biancalana took second, which was followed by a walk to Smith. Wilson then tripled them both home, as Horton was brought in to relieve Forsch. Horton was able to get Brett to ground to Clark, but the Royals had sprinted out to a 4–1 advantage.

Jackson settled in with the lead, and like Saberhagen became an enigma for the St. Louis hitters. He kept them off the board through the third and fourth innings, and then later retired 10 straight Cardinal batters into the ninth. His men were literally going to the mat for him, as exemplified by Brett in the Cardinals' half of the seventh inning. He chased a pop foul off the bat of Nieto towards the third base dugout, but was unable to make the play. Nonetheless, he emerged from his collision with the dugout railing with a black eye, as he popped his glove and cheerfully returned to his position at the hot corner. Worrell entered the game for the Cardinals, and tried to rally them by tying a World Series record in striking out six straight Royals. Jackson picked up two insurance runs towards the end of the game, however, and the result was a convincing 6–1 win that would send the series back to Royals Stadium.

The Cardinals were concerned about their lack of offensive output. The team had managed only 12 runs in the first five games while batting a weak .196 over the same span. "They say we're not running," Herzog noted about the criticism of his club. "Well, we're not getting on." Smith and the two catchers—Porter and Nieto—were hitting a combined 2-for-30, and several others were struggling as well. To try and jump-start things, Herzog put Smith in the lead-off spot and moved McGee to the number-two position. The Royals were enjoying better numbers at the plate, due in part to the performance of the surprising Biancalana. Biancalana, whose diminutive stature and normally-harmless hitting gained him an appearance on the *Late Show with David Letterman* late in the regular season, had a robust .333 mark going into Game Six, in addition to an impressive .500 on-base percentage. He also had yet to make an error at shortstop in the series.

The Cards were looking for Cox to give them another big performance in a big game, and the young right-hander did everything he could to focus on his job. He skipped a midday press conference, as he holed himself up in his Overland Park, Kansas, hotel room with a "DO NOT DISTURB" sign on the door. Cox had been the Cardinals' scheduled representative for the press conference, but Pendleton went in his place. Pendleton explained to the media that the team felt, as a whole, the club didn't get a fair shake from the papers down the stretch of the pennant drive. He described how the top of each day's paper would say, "Mets Lose," while one had to scan to the bottom to find the words, "Cards Win." "I think that's what upset the guys the most," said Pendleton.

Leibrandt was slated to be the man in Game Six for the Royals, as he was looking to duplicate his fine performance in his Game Two loss to Dayley which Cox started for the Cardinals.

What worried some forward-thinking Cards insiders, such as Bob Broeg, was the prospect of a seventh game—for one reason in particular. "If the series goes seven games," Broeg noticed, "Tudor will be working Game Seven with the same plate umpire—Don Denkinger of the American League—he had a week ago when he seemed to have trouble getting strikes on pitches important to a thinking man's left-hander. That is, the inside-corner fast ball that counteracts his breaking ball, and especially the change-up away."

But everyone tried to think happy thoughts, like the Cards' simply winning Game Six behind Cox and going home champions, as the crew chief Denkinger spent the evening at first, with fellow American Leaguers Jim McKean at third and John Shulock down the right field line. Behind the plate for the sixth game was Jim Quick of the National League, along with Billy Williams at second base and Bob Engel on the left field line, also from the Senior Circuit.

Both Leibrandt and Cox were up to the task, but Leibrandt was espe-

11. A Collision on the Interstate

cially hard to crack. By the time Cedeno dropped a single into left to start the sixth inning with the score still tied 0–0, Leibrandt had become the first World Series pitcher since Boston's Jim Lonborg in 1967 to set down the first 15 batters in a game. Cedeno's hit looked like it was going to be the rock that broke the dam, as the slumping Porter then lined a single to right, with Cedeno stopping at second. Next was Cox, with a chance to put a pair of runners in scoring position. But his bunt attempt wallowed in the air long enough for Brett to catch it on the fly, and the runners held. Next, Smith rolled a double-play ball to Biancalana, and Leibrandt left the promising St. Louis inning in the dust.

Cox was tough also, as Ozzie returned the favor in being the middle man in a double play from Herr to Clark, and the Royals were turned away in their half of the sixth. Each pitcher retired the other club effectively in the seventh, too, as the tension mounted.

After Landrum flied out to Wilson in center to start the Cardinals' eighth, Pendleton stroked a single right, which caused Howser to charge up Quisenberry and Black in the bullpen. Cedeno then walked, but Porter was called out on strikes as Pendleton stood 180 feet away from a possible World Series title at second base with two out. At that point Brian Harper, who had been a relative no-name on the Cards' bench the whole season, popped a looping single over the second base bag to score Pendleton and give the Cardinals the lead. Smith then walked to load the bases, as Howser emerged from the dugout to retrieve Leibrandt in favor of Quisenberry. As the lefty walked off, the Kansas City faithful of 41,628 gave him a thunderous ovation for his efforts. Quisenberry quickly got McGee to ground out to Biancalana, as St. Louis took the field in defense of a 1–0 lead. Six outs were needed.

Dayley was brought in by Herzog to relieve Cox, and he got Lonnie Smith swinging on a foul tip that Porter held on to for strike three. Wilson then walked, but the speedster was unable to get a jump off the bag due to the crafty pickoff move of the Cardinal lefty. Dayley then got Brett to strike out swinging, and White followed with a harmless fly to McGee in center. The Redbirds were three outs away from the title, as it looked as if the battling Leibrandt would be a hard-luck loser once again.

It was as if the Cardinals were anxious to get through their batting turns, for Herr grounded out to Balboni, Clark struck out swinging, and Pendleton flied out to Wilson to pose no further threat to the Royals. Landrum did mix in an infield single before Pendleton's final bow, but the club appeared bent to get the three outs and celebrate.

Howser started the Kansas City ninth by sending up the right-handed-hitting Motley for Sheridan, which prompted Herzog to bring in

Worrell from the bullpen. Worrell had proven his worth in his month with the club, and Herzog had full confidence in him. Countering the move, Howser came back with Orta, a left-handed batter who was adept at being a "slap" hitter and getting on base, which was exactly what the club needed. He flailed at a steaming Worrell fast ball, and pushed a dribbler towards the right side of the infield. Clark went to his right to cleanly field the ball, but was too far from the base to make the play unassisted. Worrell covered the base, and took the throw from Clark as he worked to get his feet in the proper position on the bag. As Orta touched down on the base, Worrell already had the ball in his glove, but Denkinger threw both arms up in a "safe" call, claiming the Worrell's foot never came in contact with first. Worrell turned in disbelief at Denkinger, which was followed with visits by Clark, Herr, and then Herzog jogging over from the Cardinals' dugout. As usual, the players' protests did nothing to change the umpire's mind, and the game continued with the tying run on first. Clark would later say, "I thought he was out, but to be honest, I was kind of blocked on the play. Worrell is much bigger than Orta, although it looked like Todd beat him to the bag."

Balboni was next in the order after Orta had reached, and it appeared his slump was continuing as he lifted a soft pop foul towards the first base dugout. Clark circled under it, but lost it at the last second as the ball fell to the ground. Balboni took advantage, and subsequently broke out of his doldrums with a single to left. Sundberg then attempted a sacrifice bunt to move the runners along. Worrell hopped off the mound and fired a shot to Pendleton at third to get the lead runner. With a 1–0 count to McRae, who was pinch-hitting for Biancalana, Porter allowed a pitch to sneak by him for a passed ball, as the winning runs moved up to second and third. At that point McRae meant nothing, so Herzog ordered him walked to get to the pitcher's spot in the order. Howser's choice to bat was Iorg, the Cardinals' familiar face from the '82 club who had become a dangerous pinch-hitter. He turned on a pitch inside from Worrell, and knocked a base hit into right. Van Slyke came up charging and throwing, hoping to cut off Sundberg, who was trying to bring home a win and a tied series for the Royals. The throw was right on the money to Porter, but Sundberg was able to scoot across on an open corner of the plate, as he jumped joyously into the arms of on-deck hitter Lonnie Smith. The Royals had come back to win in dramatic fashion, 2–1, setting up a winner-take-all finale the following evening.

It was the first time all year that the Cardinals lost a game they had led going into the ninth inning. Before this game, they had a record of 84–0 when leading after eight.

11. A Collision on the Interstate

In the Cardinals' clubhouse, much of the dejection and anger centered around Denkinger and his call on Orta's hit. Herr and McGee sat on the floor in disgust, ignoring not only reporters' questions but also steaming plates of barbecue beef that had been placed before them. Some had suggested that the umpiring had been poor throughout the series, and Herzog was asked if he himself thought the work of the men in blue had been sub-par.

"[It has been] by the American League umps," he angrily replied. "It looks like they're prejudiced. We've haven't got one call yet from those [expletive]. And I don't care what they say, the guy [AL umpire Jim McKean] missed a lot of strikes the other night on Joaquin." It was one of the few times all year that Herzog agreed with Andujar when the pitcher complained of a small strike zone.

"I went out and asked him [Denkinger] what the hell was going on," Herzog continued. "If he had told me that Todd had pulled his foot off the bag, I wouldn't have said anything. But he told me he [Orta] beat it, and that's BS." Then the writers shuffled over to Worrell, a participant and first-hand witness on the scene. "He [Orta] came down on the back of my foot, which was on the bag, after I had the ball in my glove," Worrell described. "When Whitey was arguing with him, [the umpire] said my foot was up off the top of the bag when I caught the ball. "I don't know how I can have my foot in the air and still have somebody step on it."

"Let me just say this," Herzog added. "The two best teams in baseball are supposed to be in the World Series. They ought to have the best umpires from the two leagues, too. I think it's a disgrace."

Kevin Horrigan suggested that Denkinger, in the day's preparation for Game Seven the next evening, ought to take a drive up the road to Liberty, Missouri — the boyhood home of notorious robber Jesse James.

Despite complaints, protests, and even threats, the reality was that the series was indeed tied, with the clubs' two aces to set to twirl in the final game of the 1985 season. The Cardinals, despite their disappointment from Game Six, had their contingency plan in place with Tudor taking the mound. It was Saberhagen again for the Royals, who looked forward to the final game in front of the home crowd. Saberhagen had just welcomed the birth of his son the day before, as the newly-arrived Drew William Saberhagen gave the young righty an extra inspiration for the game of his life.

The most positive of thinkers wished that the Cards had a chance. It was hoped that Tudor would continue on his winning ways, and that the offense would finally wake up and return to its exciting, thoroughbred form from the regular season. Perhaps Game Six had been too much of a crushing blow, however, as Tudor collapsed along with his teammates all

After being thrown out of Game Seven of the World Series by umpire Don Denkinger, Andujar still had a few thoughts to share with him. *(From the collections of the St. Louis Mercantile Library at the University of Missouri–St. Louis)*

around him. The Royals jumped on him for five runs within the first three innings. The assault began in the second stanza, as Motley nailed a two-run homer just inside the left field foul pole to send Kansas City on its way. Tudor started out the third with a walk to Smith, followed by a single by Brett and two more walks to White and Sundberg, which made it a 3–0 game.

Campbell was brought in at that point, as Tudor injured his hand by punching a fan in the Cardinals' dugout ("The kind that blows air; *not* the kind that cheers," it was made clear in a press box announcement). Tudor's 2⅔ inning stay was his shortest of the year, the previous being a three-inning excursion against the Mets way back on April 22. Campbell's first opponent, Balboni, proved that he was fully recovered from his hitting problems by singling home Brett and White, blowing the game open, 5–0.

As scheduled, Denkinger was behind the plate for Game Seven, and as expected, he became a receptacle for Cardinal slurs throughout the game. After brief stints by Lahti and Horton in the fifth, Andujar was brought in after another Royals onslaught had raised their advantage to 9–0. Andujar almost cheerfully took the mound, realizing the pressure was off and that he could just pitch. He would only face one batter of record. It was White, who drew a walk that scored Wilson for a 10–0 KC lead.

After Sundberg, the next batter, took a called ball, Andujar strolled halfway to the plate and started chirping at Denkinger — first in Spanish, then in half–English, and then back to Spanish again. Herzog yelled something after charging toward the plate from the dugout, and Denkinger ejected him. A moment later, Andujar was asked to leave the premises as well, as Pendleton, Roarke, Nick Leyva, and Hal Lanier all tried to restrain him.

Denkinger had thought that Andujar had made an obscene gesture at him, but Andujar later claimed that he was only beckoning Porter to come out to the mound. Denkinger also had a side to it. "Andujar came off the mound screaming," he told a reporter. "I told him one more [outburst] and he's gone. Whitey came out and started yelling. He was using vulgarity. He was gone.

"We got settled down, started again, one pitch, and Andujar starts again. He's gone."

Andujar became the first player kicked out of a World Series game since Cincinnati pitcher Clay Carroll got heaved in 1970.

Forsch then entered and threw a wild pitch to plate the Royals' 11th run before getting Balboni to fly out to McGee to end the mess. The six-run fifth had demoralized the Cardinals, and even though there were four more frames left to play, the game was effectively over at that point.

That was due in part to the slick Saberhagen, who exercised pinpoint control in not walking a St. Louis batter the entire evening. He blasted his way through the sixth, seventh, and eighth, and the crowd of over 41,000 at Royals Stadium rose in expectation as he took to the hill in the ninth.

Herr commenced the ending with an easy grounder to his counterpart White at second. Clark flew out to Wilson in center, and Van Slyke closed the story by chasing Motley to the warning track in right, nearly spoiling the shutout bid of Saberhagen. The new father, all of 21, had just won his second World Series game in as many tries, allowing only five hits. Shortly thereafter, he would be named the series MVP.

The 11-0 score was the most lopsided World Series game since the Cards beat up on the Brewers, 13-1, in Game Six in 1982. And in spite of his fantastic run since the end of May, all of the good memories were erased for John Tudor. "Call it choke, call it whatever you want," he told reporters about his troubles in Game Seven. "I didn't come through when my teammates needed me the most."

Baseball's world championship belonged to Kansas City.

"The Royals just outplayed them Cardinals," Horrigan concluded. "They won more graciously — no whining was heard from them about not getting any national recognition — and they lost more graciously — and one less frequently." John Sonderegger also chipped in his thoughts. "Left for dead at every other turn in the road this season, the Royals kept throwing back the stone and rising, much to the disbelief of nearly everyone, especially the Toronto Blue Jays and the Cardinals."

The Royals had spent every dime of energy they had, which left them on top at the end. "We couldn't have taken another close game," Brett admitted. "These two series killed us. We were emotionally and physically drained. Getting two runs in the second and three in the third and knocking their best pitcher out took a lot of pressure off us."

Understandably, Horrigan and other witnesses had difficulty stomaching the ugly scene unfolding for the Cardinals down on the field, saying that many people had their hand in the demise. "But it was left to Joaquin Andujar to put the cap on it," he wrote, "to put an indelible scar on the proud legacy of the St. Louis Cardinals. Brought in from the bullpen, where he had been justifiably exiled, he was handed the ball in a 9–0 game and told to finish up. But he couldn't handle it. All he had to do was pitch and handle himself with dignity. But he wanted to show off. He pouted and slammed the resin bag, and then he tried to storm Denkinger when he thought the umpire didn't give him a pitch. 'What the hell,' Andujar said. 'I didn't kill nobody.'... He's the laughingstock of baseball, and he drags all St. Louis down with him."

"A red face for performance and a black eye for conduct," United Press International decided about Andujar and the Cardinals, in agreement with Horrigan's thesis.

Horrigan's point was well-taken — that Andujar could have saved some face, not only with St. Louis fans but baseball people everywhere who had endured him over the season — by simply holding his head high and pitching the best he could. Whether it was the pressure from the drug inquiry, his late-season collapse, his constant feud with the media, or whatever else, something inside him boiled over in the fifth inning of the last game of the year.

In their morbid locker room, the Cardinals did receive a consoling phone call from President Reagan. "We stunk it up," Herzog told the President as he handed the receiver to somebody else, not feeling like saying anything more. The Cards became the first team in history to win the first two games on the road of a seven-game World Series and not win the title. The offense had totally gone in the tank, as their team batting average of .185 was the lowest all-time for a seven-game showdown. "Thirteen runs in seven games is almost a disgrace," Herzog muttered.

Mike McKenzie of the *Kansas City Star* smugly wrote that, for their troubles, "The Cardinals are a sadder Bud-weiser team."

So truth be told, Denkinger or no Denkinger, the Cardinals had beaten themselves during the 1985 World Series. It did not tarnish, however, the grand accomplishments by Herzog and his charges in one exciting summer. As Bob Forsch would call it later, "It was a heckuva year."

Skies were sunny once again in the best baseball city in the world, as loyal Cardinal fans — also the best in the world — were rewarded with a lightning bolt of a team that came from nowhere.

Epilogue

The postseason awards in the National League turned out as expected. McGee was named Most Valuable Player, Coleman was the Rookie of the Year, and Tudor was beaten out for the Cy Young by Gooden. Over in the American League, first baseman Don Mattingly of the Yankees was the MVP with his league-leading 48 doubles and 145 RBIs, to go with 35 home runs and a .324 batting average. McGee's MVP award was the first by a position player in 12 years with the winner hitting as few as 10 home runs; it was also something that had been done only five times ever before. The biggest surprise, of course, was Coleman, who during the 1985 season had stolen second and third base ten times in the same inning. "Coleman was better at stealing third than anyone in history," Herzog stated years later. And Whitey got his due, too, as he was named the National League Manager of the Year in one of the greatest orchestral jobs in the history of the game. Toronto's Cox got the honor in the AL.

It is easy to see how some thought Herzog's job would have been in jeopardy at the start of the season, with everything that surrounded him starting to crumble. Horrigan remembered that "the seers saw his Bruce Sutter–less Cardinals finishing sixth and last in the National League East ... they noted that Joe McDonald, Herzog's handpicked general manager and erstwhile aide-de-camp, had been sacked last winter. It was a simple matter to deduce that Herzog would be next." Fortunately, Gussie Busch had the wisdom to hold on to him, and he and Cardinal fans were rewarded with the shrewdest mind in baseball leading the way. Horrigan went on to write that Busch, before 1985 was out, had already made it a priority to extend Herzog's contract. "In other words, if Gussie Busch's word is good — and there aren't many men whose word is as good as Gussie's — the brewery will have to re-sign Herzog this year." And they did. For the 1985 season, Herzog was in the middle of a three-year contract he had finalized at the end of 1983, and it was worth $250,000 a year. He got the contract extended with little trouble from management. "We sincerely believe that he is the best manager in the game today," Dal Maxvill said unconditionally. "I think he's one of the best evaluators of talent I've ever seen."

The Cardinals would finish third in the National League East in 1986, three games below .500 at 79–82. Reasons for the decline were many, but they centered around Tudor and Cox coming back down to earth after spectacular numbers in 1985, although each still posted a solid season. Another important factor was the anemic nature of the team's power hitting, accounting for a scant 58 home runs during the entire season. Van Slyke was the only player in double figures with 13, as Clark was injured again, hurting a finger that limited him to 232 at-bats. Herr's knees continued to be a problem for him, as he had undergone three surgeries on them in the past year. McGee was also slowed by injury, but a bright spot was the emergence of Worrell as a dominant closer out of the bullpen. He followed up Coleman's prize the previous season by taking home the 1986 Rookie of the Year award, thanks to 36 saves and a 2.08 ERA. And with Coleman, Van Slyke, and a healthy McGee, the Cards continued to have supreme fly chasers covering every inch of the pasture. In all he had seen, Broeg's words spoke volumes. "In this judgment, there hasn't been an outfield since the famed one of Stan Musial, Terry Moore, and Enos Slaughter that could match this one defensively," he believed.

There are two sides to the argument on the running game in baseball, and each side has its own cliché. One side says that "speed never goes into a slump"; that despite the mental stress that a lack of hitting success can do to a player, his speed does not leave him, and thus remains a perpetual factor in the game. The other side to the argument boldly asserts that "you can't steal first base"; for no matter how fast a player might be, he still needs a certain degree of batting skill to utilize his speed. The St. Louis Cardinals of the 1980s satisfied both sides of the argument.

It is often remembered that the Cardinals stole a lot of bases in the '80s, which they certainly did. They were able to do this, however, because of quality batsmen at the plate. In the Cardinals' pennant-winning years of 1982, 1985, and later in 1987, they led the National League in on-base percentage in each of those years: .337, .338, and .343 respectively, as well as another top mark of .323 in 1989. The Cardinals finished first in the league in runs scored in 1985 with a total of 747, a telling final figure for a team that jetted around the bases all summer long.

Writer David Schoenfield summarized the era most appropriately. "The Cardinals didn't win because they stole lots of bases—they always stole lots of bases and finished under .500 sometimes—but they won when they scored enough runs." Schoenfield also pointed out that, during a nine-year stretch from 1982 to 1990, the Cardinals finished last in the National League in home runs in eight of those seasons, and second-to-last in the other (which was 1985, in fact).

In another vein, the impact of the defensive skill of the 1985 club cannot be underestimated. The Cardinals finished with a team fielding percentage of .983, which was not only the best in the National League, but was also the best mark in club history. And Herzog took Broeg's thought a step further in saying that "Coleman, Van Slyke, and McGee might be the best defensive outfield in the history of the game." Regardless of opinions, one would be hard-pressed to find a trio that covered more ground. When the three shot toward the gaps on a batted ball, they gulped up the Astroturf at Busch Stadium in waves. And not too many balls were hit beyond their reach either, as Cardinal pitchers allowed a league-low 98 home runs in '85.

Several notable items occurred after the 1985 season that would impact the game for some time to come. Bobby Cox left the division-winning Blue Jays to accept the general manager's position with the Atlanta Braves, beginning a run of success with that organization that continues into the twenty-first century. Second Street in Cincinnati, which runs in front of (then) Riverfront Stadium, was re-named Pete Rose Way in honor of the world's hit leader. And Curtis Strong was ultimately convicted in the drug saga, and sentenced to 4 to 12 years in federal prison. All of the players who testified in the trials received their promised immunity.

Some interesting developments took place with members of the 1985 Cardinals as well. It turned out to be true that Andujar's days in St. Louis were numbered, as he was traded to the Oakland A's before the '86 season after winning only once in 1985 after August 23. In addition, he was fined $500 and suspended for the first ten games of 1986 for his tirade in the seventh game of the World Series. He would spend two mediocre seasons there while sustaining injuries to his elbow and leg. He finished his career in 1988 with the club he started with, the Houston Astros. Pendleton, who some considered a disappointment on the '85 club after his stellar rookie year in 1984, went on to win a couple of batting titles with the Braves. Van Slyke would move on in the early 1990s to form a dynamic trio in the Pittsburgh outfield with Barry Bonds and Bobby Bonilla. The stolen base records would continue to pile up for Coleman, as he would steal 100-plus bases in his first three seasons in the league. In 1990, McGee won his second batting title—though it was in absentia. Despite being traded to Oakland for Felix Jose, Daryl Green, and Stan Royer on August 29, McGee left town with enough plate appearances to qualify for the title in the National League. Ozzie Smith continued to live in the St. Louis area after he retired in the mid–1990s, becoming a restaurant owner and a commentator on the Cardinals' television broadcasts. And of all people, Jack Clark was named the hitting coach for the Los Angeles Dodgers for the 2001 season.

Cedeno had served much the same purpose as Will Clark did in the Cardinals' playoff run in 2000. Both the player and the club knew that a relationship past the given season was not likely, but both "hired guns" provided veteran leadership and played key roles in both cases—in addition to the on-field production they offered. Cedeno spent one more season in the majors in 1986 with the Dodgers.

The sun appears to be setting for Busch Stadium, as different factions around St. Louis are calling for its replacement. Nonetheless, it will be a long time before fans forget the hot summer nights of the 1980s, when hot feet tore up the base paths at the ballpark down by the river.

Appendix A: 1985 Final Standings

National League

Eastern Division	W	L	Pct.	GB
St. Louis	101	61	.623	—
New York	98	64	.605	3
Montreal	84	77	.522	16½
Chicago	77	84	.478	23½
Philadelphia	75	87	.463	26
Pittsburgh	57	104	.354	43½

Western Division	W	L	Pct.	GB
Los Angeles	95	67	.586	—
Cincinnati	89	72	.553	5½
Houston	83	79	.512	12
San Diego	83	79	.512	12
Atlanta	66	96	.407	29
San Francisco	62	100	.383	33

American League

Eastern Division	W	L	Pct.	GB
Toronto	99	62	.615	—
New York	97	64	.602	2
Detroit	84	77	.522	15
Baltimore	83	78	.516	16
Boston	81	81	.500	18½
Milwaukee	71	90	.441	28
Cleveland	60	102	.370	39½

Western Division	W	L	Pct.	GB
Kansas City	91	71	.562	—
California	90	72	.556	1
Chicago	85	77	.522	6
Minnesota	77	85	.475	14
Oakland	77	85	.475	14
Seattle	74	88	.457	17
Texas	62	99	.385	28½

Appendix B: 1985 St. Louis Cardinals' Batting Statistics

	G	AB	R	H	2B	3B	HR	RBI	SB	AVG
Ford	11	12	2	6	2	0	0	3	1	.500
Cedeno	28	76	14	33	4	1	6	19	5	.434
McGee	152	612	114	216	26	18	10	82	56	.353
Herr	159	596	97	180	38	3	8	110	31	.302
Clark	126	442	71	124	26	3	22	87	1	.281
Landrum	85	161	21	45	8	2	4	21	1	.280
O. Smith	158	537	70	148	22	3	6	54	31	.276
Coleman	151	636	107	170	20	10	1	40	110	.267
L. Smith	28	96	15	25	2	2	0	7	12	.260
Van Slyke	146	424	61	110	25	6	13	55	34	.259
Harper	43	52	5	13	4	0	0	8	0	.250
Pendleton	149	559	56	134	16	3	5	69	17	.240
Braun	64	67	7	16	4	0	1	6	0	.239
Nieto	95	253	15	57	10	2	0	34	0	.225
DeJesus	59	72	11	16	5	0	0	7	2	.222
Porter	84	240	30	53	12	2	10	36	6	.221
Lawless	47	58	8	12	3	1	0	8	2	.207
Jorgensen	72	112	14	22	6	0	0	11	2	.196
Hunt	14	19	1	3	0	0	0	1	0	.158
LaValliere	12	34	2	5	1	0	0	6	0	.147
Howe	4	3	0	0	0	0	0	0	0	.000

Appendix C: 1985 St. Louis Cardinals' Pitching Statistics

	W–L	G	GS	CG	IP	H	BB	SO	Sho	ERA
Perry	1–0	6	0	0	12	3	3	6	0	0.00
Bair	0–0	2	0	0	2	1	2	0	0	0.00
Hassler	0–1	10	0	0	10	9	4	5	0	1.80
Lahti	5–2	52	0	0	68	63	26	41	0	1.84
Tudor	21–8	36	36	14	275	209	49	169	10	1.93
Dayley	4–4	57	0	0	65	65	18	62	0	2.76
Cox	18–9	35	35	10	241	226	64	131	4	2.88
Horton	3–2	49	3	0	90	84	34	59	0	2.91
Worrell	3–0	17	0	0	22	17	7	17	0	2.91
Andujar	21–12	38	38	10	270	265	82	112	2	3.40
Campbell	5–3	50	0	0	64	55	21	41	0	3.50
Forsch	9–6	34	19	3	136	132	47	48	1	3.90
Boever	0–0	13	0	0	16	17	4	20	0	4.41
Keough	0–1	4	1	0	10	10	4	10	0	4.50
Kepshire	10–9	32	29	0	153	155	71	67	0	4.75
Allen	1–4	23	1	0	29	32	17	10	0	5.59

Saves: Lahti 19, Dayley 11, Worrell 5, Campbell 4, Forsch 2, Allen 2, Horton 1

Appendix D: 1985 St. Louis Cardinals' World Series Statistics

Batter	G	AB	R	H	2B	3B	HR	RBI	SB	AVG
Landrum	7	25	3	9	2	0	1	1	0	.360
Pendleton	7	23	3	6	1	1	0	3	0	.261
McGee	7	27	2	7	2	0	1	2	1	.259
Harper	4	4	0	1	0	0	0	1	0	.250
Clark	7	25	1	6	2	0	0	4	0	.240
Herr	7	26	2	4	2	0	0	0	0	.154
Cedeno	5	15	1	2	1	0	0	1	0	.133
Porter	5	15	0	2	0	0	0	0	0	.133
Van Slyke	6	11	0	1	0	0	0	0	0	.091
O. Smith	7	23	1	2	0	0	0	0	1	.087
Nieto	2	5	0	0	0	0	0	1	0	.000
Jorgensen	2	3	0	0	0	0	0	0	0	.000
Braun	1	1	0	0	0	0	0	0	0	.000
DeJesus	1	1	0	0	0	0	0	0	0	.000
Lawless	1	0	0	0	0	0	0	0	0	—
Pitchers	7	12	0	0	0	0	0	0	0	.000

Appendix D: Cardinals' 1985 Statistics

Pitcher	W–L	G	GS	CG	IP	H	BB	SO	Sho	ERA
Dayley	1–0	4	0	0	6	1	3	5	0	0.00
Cox	0–0	2	2	0	14	14	4	13	0	1.29
Campbell	0–0	3	0	0	4	4	2	5	0	2.25
Tudor	2–1	3	3	1	18	15	7	14	1	3.00
Worrell	0–1	3	0	0	4.2	4	2	6	0	3.86
Horton	0–0	3	0	0	4	4	5	5	0	6.75
Andujar	0–1	2	1	0	4	10	4	3	0	9.00
Forsch	0–1	2	1	0	3	6	1	3	0	12.00
Lahti	0–0	3	0	0	3.2	10	0	2	0	12.27

Saves: Worrell 1 (Game One), Lahti 1 (Game Two)

Appendix E: 1985 Kansas City Royals' World Series Statistics

Batter	G	AB	R	H	2B	3B	HR	RBI	SB	AVG
Jones	6	3	0	2	1	1	0	0	0	.667
Iorg	2	2	0	1	0	0	0	2	0	.500
Brett	7	27	5	10	1	0	0	1	1	.370
Wilson	7	30	2	11	0	1	0	3	3	.367
Motley	5	11	1	4	0	0	1	3	0	.364
L. Smith	7	27	4	9	3	0	0	4	2	.333
Orta	3	3	0	1	0	0	0	0	0	.333
Balboni	7	25	2	8	0	0	0	3	0	.320
Biancalana	7	18	2	5	0	0	0	2	0	.278
White	7	28	4	7	3	0	1	6	0	.250
Sundberg	7	24	6	6	2	0	0	1	0	.250
Sheridan	5	18	0	4	2	0	0	1	0	.222
McRae	3	1	0	0	0	0	0	0	0	.000
Wathan	2	1	0	0	0	0	0	0	0	.000
Concepcion	3	0	1	0	0	0	0	0	0	—
Pryor	1	0	0	0	0	0	0	0	0	—
Pitchers	7	18	1	0	0	0	0	0	0	.000

Appendix E: Royals' 1985 Statistics

Pitcher	W–L	G	GS	CG	IP	H	BB	SO	Sho	ERA
Beckwith	0–0	1	0	0	2	1	0	3	0	0.00
Saberhagen	2–0	2	2	2	18	11	1	10	1	0.50
Jackson	1–1	2	2	1	16	9	5	12	0	1.69
Quisenberry	1–0	4	0	0	4.1	5	3	3	0	2.08
Leibrandt	0–1	2	2	0	16.1	10	4	10	0	2.76
Black	0–1	2	1	0	5.1	4	5	4	0	5.06

Saves: None

Index

A's (Kansas City) 8
A's (Oakland) 17, 34, 113, 119, 140, 153, 189
Aaron, Hank 137
Abbott, Jim 64
ABC Television Network 69
Aguayo, Luis 116
Aguilera, Rick 92, 150
Alexander, Doyle 163
All-Star Game (1966) 7; (1971) 107; (1983) 17, 107; (1985) 57, 67, 80, 96, 99–107, 111, 125
Allen, Neil 12, 27, 40–42, 45, 51, 60, 62, 65–66, 76–77, 89, 101, 108
Alvin, TX 61
Amalfitano, Joey 159
American League Championship Series (1982) 11–12; (1983) 30; (1985) 155, 157–158, 163, 167, 175
Anderson, George "Sparky" 32, 106–107
Andujar, Joaquin 2, 9, 34, 38, 43, 45, 47–48, 50, 62, 64–66, 71, 73, 79–80, 83, 89–90, 92, 96–97, 99–101, 106, 108–109, 111, 114, 119, 121, 124–127, 129, 132, 134–135, 138, 140–142, 145, 148–150, 152–153, 155–156, 158, 161, 163–164, 175–177, 183–186, 189
Angels (California) 12, 29, 64, 77, 91, 116–117, 131, 144, 150, 154
Anheuser-Busch Brewery 19, 43
Arcadia, CA 128
Arizona, University of 63

The Astrodome (Houston) 60–61, 100
Astros (Houston) 25, 38, 60–62, 64, 71–72, 100, 125, 129, 131, 189
Auburn, NY 90
Auburn, University of 64

Backman, Wally 138, 149–150
Bailey, Mark 72, 125
Baines, Harold 105
Bair, Doug 128
Baker, Dusty 156
Balboni, Steve 169, 171–172, 178, 181–182, 184–185
Baller, Jay 136, 152
Banks, Ernie 5
Barker, Len 127
Baylor, Don 155
Bears (Chicago) 69, 79
Beazley, Johnny 152
Bedrosian, Steve 66, 135
Belanger, Mark 131
Benedict, Bruce 134
Berenyi, Bruce 42, 86
Bergesch, Bill 32
Berra, Dale 76, 108
Bettencourt, Dave 77
Biancalana, Buddy 171, 173, 176, 178–182
Bidwell, Bill 35
Black, Bud 170, 177, 181
Blair, Paul 131
Blue, Vida 34, 41, 99
Blue Jays (Toronto) 63, 77, 129, 131,

144, 150, 154–155, 157–158, 163, 167, 179, 185, 189
Blyleven, Bert 76, 81, 105
Boever, Joe 108–109, 117, 128–129
Boggs, Wade 23, 105, 119, 155
Bonds, Barry 189
Bonilla, Bobby 189
Bosley, Thad 85
Boston College 14
Bowa, Larry 10–11, 28–29, 57, 83, 114, 122
Boyer, Ken 8
Bradley, Phil 105
Braun, Steve 30, 86, 109–111, 119, 145, 153, 164
Braves (Atlanta) 1, 10, 12, 16, 20, 26–27, 41, 50, 54, 60, 62–63, 65–66, 68, 119, 125, 127, 134–135, 143, 189
Brenly, Bob 97
Brett, George 17–18, 32, 105, 107, 155, 169–172, 174–175, 178–179, 181, 184–185
Brewers (Milwaukee) 9, 11–12, 41, 169, 179
Brinkley, Christie 97
Brock, Greg 108, 156, 162, 164, 172
Brock, Lou 7, 22, 46, 72, 112, 128, 142, 146
Brocklander, Fred 149
Broeg, Bob 8, 13, 38, 46, 102, 104, 180, 188–189
Brooks, Hubie 39, 143
Brown, Bobby 151
Brown, Gates 110
Brown, Joe 74, 116
Browning, Tom 132, 137
Browns (St. Louis) 7, 64
Brummer, Glenn 24
Brunansky, Tom 105, 118
Brusstar, Warren 113
Buck, Jack 10, 13, 45, 162
Buckner, Bill 37
Budweiser Clydesdale Horses 176–177
Bulls (Chicago) 79
Bumbry, Al 111
Burroughs, Jeff 154
Busch, August A., Jr. 5–8, 11, 153, 176–177, 187
Busch Stadium (St. Louis) 6–7, 12, 14–15, 17–18, 47, 56, 66, 78, 82–84, 90, 97, 100, 115, 117–119, 123–124, 130–131, 133–134, 144–145, 148–150, 153, 160–161, 166, 175–176, 178, 189–190
Bush, Vice President George 40
Butera, Sal 124

Cabell, Enos 166
Cal Poly–San Luis Obispo 10
Campanis, Al 156
Campbell, Bill 37, 41, 47, 62, 66, 72–73, 80–81, 101, 108, 117, 123, 128, 141, 143, 150, 152, 161, 166, 184
Candelaria, John 45, 75–76, 116
Candlestick Park (San Francisco) 20
Caray, Harry 7
Cardinals, St. Louis (football) 34–35, 72
Carew, Rod 104, 117, 138
Carlton, Steve 7, 41, 82, 90–91, 100, 116–117
Carman, Don 82
Carroll, Clay 185
Carter, Gary 39, 42, 89, 92, 105–106, 121, 136, 148–150, 153
Cashen, Frank 122
Cedeno, Cesar 129, 133, 136–138, 141–144, 163, 166, 171–172, 174, 181, 190
Cey, Ron 11, 50, 84, 114, 153–154, 156
Clark, Jack 2, 17, 20–21, 32–33, 40–43, 46, 48, 51–53, 63, 65–66, 68, 72, 77–80, 85–86, 88, 92–94, 97, 99–101, 105, 107, 110–113, 120, 126, 128, 133, 136, 141–144, 148, 150, 158, 161, 165, 171–174, 176, 179, 181–182, 185, 188, 190
Clark, Will 190
Clearwater, FL 32
Clemente, Roberto 15
Cobb, Ty 31, 40, 65, 71, 120, 127, 132, 135, 137–138, 140
Coleman, Greg 22
Coleman, Vince 2, 22, 29, 34, 44–47, 50–53, 57–58, 62, 68, 70–72, 79–80, 82, 84–86, 88, 90–92, 94–97, 99–101, 110–111, 114, 120–121, 124, 127–128, 131–134, 136, 139–140, 142–144, 146, 148, 150, 153–154, 156, 158–161, 163, 166, 170–171, 174–175, 177, 187–189
Colliston, LA 112
Columbia University 19
Comiskey Park (Chicago) 69
Concepcion, Dave 70
Cooper, Cecil 11–12, 105
Cooper, Mort 152

Index

County Stadium (Milwaukee) 16
Cox, Bobby 154, 187
Cox, Danny 2, 25–26, 30, 43, 46, 51, 57, 60, 62, 70, 76, 80, 83, 91–92, 96–97, 99, 101, 108, 110–111, 114, 117, 121, 123, 125, 127, 133, 136, 140–141, 143, 148, 150, 152, 158–159, 163, 174, 179–181, 188–189
Crowder College 108
Cruz, Jose 71, 105–106
Cubs (Chicago) 5, 10–11, 14, 17, 28–29, 35, 37–38, 41, 44, 47, 54, 56–57, 62, 64, 66, 69, 72–78, 80–89, 94–95, 110, 112–114, 116, 118, 120–123, 133, 135, 139–141, 143, 146, 148, 151–156
Cuellar, Mike 81, 131

Dalles, OR 27
Darling, Ron 28, 42, 72, 105, 136, 141, 148–149
Davenport, Jim 20, 51
Davidson, Bob 23
Davis, Chili 52
Davis, Jody 79, 85, 114, 139
Davis, Mark 31, 110
Dawson, Andre 143–144
Dayley, Ken 2, 27, 41, 60, 62–63, 65, 72–73, 76, 81, 85, 86, 91–93, 101, 111, 114, 121, 123–125, 138, 145, 149–150, 155, 157, 159, 162, 166, 174, 181
Dean, Jay "Dizzy" 48, 83, 137
DeJesus, Ivan 10, 37, 45, 88, 92, 143, 153
DeLeon, Jose 141
Denkinger, Don 180, 182–186
Denny, John 91
Dernier, Bob 35, 68, 78, 80, 85, 112, 114, 122–123, 139
Dodgers (Brooklyn) 5, 77, 155
Dodgers (Los Angeles) 31–32, 37–38, 41, 48, 50–51, 53–54, 56, 75, 80, 94–96, 108–110, 119, 124, 128, 150, 153, 155–166, 190
Dodgers Stadium (Los Angeles) 156–157, 163–165
Doran, Bill 130
Draft, Professional Baseball (1968) 25; (1982) 29, 58, 128; (1985) 63–64
drugs, baseball and 34, 54–56, 66–67, 116, 134, 142
Duke University 9

Duncan, Mariano 164
Dunston, Shawon 28–29, 56–57, 122, 133, 140
Durham, Leon 9, 35, 86, 120
Durocher, Leo 115
Dykstra, Lenny 28, 89

Eagleton, Thomas 35
Eastern Oklahoma Junior College 30
Eastwood, Clint 32
Eckersley, Dennis 47, 81, 84, 112, 120, 151
Ellingsen, Bruce 94
Engel, Bob 180
Engel, Steve 112–113, 133, 141
Engle, Dave 77
Exhibition Stadium (Toronto) 155, 163
Expos (Montreal) 11, 39–40, 47–48, 54, 59–60, 73–74, 81, 85–86, 88, 91, 94, 97, 99, 103, 109–110, 117, 123–124, 126, 139, 143–144, 147, 152, 154–155

Face, Elroy 73
Falmouth, MA 77
Farr, Steve 170
Federal Bureau of Investigation (FBI) 54, 56
Feeney, Chub 151
Fehr, Donald 47, 64, 67, 118
Fenway Park (Boston) 22, 113
Fernandez, Sid 82, 100, 143
Fingers, Rollie 9
Fisk, Carlton 105, 155
Fitzgerald, Mike 39
Flanagan, Mike 30, 81
Flannery, Tim 111
Flint, MI 64
Flood, Curt 7
Florida A&M University 22
Fontenot, Ray 114, 136
Ford, Curt 81–82, 86, 92, 94, 153
Forsch, Bob 2, 17, 24–25, 43–44, 47, 63, 66, 70, 73, 79, 86–87, 101, 109, 117, 121, 123, 132, 139–140, 142, 151–152, 158, 161–162, 179, 185–186
Forsch, Ken 25
Foster, George 91, 136, 149–150
Francona, Terry 124
Frazier, George 79
Frey, Jim 14, 29, 57, 81, 84, 88–89, 123, 139

Index

Frisch, Frankie 115, 121, 143
Fulton County Stadium (Atlanta) 65

Galbreath, Dan 74
Garcia, Damaso 105
Gardenhire, Ron 122
Gardner, Billy 81
Garrelts, Scott 105, 109
Garver, Ned 6
Garvey, Steve 96, 99, 105–107, 126, 137, 156
Gas House Gang (1934 Cardinals) 22, 115
Gedman, Rich 106
Georgia Southern University 22
Giants (New York) 5, 77, 83, 121, 153
Giants (San Francisco) 20, 24, 34, 41, 51–53, 55, 74, 96–97, 99, 109–110, 119, 125, 156
Gibson, Bob 126, 178
Gibson, Kirk 154
Gieselmann, Gene 26
Gitto's Restaraunt (St. Louis) 96
Gladden, Dan 52
Glen Echo Country Club (St. Louis) 119
Gooden, Dwight 23, 28, 33, 40, 47–48, 73, 82, 89, 92, 100, 105, 118, 120, 125, 127, 134, 136–137, 144, 147–149, 154, 170, 187
Gorman, Tom 73
Gossage, Rich 100, 105, 107, 111
Gottlieb, Ed 37–38, 43
Granite City, IL 19
Gray, Pete 64
Green, Dallas 57, 69, 153–154
Green, Daryl 189
Green, David 9, 15, 20, 51–52, 89
Griffey, Ken 108
Gross, Kevin 83, 116
Gubicza, Mark 163, 170
Guerrero, Pedro 94, 106, 119–120, 142–143, 155, 157, 159, 166
Guillen, Ozzie 100
Guinness Book of World Records 114
Gullickson, Bill 43–44
Gura, Larry 66
Gwynn, Tony 105, 107, 137

Haas, Eddie 68, 127
Hall, Donald 23

Hands, Bill 146
Harper, Brian 21, 44, 125, 132, 181
Harper, Terry 66
Hassler, Andy 27, 41–42, 47
Hawkins, Andy 73, 100–101, 111
Hayes, Von 77
Hays, Ernie 153, 176
Hebner, Richie 79, 114
Heep, Danny 28, 42, 100
Heisman Trophy 64
Henderson, Rickey 14, 22, 51, 72, 105–106, 119
Hendrick, George 17, 21, 43, 61–62, 77, 89, 116
Henke, Tom 155
Herman, Babe 155
Hernandez, Keith 12, 40–41, 43, 54, 89, 96, 108, 134, 138, 145, 149–150
Hernandez, Willie 105
Herr, Tommy 2, 9, 23, 29–30, 33, 36, 38, 40–41, 45–46, 48, 51, 56–57, 63–64, 66–68, 73, 77, 79–86, 88, 90, 92–93, 96–97, 101, 103, 105, 107, 111–112, 114, 119–121, 123, 126, 130–131, 133, 139, 142–143, 145, 150, 152–153, 159, 161, 164–165, 174, 176, 178–179, 181–183, 185, 188
Hershiser, Orel 51, 158, 163–164
Herzog, Whitey 1–2, 7–21, 24–29, 31–34, 36–41, 43–46, 49, 51–53, 55, 58–61, 66, 71–73, 76, 78–79, 85–86, 88–90, 93, 96, 100, 108–110, 114–115, 120, 125, 128, 130–133, 136, 140–143, 148–153, 155–157, 159–160, 162–164, 166, 170–172, 174–175, 177–183, 185–189
Hesketh, Joe 44
Highland, IL 135
The Hill (St. Louis neighborhood) 96
Hodges, Gil 5
Holland, Al 47, 116
Honeycutt, Rick 96
Hood River, OR 27
Horner, Bob 10, 63, 134–135
Hornsby, Rogers 22, 143
Horton, Rick 1, 27, 42, 45, 51, 60–62, 72–73, 76, 86, 92, 94, 101, 103, 108–109, 117, 119, 121, 125, 128–129, 132, 136, 138, 140–141, 145, 150, 152, 159, 161, 176, 179, 184
Howe, Art 47
Howe, Steve 95, 142, 157

Index

Howell, Jay 105
Howell, Ken 51, 96
Howser, Dick 169–171, 175–176, 178, 181–182
Hoyt, Lamarr 100–101, 105–107, 112
Hubbell, Carl 137
Hudson, Charles 116, 146
Hunt, Randy 70, 88
Hunter, Jim "Catfish" 132
Hurdle, Clint 28
Hutchinson, Fred 6

Indians (Cleveland) 35, 41, 76–77, 85, 94, 119, 142, 168
International League 13
Iorg, Dane 173, 182

Jackson, Bo 64
Jackson, Danny 170–172, 179
Jackson, Reggie 12, 17, 91, 104
James, Jesse 183
Jeltz, Steve 37
Jenkins, Ferguson 146
Joel, Billy 97
John, Tommy 29
Johnson, Davey 39, 86, 137, 144, 148
Johnson, Howard 40, 89, 92, 136
Johnson, Walter 38, 41
Joliet, IL 43
Jones, Lynn 172
Joplin, MO 30
Jordan, Michael 79
Jorgensen, Mike 27, 126, 133, 136
Jose, Felix 189

Kaufmann, Ewing 24
Kell, George 143
Kennedy, Terry 100–102, 106–107, 111
The Kentucky Derby 53
Keough, Matt 108, 140, 143
Kepshire, Kurt 26, 42, 45, 60, 63, 65, 70, 72–73, 81, 84–85, 91, 96, 99, 101, 110, 121, 123, 125, 127, 130, 132, 135, 140, 142, 144, 152–153
Key, Jimmy 105
Kipper, Bob 144
Kissell, George 29
Kittle, Hub 18, 38
Kittle, Ron 62
Klein, Chuck 155
KMOX Radio (St. Louis) 45, 112

Knepper, Bob 60, 131
Knicely, Alan 31
Koosman, Jerry 82, 89–90, 127
Koufax, Sandy 107, 146
Kroc, Ray 10
Krukow, Mike 52, 109–110
Kuenn, Harvey 11
Kuhlmann, Fred 19, 26, 30, 56, 88
Kuhn, Bowie 34

Lahti, Jeff 27, 38, 47, 62, 66, 73, 77, 79, 82, 85, 91–93, 101, 109, 111, 123, 125–128, 132, 144, 150, 155, 175, 184
Lake, Steve 85
Lakeland, FL 32
Landreaux, Ken 51, 166
Landrum, Tito 30, 32–33, 38, 43–44, 65–66, 77, 90, 101, 124, 133, 157, 160–161, 164, 171–172, 174–175, 177, 179, 181
Lanier, Hal 13, 97, 162, 184
Lankford, Ray 17
Lapoint, Dave 20, 52–53, 89, 96–97, 109
Larussa, Tony 100
Laskey, Bill 97
Lasorda, Tommy 75, 94–96, 156, 159, 162, 164–165, 176
Laudner, Tim 77
Lavalliere, Mike 24, 42
Lavelle, Gary 24
Law, Vance 103, 124
Lawless, Tom 2, 59, 80, 82, 88, 101, 153
LeFlore, Ron 142
Leibrandt, Charlie 170, 174, 180–181
Leonard, Jeff 97
Letterman, David 180
Lewis, Johnny 13
Leyva, Nick 13, 184
Lezcano, Sixto 9
Liberty, MO 183
Lindbergh High School (St. Louis) 108
Lonborg, Jim 181
London, Dr. Stan 161, 175
Lopes, Davey 79–80, 86, 146, 156
Lynch, Ed 73, 82
Lyons, Bill 65

MacPhail, Lee 47, 104, 117
Madlock, Bill 134, 141, 155–157, 162, 164
Magrane, Joe 63
Mahler, Mickey 59, 74

Mahler, Rick 50, 63, 134
Maldonado, Candy 157, 159
Mantle, Mickey 121
Marshall, Mike 54, 156, 159, 164
Martin, Billy 144
Martinez, Carmelo 111
Martinez, Dennis 30
Martinez, Silvio 9
Mathis, Ron 62
Matthews, Gary 74, 78, 85, 112, 116, 140, 151, 153
Mattingly, Don 105, 187
Maxvill, Dal 19–20, 26, 30–31, 37, 44, 54, 58, 65–66, 76, 88, 96, 108, 126, 129, 188
Mays, Willie 55, 83, 159
McBride, Bake 70
McCovey, Willie 33
McDonald, Jim 72
McDonald, Joe 11, 15, 19, 88, 90, 187
McDowell, Roger 42, 48, 89, 136, 145, 150
McGee, Willie 2, 15–18, 33, 36, 42–46, 53, 62, 68, 70–71, 73–74, 79, 81–86, 92, 94–96, 99–101, 105, 107, 110–114, 120–121, 123–124, 126, 128, 130–133, 138–139, 142–143, 145, 150, 153–155, 158–159, 164–166, 171–172, 174, 176–178, 180–181, 183, 185, 187–189
McGwire, Mark 2
McHale, John 55
McKean, Jim 180
McLain, Denny 48
McNally, Dave 131
McRae, Hal 169, 172, 178, 182
McSherry, John 51, 124
McWilliams, Larry 76
Medwick, Joe 83
Memorial Stadium (Baltimore) 81
Meredith, Ron 112
Metrodome (Minneapolis) 104, 107
Mets (New York) 2, 8, 11, 13, 19, 28, 31, 33, 38–40, 42, 47–48, 56, 72–73, 77, 82, 85–86, 89, 91–93, 96–97, 99–100, 102, 109–110, 115–117, 121–123, 125–126, 128, 133, 136–139, 141, 143–153, 180, 184
Michigan, University of 64
Mickey Owen Baseball School 3
Miller, Ray 30, 81
Milner, John 55

Minton, Greg 119
Mize, Johnny 83
Mobile, AL 10
Molitor, Paul 12, 16, 105
Monday, Rick 37
Moore, Donnie 105
Moore, Terry 188
Moreland, Keith 79, 82, 89, 114, 120, 140
Moreno, Omar 76, 108, 140, 169
Morris, Jack 18, 32, 58, 65, 105, 107
Morrison, Jim 75
Moseby, Lloyd 129, 154
Motley, Daryl 169, 171–173, 178, 181, 184–185
Mueller, Don 83
Murphy, Dale 12, 41, 50, 96, 99, 105, 127
Murray, Eddie 105
Murtaugh, Danny 47
Musial, Stan 13, 22, 188

National Baseball Hall of Fame 112
National Football League 14, 22
National League Championship Series (1982) 11–12; (1984) 35, 69, 151; (1985) 153, 155–166, 171–172, 175
NBC Game of the Week 152
Neosho, MO 3
Nettles, Graig 105–106, 110
Nevada–Las Vegas, University of 63
New Athens, IL 8
New York University 23
Niedenfuer, Tom 32, 96, 157, 162, 164–165, 171
Niekro, Phil 113, 154
Nieto, Tom 24, 27–28, 46, 60, 72, 80, 86, 91–92, 97, 101, 109–110, 131, 133, 144, 166, 177–180
Nixon, President Richard 163
Noll, Roger 23
North Elmore, NY 58

Oakland Naval Yards 17
Oberkfell, Ken 27, 135
O'Connor, Jack 145
O'Hare Airport (Chicago) 118
Oliver, Al 158
Olympics (1984) 104
O'Malley, Walter 5
Oquendo, Jose 31
Orioles, Baltimore 11, 15, 30, 47, 81
Orosco, Jesse 92, 137, 141, 146, 149

Orta, Jorge 172, 182–183
Orza, Gene 118
Osteen, Claude 146
Overland Park, KS 180
Ownbey, Rick 12, 25, 108
Oxnard, CA 29

Padres (San Diego) 9–10, 32, 35, 41, 53–54, 74, 95–96, 99–102, 109–111, 124, 126, 151, 168
Pallone, Dave 22–23
Palmer, David 54
Palmer, Jim 81, 146
Parker, Dave 32, 55, 65, 105, 132, 134
Parrish, Lance 105–106, 155
Patterson, Reggie 135
Payton, Walter 79
Peabody, MA 22
Pena, Tony 43, 105, 119, 121
Pendleton, Terry 29, 33, 36, 38, 40–44, 47, 53, 63, 73, 80, 82, 88–89, 94–97, 101, 109, 111–112, 120, 131, 133, 143, 145, 147, 149, 150, 157–161, 172, 174, 177–178, 180–181, 184, 189
Perez, Pascual 119
Perez, Tony 128, 132
Perry, Pat 136, 138, 141, 150
Peterson, Pete 59, 74
Petry, Dan 105
Phillies (Philadelphia) 6, 11, 13, 22, 24, 32, 37, 41, 47, 67–68, 77, 82–83, 90, 95, 106, 116–117, 120–123, 142–143, 146, 154–155, 168
Phillips, Richie 34, 151
Piniella, Lou 17
Pipp, Wally 16
Pirates (Pittsburgh) 21, 31, 41–43, 45–47, 52, 54–55, 59, 61–62, 73–78, 91, 103–104, 116, 119, 121–123, 134, 140–142, 144–145, 156, 189
Polo Grounds (New York) 77
Porter, Darrell 9–10, 24, 42, 52, 59–60, 65, 70, 77, 81–82, 85, 89, 96, 101, 109–110, 112, 125, 142, 149, 157–158, 164, 169, 172, 176, 180–182, 185
Portland, University of 27
Portland State University 27
Puckett, Kirby 23

Quick, Jim 180
Quisenberry, Dan 170, 174, 176, 181

Rader, Doug 59
Raines, Tim 11, 54, 105, 124, 144–145
Rajsich, Gary 20, 52, 108
Ramirez, Rafael 134
Ramsey, Mike 59
Rangers (Texas) 8, 27, 54, 59, 95
Rapp, Vern 59
Rawley, Shane 91, 117, 121
Ray, Johnny 123
Rayford, Floyd 30
Reagan, President Ronald 138, 186
Reardon, Jeff 54, 105, 107
Red Sox (Boston) 13, 28, 105, 113, 119, 170
Reds (Cincinnati) 10, 27, 40, 50, 59, 65–67, 70, 120, 124, 127, 129, 131–132, 143, 150
Redskins (Washington) 22
Reitz, Ken 9
Rennert, Dutch 150
Reuschel, Rick 76
Reuss, Jerry 45, 50, 160–161
Rice, Jim 105
Ricketts, Dave 13
Rickey, Branch 4, 13, 102
Ripken, Cal, Jr. 105, 107
Riverfront Stadium (Cincinnati) 127, 189
Rivers, Mickey 18
Roarke, Mike 13–14, 42, 62, 125, 173
Robinson, Brooks 131
Robinson, Don 121
Rogers, Steve 45, 64, 176
Rose, Pete 25, 31–32, 40, 42, 59, 65, 67, 70–71, 105, 119–121, 127–129, 131–133, 135, 137–138, 143, 148, 189
Rose, Pete, Jr. 32
Ross, Mark 60–61
Royals (Kansas City) 8–9, 11, 17–18, 24, 32, 58, 116, 131, 144, 150, 154–155, 158, 163, 167–186
Royals Stadium (Kansas City) 168, 179, 185
Royer, Stan 189
Rucker, Dave 37, 143
Runge, Paul 159
Russell, Bill 51, 150
Ruth, George Herman "Babe" 6, 137, 170
Ruthven, Dick 88, 120
Ryan, Nolan 25, 38, 41, 60–61, 100, 105, 107, 117

Saberhagen, Bret 170–171, 175–176, 179, 183, 185
Salazar, Argenis 31
Samuel, Juan 111, 114, 116
Sandberg, Ryne 10–11, 17, 78–79, 85, 96, 99, 105, 112–113, 122, 140, 152
Sanderson, Scott 78, 112, 120, 153
Santana, Rafael 42, 100, 122
Sax, Steve 157
Schatzeder, Dan 44
Schaumburg, IL 69, 95
Schenectady, NY 22
Schiraldi, Calvin 73
Schmidt, Mike 32, 59, 90–91, 104, 121
Schoendiest, Albert "Red" 8–9, 12–13, 145
Schott, Marge 32, 40, 67
Schu, Rick 90
Schuerholz, John 58, 168–169
Schulze, Don 91
Scioscia, Mike 156, 159
Score, Herb 125
Scott, Mike 130
Scott, Tony 9
Seaver, Tom 41, 113, 116, 127
Seton Hall University 58
Shannon, Mike 22, 45
Shea Stadium (New York) 11, 55, 72, 91, 121, 124, 136, 144, 146, 152
Sheridan, Pat 172, 176, 181
Sherman, General William 127
Show, Eric 110, 137
Shulock, John 180
Simmons, Ted 9
Singer Bill 146
Sisk, Doug 73
Skinner, Bob 103
Slaughter, Enos 112, 188
Smith, Dave 129
Smith, Lee 84, 86
Smith, Lonnie 9–10, 22–25, 33–34, 40, 46, 51, 53–55, 57–59, 65, 89, 134, 169–170, 172, 179, 182, 184
Smith, Ozzie 2, 10, 17, 21, 29–31, 36–38, 41–43, 45, 53, 60, 63, 83, 86, 90, 92, 96–97, 99, 101, 105, 107, 111, 116, 121–122, 124, 128, 131, 136, 138–140, 142–143, 148, 150–151, 153, 160, 162–166, 171–172, 174, 176, 180–181, 190
Sorensen, Lary 9, 123
Sorter, George 23

Sosa, Sammy 94
Speier, Chris 57, 98, 114
Spinks, Michael 72
Sport magazine 34
The Sporting News 19
Sportsman's Park (St. Louis) 5–6, 112
Springfield, IL 95, 136
Springfield, MO 72
Stanford University 23
Stanky, Eddie 13
Stargell, Willie 47
Steinbrenner, George 108
Stengel, Casey 7, 13
Stewart, Dave 95
Stieb, Dave 105, 155
Stockslek, Bill 7
Stone, Mike 54
Stone, Steve 81
Stoneham Horace 5
Stottlemyre, Mel 63
Stottlemyre, Todd 63
Strawberry, Daryl 40, 105–106, 117, 149
strike, baseball (1981) 3, 10, 15, 23, 25, 67, 71, 117, 154; (1985) 3, 118–120; discussion of possible 23, 47, 64, 67–68, 102–104, 108–109, 112, 115–117, 151
Strong, Curtis 67, 134, 189
Stuper, John 70
Sundberg, Jim 169, 172, 176, 178–179, 182, 184
Susman, Lou 19, 30, 37, 43, 56, 88, 108
Sutcliffe, Rick 41, 62, 69, 74, 78, 85–87, 95, 103, 112–113, 120, 133, 157
Sutter, Bruce 1, 9, 17, 26–27, 62–63, 79, 85, 89, 108, 125–126, 163, 187
Sutton, Don 113, 119
Sykes, Bob 15

Tanner, Chuck 47, 141
Taos, MO 155
Taylorville, IL 136
Tekulve, Kent 47
Templeton, Garry 10, 20, 105, 145
Tenace, Gene 17
Teufel, Tim 77
Texas, University of 79
Thomas, Gorman 12, 16, 62
Thompson, Jason 75, 77
Thompson, Governor Jim 95
Thon, Dickie 71

Index

Three Rivers Stadium (Pittsburgh) 54–55, 74–75
Thurmond, Mark 100
Tibbs, Jay 70, 127
Tigers, Detroit 14, 32, 48, 53, 107, 110, 123, 131, 140, 143, 154
Toomey, Jim 132
Torrez, Mike 71
Trammell, Alan 105
Trans World Airlines (TWA) 44
Trout, Steve 35, 62, 66, 69, 78, 88, 112, 120, 139, 152
Tudor, John 2, 21, 41–42, 44, 52, 61, 71, 73, 76–77, 82, 87–88, 91–92, 94, 96, 99, 101, 109–110, 112, 116, 120–121, 123–125, 127–128, 131, 134, 136–138, 140–141, 144, 146–149, 152–153, 155, 157, 160–161, 163, 171–173, 177–179, 183–185, 187–188
Turner, Ted 68, 127
Twins (Minnesota) 81, 95, 117–118, 142
Tyler, TX 3

Ueberroth, Peter 34–35, 40, 54–55, 66, 104, 118, 163, 177
Union, MO 26
Uribe, Jose 20, 52

Valenzuela, Fernando 38, 75, 97, 105, 107, 109–110, 153, 157–158, 161–162, 175
Van Slyke, Andy 2, 29–30, 32–33, 43–46, 48, 53, 57, 62, 65–66, 71, 78–80, 84, 86, 88, 92, 101, 111, 120, 131, 133, 139, 141, 143, 145, 147, 150–152, 165, 171–173, 182, 185, 188–189
Vaughan, Arky 112
Veterans' Stadium (Philadelphia) 68
Viola, Frank 117
Virgil, Ozzie 83, 91, 105, 146
Vuckovich, Pete 9, 16

Wagner, Honus 138
Wallach, Tim 105–106, 143
Waller, Ty 9
Ward, Gary 105
Washington, Harold 69
Washington University (St. Louis) 19
Wathan, John 11, 169
Weaver, Earl 15, 81
Welch, Bob 159
West, Joe 97
Weyer, Lee 137
Whitaker, Lou 105, 107
White, Frank 169–170, 172, 174, 176–177, 179, 181, 184–185
White Sox (Chicago) 17, 41, 62, 69, 100, 113, 117–118
Whitfield, Terry 96
Whitson, Ed 144
Whitt, Ernie 105
Wiggins, Alan 54
Wilhelm, Hoyt 112
Williams, (Umpire) Billy 114–115, 180
Williams, Dick 99–101, 106, 111
Williams, Ted 68
Wills, Maury 142, 146
Wilson, Glenn 105–106
Wilson, Mookie 91–92, 138, 150
Wilson, Willie 58, 169, 172, 174, 181, 184–185
Wine, Bobby 127, 135
Winfield, Dave 15, 17, 105
Winningham, Herm 39
Winter Leagues, Baseball 55
World Series (1954) 159; (1964) 6–7; (1967) 181; (1970) 185; (1971) 160; (1982) 16–17, 19, 22, 62, 70, 128, 179, 185; (1984) 53, 107; (1985) 168, 170–186, 189
World War Two 11
Worrell, Todd 2, 128, 132, 141, 143–144, 150–151, 159, 162, 164–165, 172, 175, 179, 182, 188
Wrigley, Phil 5
Wrigley Field (Chicago) 28, 35, 69, 74, 77–81, 84, 89, 95, 110, 112, 114, 123, 135, 138, 141, 146, 154
Wynegar, Butch 154

Yakima Valley (WA) College 63
Yankees (New York) 6–8, 15, 17, 31, 64, 76, 95, 108, 113, 117, 119, 131, 144, 150, 154–155, 157, 168–169
Yastrzemski, Carl 105, 143
Yeager, Steve 156
Youmans, Floyd 39
Young, John 31
Young, Larry 22–23, 25
Youngblood, Joel 55
Yount, Robin 11

www.ingramcontent.com/pod-product-compliance
Ingram Content Group UK Ltd.
Pitfield, Milton Keynes, MK11 3LW, UK
UKHW042002140426
5217IPUK00015B/936